LITERARY/CULTURAL THEORY

QUEER STUDIES

Literary/Cultural Theory provides concise and lucid introductions to a range of key concepts and theorists in contemporary literary and cultural theory. Original and contemporary in presentation, and eschewing jargon, each book in the series presents to students of humanities and social sciences exhaustive overviews of theories and theorists, while also introducing them to the mechanics of reading literary/cultural texts using critical tools. Each book also carries glossaries of key terms and ideas, and pointers for further reading and research. Written by scholar-teachers who have taught critical theory for years, and vetted by some of the foremost experts in the field, the series Literary/Cultural Theory is indispensable to students and teachers.

Also in the series

Psychoanalytic Theory and Criticism
Feminisms
Jacques Lacan
Dalit Literature and Criticism
Ecocriticism
Postsecular Theory
Nations and Nationalisms
Periyar
Popular Culture
Life Writing
Marxist Literary and Cultural Theory
Frantz Fanon
Mikhail Bakhtin
Deconstruction and Poststructuralism
Edward Said
Diaspora Theory and Transnationalism
Subaltern Studies
Postcolonialism Now

LITERARY/CULTURAL THEORY

QUEER STUDIES

TEXTS, CONTEXTS, PRAXIS

KAUSTAV BAKSHI
Jadavpur University, Kolkata

ROHIT K. DASGUPTA
Loughborough University, UK

Orient BlackSwan

Cover photograph by Arnab Adak.

Arnab Adak's photographic work focuses primarily on various cultural, social and environmental concerns, and aims at raising awareness among people. He explores themes surrounding gender, climate, caste and religion. He is currently associated with a management consulting firm.

QUEER STUDIES

ORIENT BLACKSWAN PRIVATE LIMITED

Registered Office
3-6-752 Himayatnagar, Hyderabad 500 029, Telangana, India
Email: centraloffice@orientblackswan.com

Other Offices
Bengaluru, Chennai, Guwahati, Hyderabad,
Kolkata, Mumbai, New Delhi, Noida, Patna

First published 2019
Reprinted 2024

ISBN 978 93 5287 584 9

039298

Typeset in Aldine 401 BT 10.5/13 *by*
Akhil Offset Printers, Hyderabad 500 020

Printed at
Shree Maitrey Printech Pvt. Ltd., Noida

Published by
Orient Blackswan Private Limited
3-6-752, Himayatnagar, Hyderabad 500 029, Telangana, India
Email: info@orientblackswan.com

Contents

Acknowledgements

We are immensely grateful to Ruth Vanita (University of Montana), Nivedita Menon (Jawaharlal Nehru University), Mary E. John (Centre for Women's Development Studies), Paromita Chakravarti (Jadavpur University), Madhavi Menon (Ashoka University), Pushpesh Kumar (University of Hyderabad), Navaneetha Mokkil (Jawaharlal Nehru University), Mallarika Sinha Roy (Jawaharlal Nehru University), Veena Hariharan (Jawaharlal Nehru University), Shohini Ghosh (Jamia Millia Islamia), Swati Ganguly (Visva Bharati), Sumanyu Satpathy (University of Delhi), Anu Aneja (IGNOU), Shivaji K. Panikkar (Ambedkar University), Panchali Ray (Jadavpur University), Akshay K. Rath (NIT Rourkela), Nithin Manayath, Niladri R. Chatterjee (Kalyani University), Jo Tacchi (Loughborough University), Patria Roman (Loughborough University), Graham Murdock (Loughborough University), Rachel Dwyer (SOAS), Paul Boyce (University of Sussex), Lipi Begum (University of Southampton), Kareem Khubchandani (Tufts University), Rajinder Dudrah (Birmingham City University), Reina Lewis (London College of Fashion), Sunil Gupta (UCA), Sharif Mowlabocus (Sussex), Sara Davidmann (London College of Communication), William Raban (London College of Communication), Unmesh Desai AM (London Assembly), Pawan Dhall (Varta Trust, Kolkata), the Late K. Moti Gokulsing, Debanuj Dasgupta, Nazli Alimen, and Nilanjana Gupta (Coordinator, Department of English, CAS, Jadavpur University).

Kaustav is immensely grateful to his mother, Ashima Bakshi, and his supervisor and colleague, Nilanjana Deb (Jadavpur University); and Rohit to his parents, Joyasree Dasgupta and Mukut Dasgupta, and Rittika Dasgupta and Tim.

Introduction

Queer Studies is an extremely dynamic field which is expanding almost every day to include new histories, new cultures of intimacy and kinship, and new ways of being queer. It is impossible to satisfactorily deal with the multiple facets of queer cultures and politics in a single book. Our attempt in this book is to rethink and recalibrate what Queer Studies means in this contemporary moment. In doing so, this book pushes the boundaries of conceptualising 'queer', and moves towards a context and praxis of interrogating the term by using texts which have not been analysed in such a way before. Methodologically too we turn and overturn boundaries of cultural studies, social sciences and participatory research to situate the importance of Queer Studies in the present moment. At the heart of this project is a constant discomfort which Teresa de Lauretis and others had anticipated: the more Queer Theory gets appropriated within mainstream academia, the more it loses its radical edge and runs the risk of turning into a normative discipline. To quote de Lauretis, 'As for "queer theory" . . . since I proposed it as a working hypothesis for lesbian and gay studies in this very journal (*differences*, 3.2), has very quickly become a conceptually vacuous creature of the publishing industry' ('Habit Changes' 296). This is unavoidable, given the manner in which Queer Studies has been appropriated in the academia in the West, if not so much in South Asia.

The only possible way to keep on queering Queer Studies is to explore and expand its immeasurable potential to challenge and dismantle norms. This book, while drawing a historiography of how Queer Studies came into being in the academia, deals with the prospects of reading and seeing queerly which are becoming progressively more popular in the field of cultural studies. While looking back, the book also takes into account the current discourses of queer politics which concerns itself with the emergence of consumerist gay and lesbian cultures and the alarmingly increasing popularity of homonormativity. In addition, we also raise concerns around issues of homonationalism, pinkwashing and migration, whilst offering different conceptual understandings of the same with ample examples. The importance of locating the understanding of queer lives within specific geographical areas, discourses of racism, ethnic xenophobia and immigration policies has also been a central part of this project. Finally, this book makes a significant intervention in critically analysing for the first time the emergence of Queer Studies in India. Above all, the book contributes positively to the field of LGBTQ+ politics in developing countries where dissident sexualities are still considered a criminal offence. As academic activists our politics is grounded in our scholarship, and this is our attempt to generate a critical debate and reflection in the field of Queer Studies.

QUEER: STRANGE AND CONTEMPTIBLE?

In academia, Queer Studies has emerged only very recently, with the term 'queer' gaining a positive political currency, even in the midst of much opposition to it. Any discussion on Queer Studies cannot but begin with recalling the etymological evolution of the term 'queer', and its appropriation by the lesbian, gay, bisexual and transgender movement worldwide, in order to make sense of the long struggle involved in reclaiming the term and infusing it with a political charge. Both the term and the movement have picked up incredible momentum in discourses related to sex, sexuality, and uncompromising challenges to all forms of normativity since 1990. The earliest recorded meaning of the word 'queer', according to the *Oxford English Dictionary*, is 'strange, odd, peculiar, eccentric'; for instance, the way Robert Frost used it in 1923 –

> My little horse must think it *queer*
> To stop without a farmhouse near

> Between the woods and frozen lake
> The darkest evening of the year.

Starting from the early sixteenth century, the term irredeemably degenerated into a term of opprobrium. In fact, there are only a few words in the English lexicon which have so consistently, so unfailingly, over the centuries, gone on picking up increasingly negative meanings, either as a verb or an adjective. By 1567, 'queer', as an adjective, acquired a wider range of unsavoury connotations: 'bad, contemptible, worthless, untrustworthy, disreputable'; and, by 1781, it mutated into a verb, which meant 'to spoil or ruin', while its adjectival use remained unaltered.

It is widely acknowledged that one of the first recorded usages of the term, disparagingly referring to men who love men, can be traced back to 1894, in one of John Douglas's (the ninth Marquess of Queensberry) infamous letters. In this letter, he anathematised Archibald Primrose, the fifth Earl of Rosebery, who had a brief tenure as the Prime Minister of Britain (5 March 1894 to 22 June 1895), as one of the 'Snob Queers' for 'corrupting' his son, Drumlanrig, the latter's secretary (Hoare 106). Interestingly, 'queer' now became a noun, loaded with the downbeat connotations piled on it over the past centuries, either as a verb or an adjective, and came to refer to homosexuals, linguistically unloading upon them all the negativities accumulated by the term so far. By this time, the term 'homosexual' had also entered the public domain, coined by the Austro-Hungarian journalist, travel writer and human rights campaigner Karl-Maria Kertbeny in 1869. The terms 'homosexual' and 'heterosexual' entered the English language almost simultaneously, subsequent to the translation of Richard von Krafft-Ebing's *Psychopathia sexualis* into English in 1892.

While the term 'homosexual' began to find frequent usage in emerging scientific disciplines of anthropology, sexology and psychology in the late nineteenth century, 'queer' continued to gain prominence as a slur for homosexuals in everyday parlance. By 1914, it seems that 'queer' as a descriptive term for sexually non-conforming individuals gained such popularity that it began to appear in print media. The *Oxford English Dictionary* cites an article from a 1914 edition of the *Los Angeles Times* in which a particular club is described as 'queer', where '"queer" people have a good time', identifying it as the first media articulation of the term designating people with non-normative sexual choices. It took a few decades for the term to acquire a positive currency.

A QUEER NATION: 'YOU AS AN ALIVE AND FUNCTIONING QUEER ARE A REVOLUTIONARY'

A leaflet, 'Queers Read This', distributed at the New York Pride March in June 1990 was one of the earliest and most sulphurous proclamations of 'queerness' which recuperated 'queer' from the swamp of negative associations: 'You as an alive and functioning queer are a revolutionary' (Anon. 1). Voicing unappeasable resentment against 'straight' people's abhorrence for the sexual non-conformists, the government's inaction in thwarting the AIDS epidemic, and unspeakable social harassment of gay and lesbian people, this anonymous leaflet declared that nothing short of an aggressive revolution could set them free:

> Until I can enjoy the same freedom of movement and sexuality, as straights, their privilege must stop and it must be given over to me and my queer sisters and brothers. Straight people will not do this voluntarily and so they must be forced into it. Straights must be frightened into it. Terrorized into it. Fear is the most powerful motivation. No one will give us what we deserve. Rights are not given they are taken, by force if necessary. (Anon. 1)

It advocated 'coming out' in the public as a necessary step in order to be seen and heard. Discreetness was as bad as escapism and could no longer be a survival strategy. It was a momentous call for inscribing the personal with the political; of unleashing queer love, lust and desire into the public domain and transfiguring the 'sexual geography' of New York City (2). The sexual revolution could acquire significant mileage only when queer people made themselves unapologetically visible everywhere, threatening compulsory heterosexuality:

> Being queer is not about a right to privacy; it is about the freedom to be public, to just be who we are. It means everyday

> fighting oppression; homophobia, racism, misogyny, the bigotry of religious hypocrites and our own self-hatred. (We have been carefully taught to hate ourselves.) And now of course it means fighting a virus as well, and all those homo-haters who are using AIDS to wipe us off the face of the earth. Being queer means leading a different sort of life. . . . It's about being on the margins, defining ourselves; it's about gender-fuck and secrets, what's beneath the belt and deep inside the heart; it's about the night. . . . We are an army because we have to be. We are an army because we are so powerful. (We have so much to fight for; we are the most precious of endangered species.) (Anon. 2–3)

This call for revolution wove the political with the emotional in an inspirational and provocative rhetoric, aiming to erase the stigma of the hateful other, cataloguing in detail various facets of queer othering. The leaflet expostulated with queer people about coalition-building and urged them to revolt, speak back and retaliate:

> They will beat us, rape us and kill us before they will continue to live with us. . . . Feel some rage. If rage doesn't empower you, try fear. If that doesn't work, try panic.
>
> SHOUT IT!
>
> Be proud. Do whatever you need to do to tear yourself away from your customary state of acceptance. Be free. Shout. (Anon. 4–5)

A revolution of this epic proportion could not possibly be termed 'gay', for 'gay' was too happy or mild a word to adequately underwrite the mordacious rage every sexually non-conformist individual felt. 'Queer', on the other hand, by the virtue or vice of the negative connotations it had gathered, was an infinitely more subversive expression, encapsulating the agony of suffering each gay or lesbian person experienced on a daily basis: 'Using "queer" is a way of reminding us how we are perceived by the rest of the world. It's a way of telling ourselves we don't have to be witty and charming people who keep our lives discreet and marginalized in the straight world' (Anon. 9).

As Judith Butler would later observe, queer 'derives its force precisely through the repeated invocation by which it has become linked to accusation, pathologization, insult' (226). Apart from that, 'queer' was a more expansive term to contain within it a wide range of non-normative sexualities which could not be simply categorised as 'gay' or 'lesbian'; it could be a label for the 'army' – or social, cultural and political coalition – of sexual minorities, resisting essentialist and often rigid classification of sexualities:

> We use queer as gay men loving lesbians and lesbians loving being queer.
>
> Queer, unlike GAY, doesn't mean MALE.
>
> And when spoken to other gays and lesbians it's a way of suggesting we close ranks, and forget (temporarily) our individual differences because we face a more insidious common enemy. (Anon. 9)

It was time to reclaim 'queer' as a term of empowerment, to turn it on its head, and use it as a weapon against those who had so far loaded it with derogatory meanings: '. . . QUEER can be a rough word but it is also a sly and ironic weapon we can steal from the homophobe's hands and use against him' (Anon. 9). This was also the time when Queer Nation, an activist organisation, was founded. Its first meeting was held on 20 March 1990 in New York City's West Village; and by June, hundreds had joined the group. On the day of the Pride March, when this leaflet under discussion was distributed, members of the Queer Nation joined the March under a banner which proudly proclaimed: 'Queer Nation . . . Get Used To It!'

This was a turning point in the etymological history of the term 'queer', a moment of rebirth as it were, when the term was imbued with a spirit of rebellion, dissent and radicalism that threatened to overturn the accepted 'naturalness' of heteronormativity (a term which was introduced and popularised within the discourses of queer cultures by Michael Warner in 1991). The etymological journey of 'queer' since then has been an extremely intriguing one. It went on to become the most contentious term within sexuality identity discourses, 'defined more by what it is not than what it is for' (McIntosh 365).

THEORISING 'QUEER'

As soon as the term 'queer' was reclaimed, Queer Theory as a discipline, as a tool of critical analysis and political thinking, entered the field of humanities and social sciences, following the conference organised by Teresa de Lauretis, a professor of the History of Consciousness at the University of California, Santa Cruz, in the month of February in 1990. It was indeed a defining moment in queer's dramatic odyssey; a consecration of sorts, on being linked to what David Halperin calls, 'the academic holy word, "theory"' (339–40). In the summer of 1991, de Lauretis edited a special issue of *differences*, a journal of international repute, titled *Queer Theory: Lesbian and Gay Sexualities*. Drawing from postmodernist debunking of master narratives and the idea of stable and fixed identities which was so far upheld in the European modernist discourses since the Renaissance, Queer Theory challenged essentialist notions of identity, binary oppositions, and easy equations between sex, gender, desire and even clothing. Queer Theory stems from the rejection of subjectivity as the property of the self, based on the poststructuralist notion that subjectivity is something that originates outside it. As Corber and Valocchi observes,

> [Q]ueer studies scholars claim that desires, practices, and identities do not line up as neatly as lesbian and gay studies scholarship implies. For these scholars, lesbians and gay identities are provisional and contingent rather than fixed and coherent. "The homosexual" is not a stable or autonomous category but a supplement that works to stabilize heterosexuality by functioning as its binary opposite. (3)

Although Queer Theory was to take a more radical turn later, de Lauretis's summing up of the basic purpose of inventing Queer Theory – 'homosexuality is no longer to be seen simply as marginal with regard to a dominant, stable form of sexuality (heterosexuality) against which it would be defined either by opposition or homology' (*Queer Theory: Lesbian and Gay Sexualities* iii) – set the tone for further arguments and debates. Rosemary Hennessy, who reviewed the special issue of *differences* in *Signs*, pointed out Queer Theory's affiliation with materialist feminism: 'Both refuse a politics in which identity is understood to be represented in a self-evident way through one's body and collectivity is reduced to group affiliation defined according to the standard of authentic embodiment' (964).

Queer Theory underscores the impossibility of explaining desire in terms of 'nature' (or genetic programming) or 'nurture' (or how one is reared and socialised) – rationalisations of same-sex desires the West often engaged in. Queer Theory tilts towards the constructionist idea of sexualities and sexual desires, dismantling the essentialist notions that 'homosexuality', 'bisexuality', etc., were 'real' (or even 'natural') identities. Rather it espouses and builds on the idea that, '[A] "homosexual" is someone who understands who and what she/he is as "homosexual" (or "gay") because she/he lives in a society that labels her/his behaviour in a certain way. In cultures where no such labels exist there would be no inherent categories or boundaries' (Naphy 9).

Advocating denaturalisation of sexualities, Halperin, within four years of the official foundation of Queer Theory, emphasised the infinite possibilities of the term 'queer', retrieving it from the reductive practice of associating it with only non-normative sexual identities: '. . . "queer" does not name some *natural* kind or refer to some determinate object; it acquires its meaning from its oppositional relation to the norm. Queer is by definition whatever is at odds with the normal, the legitimate, the dominant. There is nothing in particular to which it necessarily refers' (*Saint Foucault* 62; emphasis added).

The term 'queer' resists the practice of pigeonholing individuals based on their sexualities and encapsulates desires and sexual practices which elude definition or label, in fact, even language. The power of the term 'queer' lies in its uncontainable potential to discredit, challenge, and collapse all forms of normativity which dominate the realms of sexuality, erotic desires, coupledom, romance, kinship and social relations. For instance, a pederast and a *kothi* are both queer in different capacities; an asexual individual comes under the rubric of 'queer' as much as a polyamorous one. The boundary of the 'queer' has been further pushed by individuals who call themselves 'homoromantic asexuals' – people who seek romantic relationships based on companionship, deep emotions and friendship; but they may not be necessarily sexually attracted to their partners. Even a heterosexual couple resisting procreation, thereby frustrating societal expectations and familial demands, also 'queers' the concept of marriage to an uncomfortable extent.

Logically, therefore, queer politics is also radically opposed to homonormativity (that is, an unquestioning imitation of heteronormativity in order to enjoy state benefits), despite its growing popularity among sexual minorities in the West. One may cite, as an example, the radical queer activist Jordan Alexander Stein's discomposure at the legalisation of same-sex marriage in the United States in 2015:

> I have always wanted to live in a world that's committed to queer people's thriving, and today's Supreme Court decision almost certainly will help. And that is wonderful. But it's not without ambivalence. The thriving I'm imagining for the future isn't the same thriving we imagined when we were young. There is no Revolution. Property and identity aren't abolished. The institution of marriage looks, to paraphrase Justice Kennedy, strengthened. Our love is recognized legally, but in that sense we love with more rules, not fewer. (Web, n. p.)

Radical queers vociferously resist the co-opting of queer individuals by the state that threatens to sound the death knell of the queer movement's uncompromising iconoclasm. Despite a strong counter-discourse promoting queer politics as irreconcilable with any form of normativity, most First World countries, which apparently seem to provide an environment favourable for same-sex desires to thrive, champion an aggressive homonormativity as the only possible means by which sexual minorities might be meaningfully integrated into the mainstream. For instance, in the UK, at the Tory Party conference in October 2011, Prime Minister David Cameron made the most 'conservative' case about gay marriage while reasoning out the state's espousal of the same: 'Conservatives believe in the ties that bind us; that society is strong when we make vows to each other. . . . So I don't support gay marriage in spite of being a Conservative. I support it because I am a Conservative' (qtd. in Morgan, Web, n. p.).

Although legalisation of same-sex marriage or civil partnership has been welcomed by several members of the LGBT community, the moment also marked a temporary failure of queer politics. For legalisation of same-sex marriage, based on the ideals of monogamy, is seen as a compulsory step in reducing the possibility of the spread of sexually transmitted diseases of which the radical, uncommitted homosexual individual, with multiple sexual partners, is marked out and pathologised as a potential carrier. The endless moralising against the unharnessed, promiscuous queers, vulnerable to as well as carriers of life-threatening STDs, often makes a strong case in favour of the adoption of homonormativity. Interestingly, the unhitched queer, opposed to marriage or civil partnership, is very often judged and looked down upon by other members of the LGBT community who willingly submit to the state's apparently lucrative schemes of assimilating them. Currently, therefore, in First World countries, the movement has seen a bifurcation along the lines of radicalism and submission to the state's assimilative strategies, opening up spaces for further disputes and controversies over 'being queer', whereby 'queer' has become an even more fluid signifier, anticipating a wide range of indeterminable signifieds.

A QUEER 'THIRD WORLD'

Let us consider three interesting historical moments from the recent past in three postcolonial nations vis-à-vis recognition of queer identities.

Sri Lanka, 1995: The colonial law (Section 365A of the Penal Code of 1883 No. 2, Cap. 19) that criminalises homosexuality was amended to include lesbianism under the Penal Code (Amendment) Act No. 22 of 1995. The term 'man' in the colonial law was replaced by 'person' and 'carnal intercourse against the order of nature' was changed to acts of 'gross indecency with any person', whereby the law was de-gendered to make it more inclusive (read, more exclusionary) of any form of sexual act considered outside the approved heteronormative ways of (procreative) sexual associations. This was, ironically, a state response to the demand by LGBT and human rights activists that the colonial law be repealed.

India, 2013: The colonial law (Section 377 of the Indian Penal Code, which was drafted by Macaulay in 1860), which was read down in a momentous verdict by the Delhi High Court in 2009 in the historic case of Naz Foundation vs. National Capital Territory of Delhi, was reinforced by the Supreme Court of India on 11 December. One reason cited by the court was that LGBT people were a 'miniscule fraction' of the population and therefore it did not matter whether their rights were protected.

Uganda, 2014: The Uganda Anti-Homosexual Act 2014 was passed by the Parliament of Uganda and signed into law by President Museveni on 24 February. On 1 August, the law was ruled invalid by the Constitutional Court of Uganda on procedural grounds. But the debate surrounding the necessity of introducing such a law had been under consideration for a long time, creating in Uganda a virulent homophobic environment in which sexually non-conforming citizens felt and still feel constantly persecuted.

The pathologisation and vilification of the 'homosexual' as a criminal, a dangerous 'outlaw', a sick individual who engages in an 'unnatural' sexual practice, is rampant in former colonies of Britain since the nineteenth century. In fact, the arrival of colonial laws, as an important signifier of the arrival of Western modernity to the non-West, effectuated in its wake an awareness of what is licit and what is not as regards to sex and sexuality. At the same time, the increasing (scientific) knowledge production in the arena of sex, sexuality and sexual maladies in nineteenth-century Europe, which soon travelled to the non-West, brought about a transformation in the ways in which sex and sexuality were perceived in these countries. As Foucault has eloquently argued, as opposed to such non-Christian civilisations as China, Japan, India, Rome and the Arobo-Moslem societies which 'endowed themselves with an *ars erotica*' (*Discipline and Punish* 57), Anglo-European civilisation has only practised '*scientia sexualis*', or only developed 'procedures for telling the truth of sex geared to a form of knowledge-power . . .' (58). However, with the arrival of colonial laws and formation of new disciplines of knowledge which constantly pathologised any form of sexual association other than procreative sex between men and women, the magnificent cultures of *ars erotica* in the non-West soon came to be vilified as decadent, immoral and in bad taste, and therefore, in need of suppression or obliteration. The introduction of the term 'homosexual' as a label for a kind of perversion, and 'homosexuality' itself as a medical condition, threatened to wipe out all positive markers of homoerotic intimacies in relatively more tolerant pre-colonial cultures of the non-West. One example of this could be Altaf Hussain Hali's 1882 campaign for cleansing Urdu poetry of homoeroticism, especially of what is known as 'boy love' (Vanita and Kidwai 228).

The construction of the modern 'homosexual' by scientific discourses of the West had such an impact on the colonial world that it began denying having 'known' what same-sex desires at all meant, although numerous evidences to the contrary still exist. The introduction of the anti-sodomy law in the colonies led to the formation of a sexual subject who had to be eliminated or pathologised or punished. This is again best described by Foucault in his *Discipline and Punish: The Birth of the Prison* (1975): '. . . the constitution of the individual as a describable, analyzable object . . . in order to maintain him in his individual features, in his particular evolution, in his own aptitudes and abilities, under the gaze of a permanent corpus of knowledge' (190). The 'homosexual' suddenly became that 'describable, analyzable object', the production of a 'corpus of knowledge' about whom rendered him/her extremely vulnerable. The most intriguing case in point is the outlawing of lesbians in Sri Lanka, whom the colonial law, too obsessed with the act of sodomy and the perceived loss of manliness it supposedly engendered, had kept out of its purview. Interestingly, the 'homosexual' still remains an outlaw in many of the former colonies of Britain and Europe, although Britain legalised same-sex relations among adult citizens in 1967 and anti-sodomy law has been repealed in almost all European countries.

Arvin Narrain, talking about the impact that Section 377 of the Indian Penal Code has had on Indian queer lives, writes of how all-pervasive this law has become, and about how this had shrunk the possibility of legalising homosexuality in India: 'Section 377 is . . . not just a law but a worldview which remains entrenched in legal structures, medical, family and media discourses and perhaps, most strongly, in the "common sense" understanding of people' (257). One may cite what Bizay Sonkar Shastri, a spokesperson for the ruling party in India in 2016, told the press: 'Going against the nature is dangerous for human beings. This (homosexuality) is a criminal act. It must be stopped. For this purpose, we need Section 377' (Tiwari, Web, n. p.). This is precisely what constitutes the 'common sense' of the masses whose minds have been programmed into perceiving homosexuality as 'unnatural', the most debated term in the colonial law drafted in 1860. This mindset has not really changed even after the reading down of Section 377 of the IPC in 2018. In a peculiar reversal of the colonial rhetoric – that homosexuality was never part of white, Christian cultures, but was a perversion prolific in the colonies – in almost all postcolonial nations, homosexuality is now reprimanded as a Western import, alien to precolonial cultures. For example, the former Zimbabwean President Robert Mugabe has vehemently maintained that homosexuality is un-African, and has often framed his opposition to LGBTQ rights as his resistance to US imperialism: 'We reject attempts to prescribe new rights that are contrary to our values, norms, traditions and beliefs' (qtd. in Sanchez, Web, n. p.), he said in a speech to the United Nations in 2015.

The LGBTQ movement in the Third World is, therefore, faced with several obstacles and challenges: traditionalist, nationalist and religious, among many others.[1] Turning to South Asia, a recent incident in Bangladesh could reveal the precarity LGBTQ people are thrust into in that geopolitical area. The incident which shook the world involved the brutal murder of Xulhaz Mannan, founder of *Roopbaan*, the lone LGBTQ magazine in the country. He was under vigilance since he launched this magazine and had begun organising a Pride March, the Rainbow Rally, on the Bengali New Year's Day in Dhaka since 2014. He was threatened multiple times before he and his friend were killed by six men on 25 April 2016. What was mentioned in passing in many reports which carried the news was actually the key information which needs to be probed in order to make complete sense of this murder: Mannan was an employee of the United States Agency for International Development (USAid), which had already alienated him in the eyes of the fundamentalists, and whereby he had, in all probability, been perceived as an agent of US imperialism. His association with the LGBTQ rights movement and his status as an 'out' gay man were also viewed as an extension of his work for USAid – an attempt at imposing Euro-American notions of sexual liberalism on an Islamic state, which, as the popular belief goes, did not know of homosexuality and other such 'perversions'. In this murder, one can read a message similar to what Mugabe unabashedly put across in the UN meet (cited above). The state of Bangladesh is also obdurately opposed to recognising LGBTQ rights. However, in recent times, both India and Bangladesh have adopted favourable policies for *hijras* (a community of transgender women).

Within LGBTQ communities in the developing countries, there is a continuous demand to break away from the sexual identity politics of the West. The commonest rationale cited is that in the non-West, sexually divergent individuals do not necessarily understand or live their sexualities the way Americans or Europeans do. Historically and culturally, being gay, lesbian, bisexual or transgender in North America is not the same as being *kothi* or *poonaya* in India or Sri Lanka. For instance, it is not difficult to see the inadequacies of the Euro-American model of understanding queer kinship patterns in explaining the arrangement between *launda* dancers (feminine young boys who perform at local musical programmes in small towns and rural areas), their *parik*s and their wives and children in Bihar and Uttar Pradesh in India. As Dasgupta writes,

> [An] interesting facet of the *launda* community is the way in which kinship/family and desire is re-routed for economic purposes. Most of the *launda* dancers I interviewed entered the profession with the promise that they would land a *parikh* (partner/husband) in Uttar Pradesh and Bihar. They were also promised that they would be able to stay and live their lives as women during the dancing season, which was also a huge draw. Most of the *bajawalas* ended up having a relationship with one of the *launda* dancers, even though they were married. The wives were aware of this arrangement and, as I was told, they did not mind it. ('Launda Dancers' 446)

Postcolonial, Queer: Theoretical Intersections (2001), an anthology edited by John C. Hawley, has brought together reflections on queer lives from the non-West, from places as far apart as Algeria and Taiwan. Dennis Altman's article which opens the volume sets the tone of a critique of Western imperialism and globalisation of queer identities, raising questions about modernity and queer cultures, which have different histories in different locales. Further work has been done in this field, one of the most recent being akshay khanna's *Sexualness.* Centred on the emergence of the LGBTQ movement in India, and its impact in small towns and metropolitan spaces, khanna's work analyses what is at stake in anthropological approaches based on Euro-American models to make sense of 'sexualness' in the non-West. Other such works have also been produced from various other countries.

TALKING SEX: THE EROTICS OF QUEER STUDIES

It would be apt to begin this section with an extract from an article by Jon Binnie, written in 1997: 'Heterosexuals seem to cope with queer theory in its most abstract, intellectualised, disembodied form, but then to run scared when confronted with the materiality of lesbian, bisexual and gay lives, experiences and embodiments' (qtd. in Binnie 167).

Queer Studies is incomplete without talking about sex, the erotic dynamics within queer communities, cruising areas, social networking sites/apps, sex clubs, bathhouses, fetishes, pornography and prostitution. In other words, Queer Studies demands a dismantling of bourgeois taboos associated with sex acts, articulating sexual desires, and challenging the notions of decency and respectability of 'polite' society regarding anything bodily or sexual. This aspect of Queer Studies is often frowned upon even by members of the queer community, for, according to them, it tends to 'demean' queer men and women as hypersexual and promiscuous. In this view, too much attention on sexual lives, acts and practices further degrades sexually dissident individuals in the eyes of society, harming their political agenda of acquiring rights and equal citizenship. The problem with this argument is that it callously accepts society as heteronormative and 'normally' so, and locates queer individuals on its fringes, as the dangerous and, very often, the depraved 'other'. It also seems to assume that sexual transgression, erotic excess and promiscuity characterise queer folks only, and are alien to those who claim themselves heterosexuals. This discussion is allowed as long as it situates itself within morally charged discourses of safe sex practices, in the exigency to thwart the transmission of STDs, often holding the promiscuous queer individual solely responsible for the proliferation of such diseases.

The increasing normativisation of queer men and women; recurrent emphasis on embracing monogamous, domesticated, (apparently) desexualised lives which one sees in the justification for legalising same-sex marriage; adoption of, or technology-supported reproduction of, children by queer couples; and sanitised representation of queer coupledom in the popular media (for instance, in the immensely successful American TV series *Modern Family* which is currently into its ninth season), threaten to push discussions of sex, sex acts, polyamorous queers and the whole economy of sexual pleasures out of the boundary of the academia. However, it is impossible to deny the body, and sex, desires and pleasures around which the plurality of queer lives are organised; and an investigation into these will affirm the impossibility of polarising identities as homosexual and heterosexual, by inaugurating a whole gamut of desires that defy easy categorisation.

In an extremely well-argued paper, 'All Foucault and No Knickers: Assessing the Claims of a Queer-Political Erotics', Tamsin Wilton makes an important point about politicising private queer lives, for 'we are engaged with what *we* do in bed' (507; emphasis in the original). She emphasises the importance of tracing the history of the LGBTQ+ movement as having its roots in the 'sexual revolution' of the 1960s, a time when the citizens of the United States, horrified by the war images from Vietnam broadcast on television, 'turned to the theories of Sigmund Freud, Wilhelm Reich and Aleister Crowley to construct a radical discourse of erotic affiliation. Baffled and traumatised by the daily diet of real-life violence, this was a generation which set *eros* against *thanatos* and developed a radical politics of the erotic' (509). The evacuation of the erotic from the realm of feminist politics began to be seen in the works of lesbian feminists such as Sheila Jeffreys. In addition to that, the fear for promiscuous or transgressive sexual activities consequent to the AIDS endemic shrouded the discussion on the erotic with moral prescriptions.

One may cite Corber and Valocchi's interdisciplinary Queer Studies reader (2003) where they conscientiously included articles on private sex lives of genderqueer individuals, locating them within the political discourses of the LGBTQ+ movement. For example, C. Jacob Hale's 'Leatherdyke Boys and Their Daddies: How to Have Sex without Men or Women' eloquently deliberates on a particular sexual practice in which sexual and gender boundaries are shattered, and hegemonic ideas of the body, clothes, sex, gender and identity are infinitely problematised, insinuating the extremities of non-normativity queer lives can encompass. Here the focus is on a minority within the queer community: leatherdyke boys (dyke lesbian women) who perform a wide range of masculinities which are fathomable only within queer leather (SM) communities and their daddies who could be either butch leatherdykes or even gay leathermen. More importantly, age and sexual role are not compatible, as it is understood within daddy–son relationships within the gay community: for, here, the daddy may not necessarily be older than the boy. Hale articulates a wide range of sexual experiences which took her through a spectrum of desires, none of which can be simply classified as lesbian. This fluidity she experiences through her participation in various sexual acts makes her realise the impossibility of fixing an identity, which is always under erasure and always in the making:

> Is a leatherdyke daddy a woman or a man? Is a leatherdyke boy a woman or a man or a boy? These questions, I think, are badly misguided: they presuppose overly simplistic understanding of how gender categories work, and in so doing they reinscribe the hegemonic stranglehold of the dominant sex/gender/sexuality system. . . . From a broader cultural point of view, some nontranssexual, nonintersexual leatherdyke boys and daddies may not be easily classifiable if they do not clearly enough satisfy the defining criteria of the categories of woman and man. (66–67)

While Hale's unadulterated inside story of the leatherdyke subculture opens up erotic zones, unintelligible and even deeply disturbing to the dominant heteronormative prescriptions of lovemaking, Paul Boyce's work on the cruising areas in the city of Calcutta (now Kolkata), India, where men-having-sex-with-men (MSM) meet and engage in sexual acts, sexualises the city in a way it is barely ever imagined or represented in dominant cultural discourses. The revelation of these highly eroticised liminal spaces in the city, harbouring queer men in search of physical pleasures, transforms the social and cultural geography of Calcutta, investing queer lives with a power to challenge heteronormative or, in other words, only legitimate forms of sexual partnership. Boyce writes,

> The evident inter-play of male-to-male sexual life amidst ostensibly heteronormative contexts suggested that male-to-male sexuality in Calcutta was not necessarily signified by the appropriation of specific spaces, but, rather, was interlaced with a broader social context. This is not to say that cruising locales did not exist but these could not simply be mapped or perceived in respect of the presence of discretely identifiable men who have sex with men. (401)

At the time Boyce was writing his piece, men having sex with men in Calcutta (as elsewhere in India) did not necessarily identify themselves as gay, homosexual or queer – many still do not. However, in recent years, one sees an increasing awareness as regards to sex acts and their relation to identity discourses. The erotic energy of the cruising areas has of late shifted to virtual spaces of social networking sites and dating apps. These comparatively safer and hassle-free sites allow queer individuals in India to forge erotic intimacies and enter a kinship network, which was otherwise more difficult in real spaces of cruising areas. Rohit K. Dasgupta's recent book, *Digital Queer Cultures in India* (2017), draws attention to the importance of examining these digital spaces of sexual intimacies and friendships:

> Intimacy saturates queer interaction on cyberspace. Mediated by digital technology, the discourse of intimacy has not just been transformed, but has undergone a redefinition. Issues such as compassion, companionship, relationships and

> hook-ups on cyberspace remain central in understanding virtual intimacies. Mobile and digital media have defined new pathways and reconfigurations of public space. There has been a significant shift in the ways in which intimacy is played out on the public space through public postings, chatting on threads and blogs. Interactions have led to reciprocity, which is an important example of a way in which intimacy is performed on the digital screen. . . . Queer men, as everyone else, share the need for meaningful intimate contact that has allowed them to define new pathways in order to be able to express their love and sexuality. (56–57)

Queer Studies is incomplete without talking about these sites of intimacies, of sex and romance, of the erotic dimensions of these virtual as well as real spaces. Boyce's and Dasgupta's works focusing on the 'hidden' lives of Indian queer men challenge heteronormative registers of romance, and the sense of suspicion and apprehension regarding sexually active lives. These works defamiliarise known urban geographies, and debunk notions of compulsory heterosexuality, monogamous coupledom and engaging in sex only within the socially approved structure of marriage. They reveal an intriguing matrix of other forms of kinship, friendship and community lives, which threaten to shake the very foundation of heteropatriarchal society, notwithstanding its sustained refusal to acknowledge the existence of such a parallel universe.

One may ask whether these scholarly/autobiographical interventions into the erotic energies of queer relationships, mostly based on auto-ethnography, are also acts of confession, or compulsive truth-telling as Michel Foucault would put it. Even if they are, the production of this knowledge is immensely important, for it throws into disarray the concepts of legitimate and illegitimate sexual lives and sex acts, creating spaces for non-normative lives to exist. As Foucault says,

> Power is essentially what dictates its law to sex. Which means first of all sex is placed by power in a binary system: licit and illicit, permitted and forbidden. Secondly, power prescribes an "order" for sex that operates at the same time as a form of intelligibility: sex is to be deciphered on the basis of its relation to the law. And, finally, power acts by laying down the rule:

> power's hold on sex is maintained through language, or rather through the act of discourse that creates, from the very fact that it is articulated, a rule of law. (*History of Sexuality Vol. 1* 83)

These narratives involving queer sexual pleasures challenge the heteronormative power play surrounding sex and sexuality, operating through an imposition of a law of prohibition which implies renunciation of sex, and a ruthless suppression if one dares to articulate desires that are proscribed: 'Renounce yourself or suffer the penalty of being suppressed; do not appear if you do not want to disappear' (Foucault, *History of Sexuality Vol. 1* 84). As Jeffery Weeks wrote, 'The subject of sex has moved to centre stage in contemporary political and moral discourse. Through it we are expected to express our subjectivity, our sense of intimate self, our "identity". Through its grids of definition we are subjected to the operations of power, fixed in a world which tries to form us, but which we could re-form' (5). The operative term here is *re-form*; this is precisely the objective of talking about unnameable desires, of sexual practices, of bodily pleasures.

IS THERE A QUEER LANGUAGE?

Certainly there is a queer language – in fact, languages. Every culture has its own lexicon of queer language, which consists not only of words but also of non-verbal expressions such as body language, gestures or certain kinds of gaze. The first glossary of 'homosexual' language, compiled by Gershon Legman, can be traced back to 1941. It appeared as an appendix to a book, *Sex Variants: A Study of Homosexual Patterns* by George Henry. The appendix listed 329 terms often used by gay men; however, the book, as Anna Livia and Kira Hall tell us, was meant for the consumption of those who were into 'medical and allied professions only' (4). However, the discussion on queer language always begins with the controversies surrounding each term used in Queer Studies, including the term 'queer' itself. On the one hand, each and every term that has originated in the Euro-American cultures is often challenged within the West itself for their failure to encapsulate the indeterminable range of sexualities; on the other hand, as mentioned earlier, the non-West constantly resists and defies the linguistic imperialism of these terms. Despite their global usefulness, these terms are inadequate and delimiting for they fail to articulate the political, cultural and erotic economy of same-sex associations in the non-West, which, in many ways, are distinctively different from how the West understands it. Homosexual countercultures across the globe have different languages and modalities of communication, which, in many cases, are unintelligible to those even from within the same linguistic community if they are not familiar with the nuances of that language.

One is intrigued by the multiplicity of terms that were prevalent in the non-West prior to the emergence of words such as 'gay', 'lesbian', 'bisexual' or 'queer' as they are understood today. *Xanith/Khanith* (Oman), *bantut* (Indonesia), *tongzhi* (China), *kothi* (India), *travesty* (Brazil), *poonaya* (Sri Lanka) – this list may go on endlessly. All these terms are variously used to identify feminine men who have sex with other men, men desiring sexual reassignment and transvestites. Similarly, *chapatibaz* is a term often used in North India for women who are erotically involved with other women. One may note that these terms or identity markers are not frequently used in everyday parlance, and that the realisation of a certain sexual subjecthood dawns on same-sex desiring individuals on establishing contact with others who have already been ushered into understanding their sexualities on being tutored in a language which was so far not available to them. If identity is the retrospective effect of naming, as Lacan has observed, akshay khanna, in his auto-ethnographic research on the *kothi*s of Bengal, finds many of his respondents re-visioning their own personhood on learning terms and labels which they did not know of: 'I was always a *Kothi*, and just didn't know it' (104). This is also true of 'gay', 'lesbian', 'bisexual' or 'queer'. Men and women have engaged in same-sex relations in every culture without perceiving themselves as an aberrant 'sexuality type' until a certain kind of language emerged to mark them out as a special category. The invention of these terms and the political currency they gained also engendered a pathological homophobia within cultures which were so far comparatively more forbearing towards same-sex associations. Consequently, disciplinary mechanisms to punish the sexual 'other' – *named* 'gay', 'lesbian', 'transgender', etc. – became more stringent, as discussed earlier.

Homosexual countercultures across the globe have developed an alternative mode of communication, language as well as non-verbal signs. This language is often coded, and this code-switching is sometimes necessary for survival. In Bengal, for example, there is a dynamic language, known as *ulti-bhasa*, which is used by both *kothi*s and *hijra*s. Ajay Majumdar and Niloy Basu in a groundbreaking work entitled *Samaprem: samakamita bishoyok ekti samaj-monostwatik anweshan* (An Equal Love: A Socio-psychological Investigation into the Subject of Homosexuality), published in Bengali in 2005, records the details of a *kothi* dialect in Bengal – its richness, its disregard for cultivated gentility and its coded nature. This *kothi* dialect has a specifically feminine intonation, mimicking the language usually used by women, not so much by men. The *kothi*s imagining themselves as women, address each other as *bon* (sister), or *didi* (elder sister) or even *ma* (mother) while addressing those who are older. Within *kothi* communities, lovers or sexual partners are called *parik* – these *parik*s are 'straight-acting', more often than not bisexual, even married men, who engage in sexual acts with *kothi*s, without necessarily aligning their sexual identities with sexual minorities. Notably, neither *kothi* nor *parik* is easily intelligible to even those whose mother tongue is Bengali, if they are not familiar with this counterculture. A whole lot of identity markers exist within *kothi* communities across India, each having an interesting etymological history: *panthi*, *dhurrani*, *maunga*, *dupli*, etc. None of these words can be translated into English satisfactorily; every word would require a footnote elucidating its distinctiveness from its closest English synonym.

The *kothi* dialect, apart from having a series of proverbs, adages, skits and rhymes, has a whole range of words for sexual organs and sex acts, underlining a sexually vibrant counterculture. Majumdar and Basu enlist several of these words, explaining their necessity – in order to make the sexual lives of *kothi*s unintelligible to common people, *kothi*s have invented a coded language (206). For example, *likam* (penis), *forcun* (erection), *khajra* (sex worker), etc., are terms which barely have any use outside *kothi* communities. Interestingly, this language is not available or even comprehensible to *kothi*s of all classes. Within *kothi* communities, *kothi*s are further labelled according to their socioeconomic conditions, sexual behaviour, choice of clothes (as in whether they openly cross-dress or not), etc. These labels too are confined within the *kothi* counterculture, and may not make sense to an outsider. For example, affluent, English-educated, urban *kothi*s are called *kaditaler kothi*; middle-class or lower-middle-class *kothi*s with limited access to consumerist cultures or modern education are called *lahari kothi*s; and *kothi*s belonging to extremely poor sections of the society are called *bila kothi*s. *Kaditaler kothi*s, for example, are usually unfamiliar with this coded language of the *kothi* community, or for that matter, with this very label which marks them out within such communities. They maintain a studied distance from this local counterculture for its apparent disregard for bourgeois politeness and social decorum. They are more comfortable in identifying themselves as 'gay' rather than *kothi*, often citing the uncouthness of such a label. Thus, an extremely complex nexus of identity, class and language is observed within the local *kothi* counterculture of Bengal (or India at large), which, as one realises, is far from homogenous. Nonetheless, *ulti-bhasa* still survives and continues to challenge not only bourgeois notions of politeness and decency, but also denies outsiders easy access to the everyday lives of *kothi*s. The term *ulti*, meaning alternative or reverse or even upside down, encapsulates the queerness of the language, its disruptive potential, and its resistance to normative speech patterns.

One important concern with regard to queer language has been the necessity of adopting gender-neutral pronouns. In fact, there is a rising demand for abandoning binary common nouns – 'man' and 'woman' – in favour of 'person'. Transport for London (TfL), the organisation which runs the road and rail networks in Greater London, was recently in the news (July 2017) for doing away with the phrase 'ladies and gentlemen', and using 'Good morning everyone' to make passengers, notwithstanding the gender/sexuality they identify with personally, feel more welcome. The *Independent* quoted a spokesman for Stonewall who said, 'Language is extremely important to the lesbian, gay, bi and trans community, and the way we use it can help ensure all people feel included. We welcome gender neutral announcements to be rolled out across TfL, as it will ensure that everyone – no matter who they identify as – feels accounted for' (Meier, Web, n. p.).

Earlier in 2017, University of Sussex introduced a gender-neutral language policy. Rose Taylor, Postgraduate Education Officer for Sussex University Student Union, told the *Independent:* 'The gender-neutral pronoun "they" should be used as opposed to "he" or "she", and the pronoun "them" as opposed to "him" or "her". Individuals whose gender identities are not known should not be described as "men" or "women", and inclusive terms such as "person" should be used instead' (qtd. in Pells, Web, n. p.). The University of Tennessee in the United States had already issued a policy regarding the usage of gender-neutral pronouns, and in the summer of 2017, Boarding Schools' Association, UK, issued guidance for teachers to address transgender pupils as 'zie', a much-debated pronoun which has been in circulation for a while within queer circles. There is an increasing demand for doing away with 'he' and 'she' in favour of 'zie', and 'hir' in place of 'him'/'his'/'her'. While other terms have also been proposed, and no global consensus has been reached in terms of usage of gender-neutral pronouns in English, one cannot help wonder the complications that might arise if some South Asian languages, for instance Hindi, were to be emptied of gender. It must be noted here that it is not precisely in the wake of the LGBTQ+ movement and increasing awareness of the existence of multiple sexualities that the need for a gender-neutral language has been realised. One may find such debates in the nineteenth century in both the UK and the US regarding the need for non-binary pronouns in the English language (see Baron).

LGBT ACTIVISM AND KNOWLEDGE PRODUCTION

LGBT activism has no doubt played a significant role in knowledge production about the history of homosexuality, everyday lives of LGBT people, the necessity for legal protection of such lives, the AIDS epidemic which has plagued the community for years and how to prevent it, and so on. Without activist initiatives at network, alliance and awareness building, Queer Studies as a discipline could not have emerged in the academia. In fact, Queer Studies as a dynamic and politically charged discipline constantly needs to renew itself in relation to LGBT activism which deals with lives of real citizen-subjects, their everyday misgivings, anguish, and their constant struggle for achieving right to a dignified life. Queer Studies within the academia can only survive meaningfully when there are regular exchanges between academicians and social workers and NGOs. In other words, Queer Studies, which has been heavily informed and inspired by activism, should take into account the importance of doing 'public sociology' (a term proposed by Herbert J. Gans in 2002), which would ensure a more evocative methodology of dissipating knowledge as Santos says,

> Methodologically, this would imply favouring plural data generation methods and analytical techniques—triangulation—as a way to benefit from different perspectives and analytical insights, rather than making knowledge production dependent on single, top-down contributions. From an ethical point of view, a commitment to public sociology implies abiding by the guiding principles of accountability, intersectionality, reciprocity and reflexivity. . . . It would also represent a commitment to activism as a significant part of citizenship and an embracement of politics as an intended effect of knowledge production. (245)

While the continuous exchange between activism and academia is necessary, the very initiation of Queer Studies, as we shall show in greater detail in the concluding chapter of this book, could not have been possible had there not been sufficient material for framing a syllabus, material generated by activists with the agenda of making a favourable case for sexual minorities' right to a dignified life. In this connection, many organisational activities facilitating Queer Studies could be cited; and alternatively, how subjective experiences of activism have produced material – books, articles, etc. – which have proved to be extremely helpful in the academia. One such work is akshay khanna's *Sexualness* which we have referred to several times in this book. Here, we shall briefly talk about the contribution of two South Asian organisations – Kolkata's Counsel Club (founded in the early 1990s) which had the primary role in organising the first

Pride March or Friendship Walk in India (1999), and Colombo's Equal Ground (founded in 2004) which have played pioneering role in LGBT organising in the country in knowledge-production.

In Kolkata, *Pravartak*, edited by Pawan Dhall, made its appearance in 1991, just one year after the LGBT movement in the US had seen a paradigm shift with the birth of the Queer Nation, when the immediate need was to save hundreds of lives threatened by the AIDS virus. Turning the pages of *Pravartak* one is struck by the several discourses on AIDS, constructed through newspaper cuttings, instructions on safety measures against the virus, and a plea not to alienate AIDS-infected individuals. While some basic questions about homosexuality were addressed from time to time, what appeared as a major concern was to combat the AIDS epidemic. *Pravartak* in retrospection appears to be a significant project which sowed the seeds of a larger political alliance to germinate – as an outreach magazine, it not only functioned as an educator, but also helped establish an LGBT network, by providing from time to time addresses of queer-friendly organisations in India, of magazines and newsletters produced within the country or abroad, apart from bibliographies. Interestingly, it also had a segment on creative expressions in which queer short stories were published. *Pravartak*, at the very outset, made it clear that while activism should have to go back to academia – anthropological, sociological or literary documents – as underlined by the bibliographies they never failed to share, academia would also have ample scope to learn and modify its theories based on activist histories.

Pravartak belonged to the pre-smartphone era; even computers had not yet entered middle-class homes in South Asia, and everybody did not have access to the Internet, the latter being rather expensive. E-mail was yet to enter the landscape of communication systems. Therefore, unlike today when one hashtag can launch a movement in the virtual space, the mechanism of sharing, reaching out and forming collectives was not a mouse-click away. The first issue of *Pravartak*, launched in the first week of December 1991, listed four Indian organisations – Bombay Dost, Sakhi, Garden City Club and Friends India – along with complete mailing addresses. In the second issue (16–31 December 1991) one sees a listing of international publications and organisations, again with complete addresses, three of which were US-based – *Paz Y Liberacion* (Peace and Liberation), *The Barangay News* and *Shamakami*. The fourth one was Khush, an organisation based in Canada. In those times, which are only two decades behind us, it was quite a mission for an Indian LGBT person to 'find' someone like him or her. Under such circumstances, launching a political movement was an uphill task; there were not enough individuals who were out and about, and were willing to come forward to participate in a coalitional protest.

Pravartak went dormant for a few months, only to be revived by the Counsel Club founded in August 1993, as its house journal. In *Kolkata's Queer Movement: A Recollection of Media Outings – Mid-1984 to Mid-2013*, Pawan Dhall recalls the fascinating stories of the foundation of the Counsel Club which barely knew then that it would go down in history as one of the primary actors in organising the first Pride in India. However, as the Club embarked on its mission to decriminalise homosexuality, to create awareness about the 'normality' of homosexuality, and to combat the AIDS epidemic, it also became a site of coalition building. This coalition building did not only happen through outreach programmes or through physical attendance of queer people of the city, but also through letters which poured in from both queer and curious people in large numbers. Dhall recalls with a sense of exhilaration how these letters opened up a floodgate of emotions, possible love stories and plain inquisitiveness about homosexuality. He writes,

> From youth in their early 20s to the middle aged; from students and teachers to doctors and the odd housewife; from brief, hesitating, incoherent enquiries about *Pravartak*, salacious queries about access to sexual partners and space for having sex, to personal outpourings of loneliness, grief, oppression, unhappy marriages, sexual experiences and love stories – these letters were a microcosm of an India that was sexually active, liberal, inquisitive, orthodox and repressed, all at the same time. (Web, n. p.)

Just as the Stonewall Inn stands in Greenwich Village as a proud reminder of the historical moment of the riots, the Ballygunge Post Office where the Counsel Club postbag was housed became a mini iconic site where queer narratives accumulated in large numbers every week in sealed envelopes. These letters too are rich sources of affective queer lives which, when revisited with theoretical knowledge of sex, sexuality and identity politics, may reveal interesting insights into the history of the sexual minority population in India.

Therefore, *Pravartak* (and later the Varta Blog which has uploaded the older issues of the magazine) and the Counsel Club, while generating a literature for the LGBT movement to draw information from, were also enabling networking – the possibility of community formation – which was otherwise difficult. Outreach magazines which were born out of the initiative taken by LGBT activist groups became major sources of knowledge and information. And today, for an academician or an activist willing to pursue research in documenting the early history of the movement, the archives of these outreach magazines could prove to be productive resources for accomplishing such projects. These knowledge resources could now facilitate further knowledge production within the academia.

In Sri Lanka, it is Equal Ground which has done path-breaking work in securing lives of LGBT people who are under constant surveillance by the state and conservative religious groups. The civil war which continued for years further shrunk democratic spaces within the country, majorly affecting the lives of LGBT citizens. Yet, despite an extremely hostile environment and threats from various sectors, Equal Ground has worked relentlessly in order to ensure a better life for Sri Lanka's LGBT population. What role did it have in knowledge-production? Just like the Counsel Club, Equal Ground has its own magazines, *Equality* and *The Rainbow News*, which cover a wide range of issues, events and other relevant information to project queerness in a positive light. The homepage of the Equal Ground website states, 'Equal Ground feels that the dissemination of information via our publications is an integral part of sensitising the public and empowering the LGBTIQ community as well. We also engage in research activities and publish findings for better understanding of the status of LGBTIQ rights in Sri Lanka' (Web, n. p.). Amongst several of its publications, three in particular are important: *Mapping LGBT in Colombo, Kandy, Matara and Nuwara Eliya* by Kemone Brown, *Struggling against Homophobic Violence and Hate Crimes against Lesbian and Bisexual Women in the Rural Areas* – a report, and *Stepping Out: For Parents of Children with Alternate Sexual Orientations and Gender Identities*. As the titles of these publications suggest, these are meant for awareness-building and also bringing to the fore the precarious lives LGBT people are forced to live. The knowledge dissemination that these publications ensure is absolutely necessary for a movement to take root and to decriminalise homosexuality in the long run. It may be noted that Equal Ground makes it a point to go trilingual with most of its publications that enable the sensitisation of the non-English-educated citizens who are a numerical majority. This is important since the LGBT movement in South Asia has been for a long time led by an elite, English-speaking class of gays and lesbians. This initiative of Equal Ground helps to refute this allegation that is often brought against the community.

At the time of this book going to print, the Supreme Court of India has come back with their ruling on the unconstitutionality of Section 377. The five-judge constitutional bench heard the petitioner's plea and gave their verdict on 6 September 2018, where they reversed their 2013 judgement, declaring that consensual adult gay sex is not a crime. In its ruling, the Supreme Court deemed the prior law 'irrational, arbitrary and incomprehensible'. Most fittingly, they declared that majoritarian views and popular morality cannot dictate constitutional rights and that there is a need to vanquish prejudice, embrace inclusion and ensure equal rights. This heralds a major victory for queer rights in India and points again to the need for informed knowledge production and continuous civil activism.

LGBT activism is, therefore, informed by discourses on sex, sexuality and identity politics, and in turn it reinforces these discourses by interpolating them with lived histories of real people, with local cultures and environment influencing LGBT lives, and simultaneously, enabling sexual dissidence to take root and challenge state discrimination and oppression. Without relentless activism, continuous knowledge production about real people and their lived experiences, Queer Studies as a discipline cannot afford to survive.

NOTES

[1] This is not to claim that the LGBTQ movement is not confronted with the same obstacles in the West. A good example to cite in this context will be Bernadette Barton's book *Pray the Gay Away* (2012) in which she focuses on the infamous Bible Belt in the United States where homosexuals are often at the receiving end of vulgar hatred: bumper stickers claiming 'One Man + One Woman = Marriage', church billboards commanding one to 'Get right with Jesus', nightly news about homophobic attacks from the Family Foundation, and firing of gays and lesbians on account of their sexuality, are not uncommon.

REFERENCES

Altman, Dennis. 'Rupture or Continuity?: The Internationalization of Gay Identities'. *Postcolonial, Queer: Theoretical Intersections.* Ed. J. C. Hawley. New York: State U of New York P, 2001. 19–41. Print.

Anon. *Queers Read This: The Queer Nation Manifesto.* June 1990. Web. 10 June 2017. <http://www.qrd.org/qrd/misc/text/queers.read.this>.

Baron, Dennis. 'The Epicene Pronoun: The Word that Failed'. *American Speech* 56 (1981): 83–97. Print.

Barton, Bernadette. *Pray the Gay Away: The Extraordinary Lives of Bible Belt Gays.* New York and London: New York UP, 2012. Print.

Binnie, Jon. 'Rethinking the Place of Queer and the Erotic in within Geographies of Sexualities'. *The Ashgate Research Companion to Queer Theory.* Eds. Noreen Giffney and Michael O'Rourke. London and New York: Routledge, 2009. 167–80. Print.

Boyce, Paul. '(Dis)locating Male-to-Male sexualities in Calcutta: Subject, Space and Perception'. *The Phobic and the Erotic: The Politics of Sexualities in Contemporary India.* Eds. Brinda Bose and S. Bhattacharya. London and New York: Seagull, 2007. 399–414. Print.

Butler, Judith. *Bodies That Matter: On the Discursive Limits of 'Sex'.* New York and London: Routledge, 1993. Print.

Corber, Robert J., and Stephen Valocchi. 'Introduction'. *Queer Studies: An Interdisciplinary Reader.* Eds. R. J. Corber and Stephen Valocchi. Malden: Blackwell, 2013. 1–17. Print.

Dasgupta, R. K. *Digital Queer Cultures in India: Politics, Intimacies and Belonging*. London: Routledge, 2017. Print.

---. 'Launda Dancers: The Dancing Boys of India'. *Asian Affairs* XLIV. III (2013): 442–48. Print.

de Lauretis, Teresa. 'Habit Changes'. *differences: A Journal of Feminist Cultural Studies* 6.2–3 (1994): 296–313. Print.

---, ed. *Queer Theory: Lesbian and Gay Sexualities*. Spec. issue of *differences* 3 (1991). Print.

Dhall, Pawan. 'Memories in Media Outing – Part 2'. 17 June 2017. Web. 11 May 2018. <http://www.vartagensex.org/details.php?p=5947d13ba9926>.

Equal Ground. <www.equal-ground.org/>.

Foucault, Michel. *Discipline and Punish: The Birth of the Prison* (1975). Trans. Alan Sheridan. 2nd edition. New York: Vintage Books, 1995. Print.

---. *History of Sexuality* Vol. 1 (1976). Trans. Robert Hurley. Victoria: Penguin, 1984. Print.

Gans, H. J. 'More of Us should Become Public Sociologists' (2002). Web. 15 May 2018. <http://www.asanet.org/footnotes/julyaugust02/fn10.html>.

Hale, C. Jacob 'Leatherdyke Boys and Their Daddies: How to Have Sex Without Women or Men' (1997). *Queer Studies: An Interdisciplinary Reader*. Eds. R. J. Corber and Stephen Valocchi. Malden: Blackwell, 2013. 61–72. Print.

Halperin, David. 'The Normalisation of Queer Theory'. *Journal of Homosexuality* 45.2–4 (2003): 339–43. Print.

---. *Saint Foucault: Towards a Gay Hagiography*. New York: Oxford UP, 1995. Print.

Hawley, John C, ed. *Postcolonial, Queer: Theoretical Intersections*. New York: State U of New York P, 2001. Print.

Hennessy, Rosemary. 'Queer Theory: A Review of the "Differences" Special Issue and Wittig's "The Straight Mind"'. *Signs* 18.4. Theorizing Lesbian Experience (Summer 1993): 964–73. JSTOR. Web. 15 September 2018. <http://www.jstor.org/stable/3174918>.

Hoare, Philip. *Oscar Wilde's Last Stand: Decadence, Conspiracy, and the Most Outrageous Trial of the Century*. New York: Arcade Publishing, 1997. Print.

khanna, akshay. *Sexualness*. New Delhi: New Text, 2016. Print.

Livia, Anna, and Kira Hall, eds. *Queerly Phrased: Language, Gender, and Sexuality*. New York: Oxford UP, 1997. Print.

Majumdar, Ajay, and Niloy Basu. *Samaprem: Samakamita bishoyok ekti samaj-monostwatik anweshan* (An equal love: A socio-psychological investigation into the subject of homosexuality). Kolkata: Deep Prakashan, 2005 (reprint 2011). Print.

McIntosh, M. 'Queer Theory and the War of the Sexes'. *Feminisms*. Eds. S. Kemp and J. Squires. Oxford: Oxford UP, 1997. 364–67. Print.

Meier, Becca. 'London Tube Staff Ditch 'Ladies and Gentlemen' for Gender-neutral Greetings'. *The Independent*. 13 July 2017. Web. 15 July 2017. <http://www.independent.co.uk/news/uk/london-tube-underground-greeting-ladies-gentlemen-everyone-tfl-sadiq-khan-stonewall-a7839621.html>.

Morgan, Patricia. 'The Evidence that Blows apart Mr Cameron's Claim that Gay Marriage will Strengthen Families'. 22 May 2013. Web. 11 January 2017. <http://www.dailymail.co.uk/debate/article-2329294/The-evidence-blows-apart-Mr-Camerons-claim-gay-marriage-strengthenfamilies.html>.

Murphy, M. Lynne. 'The Elusive Bisexual: Social Categorization and Lexico-Semantic Change'. *Queerly Phrased: Language, Gender, and Sexuality*. Eds. Anna Livia and Kira Hall. New York: Oxford UP, 1997. 35–57. Print.

Naphy, William. *Born to be Gay: A History of Homosexuality*. Gloucestershire: Tempus, 2004. Print.

Narrain, Arvin. 'No Shortcuts to Queer Utopia: Sodomy, Law and Social Change'. *The Phobic and the Erotic: The Politics of Sexualities in Contemporary India*. Eds. Brinda Bose and S. Bhattacharyya. Calcutta: Seagull Books, 2007. 255–62. Print.

Pells, Rachael. 'Sussex University to Use Gender Neutral Pronouns as Students Request Greater Respect for Transgenders'. *The Independent*. 2 January 2017. Web. 18 March 2017. <http://www.independent.co.uk/student/news/sussex-university-gender-neutral-pronouns-transgender-lgbt-rights-brighton-sexuality-politics-a7505671.html>.

Sanchez, Nick. 'Robert Mugabe, Zimbabwe Dictator, Renounces Gay Rights in UN Speech'. *Newsmax*. 30 September 2015. Web.

7 August 2017. <https://www.newsmax.com/TheWire/robert-mugabe-zimbabwe-gay-righs-un/2015/09/30/id/694080/>.

Santos, Ana Cristina. 'Disclosed and Willing: Towards A Queer Public Sociology'. *Social Movement Studies: Journal of Social, Cultural and Political Protest* 11.2 (April 2012): 241–54. Print.

Stein, Jordan Alexander. 'Celebrating Marriage; Mourning the Queer Revolution'. *Outward: Expanding the LGBT Conversation*. 26 June 2015. Web. 1 July 2015. <http://www.slate.com/blogs/outward/2015/06/26/does_the_success_of_gay_marriage_mean_the_queer_revolution_has_failed.html?wpsrc=sh_all_mob_fb_bot>.

Tiwari, R. 'Section 377: Unlike RSS, BJP Shies Away from Taking a Stand on Homosexuality'. *The Economic Times*. 19 March 2016. Web. 7 August 2017. <https://economictimes.indiatimes.com/news/politics-and-nation/section-377-unlike-rss-bjp-shies-away-from-taking-a-stand-on-homosexuality/articleshow/51464248.cms>.

Vanita, Ruth, and Saleem Kidwai. *Same Sex Love in India: A Literary History*. Rev. ed. New Delhi: Penguin Books, 2008. Print.

Warner, Michael. 'Introduction: Fear of a Queer Planet'. *Social Text* 9 (4 [29], 1991): 3–17. Print.

Weeks, Jeffery. *Sexuality and Its Discontents: Meanings, Myths and Modern Sexualities* (1985). New York and London: Routledge, 2000. Print.

Wilton, Tamsin. 'All Foucault and No Knickers: Assessing the Claims of a Queer-Political Erotics'. *The Ashgate Research Companion to Queer Theory*. Eds. Noreen Giffney and Michael O'Rourke. London and New York: Routledge, 2009. 507–22. Print.

Chapter One

A Preamble to Queer Studies

DISCURSIVELY CONSTITUTING THE 'HOMOSEXUAL'

As discussed in the introduction, the reclamation of the term 'queer' and the proposition of the possibility of a 'Queer Theory' happened almost simultaneously in the United States, in the beginning of the 1990s. The emergence of Queer Theory and, subsequently, the discipline of Queer Studies was preceded by a long preamble in which the 'homosexual' was firmly constituted as an unnatural species in the public imagination, followed by cultural, anthropological, sexological and psychological interventions which challenged this discursive constitution of the 'homosexual', leading to the emergence of Gay and Lesbian Studies. The shift from Gay and Lesbian Studies to Queer Studies happened only in the 1990s, parallel to a poststructuralist shift in cultural, social, literary and gender theories. However, this chapter has no scope to historicise homosexuality; it will trace in brief what precisely led to the formulation of Queer Studies in the late twentieth century. This, we argue, was enabled by the increased production and circulation of writings on divergent sexualities that could be traced back to the early modern West, as print culture began to flourish. Besides, certain organised movements helped the discipline to emerge.

THE PRECARIOUS LIFE OF THE SODOMITE

The year 1868 is a landmark in the history of 'homosexuality' – it is the year in which the term came into existence. Literatures on homosexuality (and sexuality in general) became available from the second half of the nineteenth century in North America, Europe and Britain, as the white man was gradually introduced to sexual economies, which were so far unknown to him, in the New World. Although terms such as 'lesbian', 'sodomite', 'tribade', 'Ganymede', 'sapphist' and 'Uranian' were common in the West before 1848, the coinage of the term 'homosexual', and subsequently 'heterosexual', generated a hitherto nonexistent binary opposition, adding to the unending range of binaries reinforcing the Self/Other discourse on which the colonial enterprise ideologically premised itself. However, the 'homosexual' was not really a species outside the boundaries of the 'civilised' West, but very much inside it. Although the false notion that homosexuality was un-European and belonged to the 'less civilised' colonies which functioned on *natural* rather than *cultural* laws, was widely dissipated later, the homosexual at home had to be severely punished, ostracised and strategically obliterated by constituting repressive laws. The Oscar Wilde trials in England in 1895 are a case in point. As Ashis Nandy writes,

> It is well-known that Wilde's homosexuality would have been "forgiven" had he been more discreet about it; had he, for instance, not instituted criminal proceedings against the Marquess. Victorian England was willing to tolerate Wilde's sexual identity as long as it was accepted as part of the lifestyle of a marginal sect and not openly flaunted. But by demonstratively using homosexuality as a cultural ideology, Wilde threatened to sabotage his community's dominant self-image as a community of well-defined men, with clear-cut man-woman relationships . . . his blatant deviation from rigidly defined sexual roles . . . was working out meanings . . . in a colony thousands of miles away. (45)

Although Wilde's unpretentious articulations of his sexuality brought about his ruin, leading to the coinage of the abusive phrase 'friends of Oscar', a euphemism for detestable homosexuals, what the Anglo-European and American world was threatened with was the gradual yet powerful surfacing of a homosexual counterculture.

Homosexuals, even when they were not called so, had always existed as a strong subculture in the Judaic and Christian worlds. Or else, why would the *Book of Leviticus* warn against sexual intimacy between men? For instance, 'If a man lies with a man as one lies with a woman, both of them have done what is detestable. They must be put to death; their blood will be on their own heads' (20:13). For another instance, the figure of the 'sodomite' in early modern England was treated with suspicion and disgust, notwithstanding how cerebrally the 'male friend' was exalted in John Lyly's *Euphues* (1578) or Shakespearean sonnets. Although, when looked at through a queer lens, these texts seem to project homoeroticism in a positive light, it is also important to locate such male–male bonding within the neoplatonic discourse of friendship, the kind engendered by Cicero's *Laeliusde amicitia* written in 44 BC, and which became available during the English Renaissance. The 'male friend' was always distinguished from the 'sodomite', the profanity of which was incomparable to the sacred status of the former, for the 'sodomite' was a lot more than just a sexual dissident in early modern times. Sodomy, as Alan Bray observes, was not only a sexual crime but also a religious and political crime, something close to debauchery. Bray quotes the jurist Edward Coke (1552–1634) who wrote that sodomy was sinning against nature because it symbolised sinning against the king, 'celestial or terrestrial' (Bray 41–43).

While the image of the 'male friend' was being fiercely protected from being confused with that of the 'sodomite', puritans in Elizabethan England were vociferously contemptuous of the world of theatre where young boys dressed up as women to entertain. This literature when put together reveals the anxiety of a hetero-patriarchal society for any form of sexual ambiguity that could threaten to dismantle its foundation. Cross-dressing or transvestism on the streets, especially women dressed in men's clothing, had also become a phenomenon at that time. A Cecilia or a Rosalind, cross-dressing to hide their identities in *As You Like It*, obliquely alludes to this practice, and also creates a great deal of hilarious 'confusion' on stage which is resolved in the end. As long as the 'confusion' continues, it problematises questions of gender and sexuality to a great extent, sufficient to ruffle the feathers of Elizabethan puritans. Men dressed up as women on stage, or women dressed up as men on the streets, caused much 'confusion' – a word which had a layered meaning in Elizabethan England. 'Confusion', according to King

James' Bible, could connote 'abomination' and 'strange' (which also means 'queer') or any unnatural act or union (from the Latin verb *confundere*, meaning 'mingle together'). In the fourteenth century, 'confusion' also meant 'putting to shame', which can be equated with the idea of shaming the cross-dresser, as one sees in several pamphlets of those times.

In fact, the Elizabethan Sumptuary Statutes restricted sumptuousness or extravagance in choice of garments and regulated citizens' choice of clothes in accordance with their class and gender, in order to eliminate any kind of class or gender 'confusion'. The Book of Deuteronomy 22.5 was often quoted by those who were deeply troubled by the anarchic potential of cross-dressing whether on the streets or on the stage: 'The woman shall not wear that which pertaineth unto a man, neither shall a man put on a woman's garment: for all that do so are abomination unto the Lord thy God.' However, it seems the words of God and repetitive reminders of the same by earthly mortals fell on deaf ears, and those who wished to transgress the gendered dress codes did so without demur. This is evidenced by numerous pamphlets and other writings which reprimanded cross-dressing underlining the immorality and blasphemy associated with it, and also perhaps hinting at its ubiquity. Stephen Gosson's *Playes Confuted in Fiue Actions* (1582), Thomas Beard's thrice-printed *Theatre of God's Judgements* (1631), John Rainolds's *The Overthrow of Stage-Playes* (1599), Adam Hill's *The Crie of England* (1595), Philip Stubbes's *The Anatomie of Abuses* (1583) – all of these derided male cross-dressers in particular for indulging in a 'monstrous' act. The moral policing of the stage mostly voiced the anxiety that boy-actors dressed as women were capable of arousing uncontrollable feelings of lechery in male spectators.[1] The anti-homosexual discourse that would lead to and buttress the discursive constitution of the 'homosexual' in the nineteenth century was being formulated in early modern England.

The seventeenth and eighteenth centuries were even more intriguing in the sense that the mollies – men with sodomitical intent – began forming a covert subculture in various parts of London. With the founding of the Society for the Reformation of Manners in Tower Hamlets in 1690, molly districts were publicly identified, mollies were arrested and pilloried in public, and imprisoned. This subculture, in fact, contained the germs of a queer community which acquired a strong political valence in the late twentieth century. There are ample evidences of how sodomites even in the seventeenth century were developing a sense of identity based on their knowledge of great men who engaged in same-sex love in earlier periods of history. Norton cites William Walsh's satire, *A Dialogue Concerning Women*, published in 1691. In this poem, there are informed references to Socrates's love for Alcibiades, Plato's love for the boy Aster, and defences of homosexuality in the works of Plutarch, Lucian, Anacreon, Tibullus and Martial, as well as travellers' reports on homosexuality in Turkey, Italy and Spain (see Norton, Web, n. p.).

By 1720, the Society for Reformation of Manners was successful in shaming and prosecuting more than a hundred sodomites, along with prostitutes. However, the molly clubs, the cruising areas and the prosecutions were so widely written about that it facilitated the consolidation of the subculture even further. This was a paradoxical situation. Norton observes,

> The publicity given to homosexuality by the Societies—in sermons and tracts as well as the publicity attendant upon the raids and trials—must have made gay[2] men aware that a fair number of them were about town, and that they could pick one another up at the cruising grounds helpfully identified by worthy clergymen. (Web, n. p.)

By 1729, the concern about sexual immorality had become such an integral part of the public discourse that the Protestant Englishman John Disney brought out *A View of Ancient Laws against Immorality and Profaneness* in which he catalogued and reflected upon laws preventing polygamy, adultery, incest, rape, prostitution, bestiality and sodomy in bygone eras across cultures. The last two were discussed in the same chapter. Whereas *A Dialogue Concerning Women* catalogued ancient men having male lovers with a more or less positive intention, Disney countered it by cataloguing sodomy as a sin which the ancient laws, collected 'from the Jewish, Roman, Greek, Gothic, Lombard, and other laws, down to the middle of the eleventh century', did not approve of. Not all ancient societies outlawed sodomites, and Disney acknowledged how sodomy was 'shamefully' practised in some of the 'politest nations' by their philosophers and great men. But that could be a 'heathen' way of life which now was unfortunately rampant among Christians: 'this Practice (abominable as it is) has had and has its Followers in Christian Countries, and too many of them in our own' (181). He strongly recommended the 'necessity' of an anti-sodomy law. Notably, this book was written with the purpose of sycophantically asking for the king's patronage, for none other than the king, who had set an example by suppressing all kinds of (sexual) vice, could possibly endorse this book.

THE PATHOLOGISATION OF THE HOMOSEXUAL

At the turn of the nineteenth century, the 'homosexual' subculture gradually began to turn into a counterculture, when homosexual men and women began exhibiting their differences from the socially approved ways of performing one's gender. Simultaneously, anthropological explorations of the New World revealed homosexuality, transvestism and androgyny, which were indubitably perceived as sinful or unnatural divergence from the norm in the West, were so common across cultures that it was difficult to dismiss them as unusual or divergent. Michel Foucault's famous declaration, 'The sodomite had been a temporary aberration; the homosexual was now a species' (43), is perhaps the most telling aphorism on homosexuality as it began spawning new discourses, clinical or anthropological, in the late nineteenth century.

The nineteenth-century academic preoccupation with race, owing to the West's increasing political and cultural contacts with non-white populations, had body and sexuality at its centre. While genitalia were racially ranked, the non-Western primitive people were constantly projected as 'oversexed' both physically and socially. Andrew Lyons and Harriet Lyons, in their book *Sexualities in Anthropology: A Reader*, observe that evolutionary social theory had reached its acme of confidence when Victorian 'progressives' began to imagine and propagate 'a zero point of sexual promiscuity from which all peoples progressed at different paces on the road to monogamous, bourgeois marriages' (4). But soon, with an economic depression which struck the world at the *fin de siècle*, confidence in this social evolution theory began to recede.

Also, the neat structure of the Victorian family, with separate gender spheres, as marked out by the likes of John Ruskin in 'Of Queen's Gardens' (1864), began to dissemble with the emergence of the New Woman. Barbara Ehrenreich and Deidre English note, with an unmistakable tone of sarcasm,

> Men, men of the "establishment"—physicians, philosophers, scientists—addressed themselves to the Woman Question in a constant stream of books and articles. For, while women were discovering new questions and doubts, men were discovering that women were themselves a question, an anomaly when viewed from the busy world of industry. They couldn't be included in the men's world, yet they no longer seemed to fit in their traditional place. From a masculine point of view the Woman Question was a problem of control: Woman had become an issue, a social problem—something to be investigated, analyzed, and solved. (19–20)

To contend the New Woman, to deal with the racial Other, and to keep the colonisation enterprise afloat justifiably, a white Christian masculine stereotype began to appear in the nineteenth century. Mosse writes,

> The masculine stereotype was strengthened, however, by the existence of a negative stereotype of men who not only failed to measure up to the ideal but who in body and soul were its foil, projecting the exact opposite of true masculinity. Groups marginalized by society, such as Jews or blacks, fulfilled this role, and indeed racism was based upon stereotypes and stereotyping. Those who were said not to fit into settled and respectable society were transformed into countertypes to the ideals that society cherished. . . . (6)

The 'homosexual' was one of these countertypes – unmanly, effeminate, dandyish, diseased – one of the many 'perils of modernity'. According to Mosse, 'Manliness was supposed to safeguard the existing order against the perils of modernity, but it was also regarded as an indispensable attribute of those who wanted change' (3). By 'perils of modernity', Mosse means the counter-discourses which appallingly challenged normative patterns of life in western Europe. The expansion of the Empire compounded these 'perils', and at the turn of the century 'reports of varying reliability began to appear concerning male homosexuality and/or ritual transvestism among the Aztecs, the Cueva of Panama, the Timacuans of Florida, and other peoples' (Lyons and Lyons 99). Not only that, ambiguous sexualities among the Inuit, northeast Asian populations and North American tribes fascinated and alarmed the white investigator. The term *berdache*, of French and Persian origin, referring to a ritual transvestism practised by Native North Americans, entered the ever-expanding vocabulary used to identify the sexual Other.

It is not surprising how the coinage of the term homosexual and the foundation of the Anthropological Society of London almost coincided with each other. In 1863, Richard Francis Burton and James Hunt broke away from the Ethnological Society of London with the objective of collecting facts and natural laws that could rationalise and explain diversities in humankind. Burton's journal, *Anthropologia*, was launched around this time with the purpose of knowing the unknown. Burton said, 'My motive was to supply travellers with an organ that would rescue their observations from the outer darkness of manuscripts and print their curious information on social and *sexual matters* out of place in the popular book' (qtd. in Wright 65; emphasis added). Anthropological investigations were often directed at making sense of 'strange' sexual economies, and produced large volumes of literature at the turn of the century. Not all of these were negative representations of homosexuality, though. Hence, despite positive interventions, the discursive construction of the homosexual as an aberrant species was taking place in the nineteenth century through a large number of written pieces – concrete texts – scientific or cultural.

Sex, sexuality, conjugality and the human anatomy, in general, were of great interest to anthropologists, sexologists, philosophers, artists, psychologists and historians. To name a few, Havelock Ellis, Ernest Cawley, Richard Burton, Edward Westermarck and Edward Carpenter were instrumental in formulating an idea of sexualities which went beyond the neatly defined heteronormative way of understanding them. For example, Ellis, an English physician and sexologist, in his much celebrated and much reprimanded *Sexual Inversion* (1897, originally published in German 1896), shocked Victorian moralists by recording his 'psychological' account of understanding homosexuality by focusing considerably on lesbianism: 'Homosexuality has been observed in women from very early times, and in very wide-spread regions. . . . It is certain that homosexuality is by no means less common in women than in men' (118). Edward Carpenter, the English philosopher and poet, began his *The Intermediate Sex* (1908) by summing up how on the Continent the 'homosexual' was being constituted through different knowledge systems:

> The subject dealt with in this book is one of great, and one may say growing, importance. Whether it is that the present period is one of large increase in the numbers of men and women of an intermediate or mixed temperament, or whether it merely is that it is a period in which more than usual attention happens to be accorded to them, the fact certainly remains that the subject has great actuality and is pressing upon us from all sides. It is recognised that anyhow the number of persons occupying an intermediate position between the two sexes is very great, that they play a considerable part in general society, and that they necessarily present and embody many problems which, both for their own sakes and that of society, demand solution. The literature of the question has in consequence already grown to be very extensive, especially on the Continent, and includes a great quantity of scientific works, medical treatises, literary essays, romances, historical novels, poetry, etc. And it is now generally admitted that some knowledge and enlightened understanding of the subject is greatly needed for the use of certain classes – as, for instance, medical men, teachers, parents, magistrates, judges, and the like. (1–2)

Several European travellers of the nineteenth and early twentieth centuries began reporting curious cases of sexual intimacies and kinship patterns, all of which, in a way, contributed to 'naturalising' homosexuality, or alternatively, worked towards compounding the coloniser's anxiety of the native's sexually promiscuous and immoral lives. Burton (in the 1840s) wrote about male brothels in Karachi, while also declaring that homosexuality was common worldwide; Carpenter (1914) wrote about shamans in the Arctic, the 'two-spirit' people or *berdache*s of North America, and male prostitutes in temples of Palestine; Westermarck (1917) wrote about rampant homosexual practices in the neighbourhood of Behring Sea, especially the fascinating story of young feminine boys who were married off to wealthy men and came to be known as *achnuchik* or *shoopon*; Elsie Clew Parsons (1916) introduced to Europe and America stories of the 'man–woman' or ła'mana among the Zuňi, and so on and so forth. The literature produced was so vast that it appeared that the white Christian model of the monogamous, heterosexual family was perhaps the most unusual form of conjugality and sexual life in the world. But this model, ironically, came to be the dominant model of kinship, replacing most other precolonial ideas of the family and sexuality in the 'non-West'.

'GERMANY IS THE ONLY PLACE FOR SEX. ENGLAND IS NO GOOD'[3]: THE WEIMAR REPUBLIC AND THE HOMOSEXUAL COUNTERCULTURE

The celebrated British writers, W. H. Auden, Christopher Isherwood, Stephen Spender, A. E. Housman, and several others came to understand their sexuality and found a new lease of adventurous sexual life in the Weimar Republic. No historical account of the Republic's homophilic disposition could match up to two fascinating novels – *Christopher and His Kind* (1976) and *The Temple* (1988) – two seriously deferred autobiographical accounts of Isherwood's and Spender's erotic lives and engagement with the politics of sexual identities during their stay in Germany in the first half of the twentieth century. In *Christopher and His Kind*, Layard and Lane, the two anthropologists to whom Auden introduced a very young Christopher, appalled and fascinated the latter with their radicalism and reinterpretation of God:

> There is only one sin: disobedience of the inner law of our own nature. This disobedience is the fault of those who teach

> us, as children, to control God (our desires) instead of giving Him room to grow. The whole problem is to find out which is God and which is the Devil. And the one sure guide is that God appears always unreasonable, whereas the Devil appears to be noble and right. God appears unreasonable because He has been put in prison and driven wild. The Devil is conscious control, and is, therefore, reasonable and sane. (Isherwood 2)

This is only a little tip of the iceberg as regards the massive revolution that was underway, and was cut short by the rise of the Nazis in the 1930s in Germany's Weimar Republic. A page from Spender's (masquerading as Paul in *The Temple*) notebook, written during his Berlin days, reads,

> I feel as if a new life had begun here in Germany. I do not know precisely in what the newness consists, but perhaps the key to it is in these young Germans having a new attitude toward the body. Although I have never been puritanical in my outlook, I confess that till now, whatever I may have pretended to myself, I have always regarded my body as sinful, and my own physical being as something to be ashamed of. . . . Now I am beginning to feel that I may soon come to regard my body as a source of joy. (Spender 54)

While a radical challenge to puritanical Christian notions of the body, soul, God and Devil is more than apparent in the above two extracts, bodily pleasure, extricated from the realm of the sinful, was placed centre-stage, as evidenced by the Institut für Sexualwissenschaft, or the Institute for Sexual Science, founded by Magnus Hirschfeld and Arthur Kronfeld in 1919 in Berlin's Tiergarten Park. The institute was founded in the wake of the fall of the monarchy, and Germany's coming of age as the most modern, democratic welfare state of Europe. Hirschfeld, a homosexual Jewish sexologist, was already well-known for his leadership of the homosexual emancipation group Wissenschaftlich-humanitäres Komitee (Scientific-Humanitarian Committee), which he had co-founded with Kurt Hiller, a Jewish doctorate in law, in May 1897. The Institute for Sexual Science housed a museum which put on display a whole range of objects, information and images related to 'sexual abnormalities' (as psychologists called them so). From photographs of sexual organs of hermaphrodites to whips and chains used for S&M sex – everything was on exhibition. It showed an urgency to locate divergent sexualities within a scientific-empirical discourse.

As Laurie Marhoefer claims, 'It was in the Weimar era that several characteristic components of twentieth century gay and lesbian liberation were first put to use in the context of mass democracy' (8). However, it would be interesting to briefly consider the differences in opinion between Hirschfeld and Hiller, the latter calling for a more radical politics as against Hirschfeld's repeated emphasis on science as the only possible way to liberation for sexual minorities. Hiller believed that taking to the streets was important for homosexual emancipation – that is, a mass movement that ensured more visibility within the public domain was a more effective way of finding acceptance. Hirschfeld thought that mass denunciation was a Utopian idea, which would do more harm than good to the movement. But, as we have seen already, the queer movement which emerged in the 1990s in New York City actually followed the path suggested by Hiller, challenging more conservative movements which did not amply intimidate compulsory heteronormativity. The Weimar Republic provides several interesting examples of consolidating the movement, one of which was the Café Zehner incident. The Stonewall Inn Riots in 1969 would have given a sense of *déjà vu* to those who were familiar with this 1921 incident, which led to the formation of the Munich Friendship League led by Richard Linsert. When Café Zehner, a meeting spot for homosexual men, was closed down by the police, Linsert took the assistance of law to prove that homosexuals, in the German Reich, had the right to equality and could certainly congregate to assert their struggle for justice.

Notwithstanding the opposing views of what a good movement entailed, the movement, as one can see, was not confined within Berlin alone; it crossed the borders of the metropolis and spilled over into small towns. A high literacy rate, cheap travel and a proliferation of print media gave small-towners easy access to the 'homosexual' material produced in Berlin. Since the late nineteenth century, numerous magazines and periodicals dedicated to the cause had been in circulation in Germany. *Der eigene* (The Self-Owning), which began appearing in 1896, was the first of these magazines, to be followed by many more. *Die freundin*, dedicated to female homosexuals, was one of the most circulated of these. Other publications included *Die garçonne*, *Frauenliebe*, *BIF – Blätteridealerfrauenfreundschaft*, *Ledigefrauen*, *Frauen liebe und leben* and *Liebendefrauen*. Several cultural texts – novels, plays, poems, paintings, pop songs and films – were also in circulation. In other words, a counter-discourse to the pathologisation of homosexuality was firmly in place by the end of the 1920s.

However, there was a major problem with nomenclature, notwithstanding how progressive the German reformers were. While conservatives vilified the movement as morally degenerate, the reformers too did not find it necessary to invent a term for all forms of non-normative sexualities they were trying to reclaim as natural; instead, they often used the term 'abnormal sexualities', failing to dissociate the negative currency underlining the expression. As Marhoefer correctly notes, the use of this expression held 'immorality' or sexual deviance as a 'social problem' which needed to be addressed (9). In fact, most of Sigmund Freud's reflections on homosexuality, especially earlier ones, are couched in similar rhetoric, notwithstanding the affirmative stance he generally took in psychologically explaining homosexuality. Sample this famous letter he wrote to a mother panicking over her son's homosexuality:

> Homosexuality is assuredly no advantage, but it is nothing to be ashamed of, no vice, no degradation; it cannot be classified as an illness; we consider it to be a variation of the sexual function, produced *by a certain arrest of sexual development*. Many highly respectable individuals of ancient and modern times have been homosexuals, several of the greatest men among them (Plato, Michelangelo, Leonardo da Vinci, etc.). It is a great injustice to persecute homosexuality as a crime – and cruelty, too. If you do not believe me, read the books of Havelock Ellis. (423; emphasis added)

Though Freud's ideas changed over time, his assertion that homosexuality was an outcome of an incomplete or truncated process of sexual development appears deeply problematic. In this letter, despite his affirmation of homosexuality as 'nothing to be ashamed of', he manages to project it as something inferior to heterosexuality, a form of sexual retardation. For Freud, changing an individual's same-sex orientation to a heterosexual one meant helping them mature, rather than a 'cure' (Drescher). Yet, the positivity Freud showed in his interpretation of homosexuality was of immense value to the homosexuals of those times, for he managed to overturn widely publicised views of Richard von Krafft-Ebing (1840–1902) and others who pathologised homosexuality (as well as bisexuality) as a congenital disease which had its roots in some genetic abnormality, the genesis of which could be discovered if family histories were investigated. Especially, Freud's declaration that humans were by nature bisexual helped, to some extent, in alleviating homo- and biphobia prevalent in Western cultures:

> It is well known that at all times there have been, as there still are, human beings who can take as their sexual objects persons of either sex without the one trend interfering with the other. We call these people bisexual and accept the fact of their existence without wondering much at it. . . . But we have come to know that all human beings are bisexual in this sense and their libido is distributed between objects of both sexes, either in a manifest or a latent form. (qtd. in Young-Bruehl 179)

Freud's commentary on homosexuality was of immense importance to post-Weimar Germany which saw the rise of the Nazis that brought an abrupt end to the progressive reformist movement, widely perceived as decadence by the conservatives all along. Alex Ross sums up this tragic end in these words:

> Nazism brought Berlin's gay idyll to a swift, savage end. Hirschfeld had left Germany in 1930, to undertake a worldwide lecture tour; wisely, he never returned. In May, 1933, a little more than three months after Hitler became Reich Chancellor, the Institute for Sexual Science was ransacked, and much of its library went up in flames during Joseph Goebbels's infamous book-burning in the Opernplatz. Röhm, who became less indispensable once Hitler took power, was slaughtered in 1934, during the Night of the Long Knives, the first great orgy of Nazi bloodlust. Hirschfeld, who had watched the destruction

> of his life's work on a newsreel in Paris, died the next year. . . . Vestiges of Paragraph 175[4] lingered in the German legal code until 1994. (Web, n. p.)

THE STONEWALL RIOTS AND THE SEXUAL REVOLUTION IN AMERICA: QUEERING THE STREETS

Another landmark moment in the discursive constitution of the 'homosexual' is the Stonewall Inn Riots, a series of disruptive demonstrations that took place in the Greenwich Village, a neighbourhood in New York City, in 1969. It was considered an important moment for LGBT organising as it was a confrontational encounter with a largely homophobic police force. The Stonewall Inn, where the riots took place, was one of the very few venues which catered to the LGBT population and was also quite diverse in its clientele, being popular with gay men, trans people, sex workers, drag queens and homeless youth. Police raids were quite common here during the 1960s but on this occasion, the police had quickly lost control when a series of riots began. LGBT people came together to organise and protest the police raid and brutality. On the night of Friday 27 June 1969 around 1:20 a.m. (officially 28 June), the police raided the Inn, in an effort to seize illegal liquor and to arrest the management and workers. As they started checking identification papers, kicking people out and arresting the 'most obvious looking homosexuals' (mostly drag queens and people of colour), a crowd of ejected patrons, nearby residents and passers-by gathered outside. This was unusual; people usually tried to slip away from bar raids (Carter 143). The growing crowd posed a problem for the police. As they loaded the van with arrestees, the crowd grew angry and started throwing pennies, beer cans, bottles and bricks.

Armstrong and Crage argue that the Stonewall Riots did not mark the origin of gay liberation in the United States. There were other events which had occurred prior to this, but they did not acquire the same mythic status and thus were forgotten. Betsy Kuhn argues that the Stonewall Riots acted as a catalyst for a meeting on 16 July to organise around gay liberation. By the end of July, the Gay Liberation Front was born as a radical movement. There were hurdles within this as some members wanted to forge ties with other radical groups to organise against the establishment, while some believed it should be based on a single issue. It should be noted that the term 'liberation' itself is loaded with meaning. It is used as a term for emancipation to procure civil, political and social rights for disenfranchised groups.

The sexual revolution which was part of the women's counterculture and gay movement advocated acceptance of non-procreative sex and sex outside marriage including non-normative forms of sexuality. While a large part of the movement was heralded through films and books, it was also largely supported through radical feminist discourses. Coinciding with women's liberation movements initiated in the early 1960s, the sexual liberation movement was aided by feminist ideologues in the struggle to challenge traditional ideas regarding sexuality and reproduction. From a feminist perspective, reducing favourable bias towards men, questioning the objectification of women, and asserting free agency and rights of women to choose sexual partners without judgement were the main goals to be achieved. Many feminist thinkers such as bell hooks (149) believed that assertion of the primacy of sexuality would constitute a major step towards the ultimate goal of women's liberation, when women were urged to initiate and experiment with all forms of sexuality.

Another social movement that began to take root during this time was 'Free Love', a form of libertarian socialism associated with the counterculture movement. It was a movement that believed in reducing the interference of the state and society (including religious organisations) in matters of personal relationships. Spurlock has argued that free love is also linked with radical social change, depicting it as a new form of anti-authoritarian and anti-repressive sensibility.

Free Love, sexual revolution and the Stonewall Riots have all been depicted in popular culture through films, documentaries and literature. Isaac Asimov's novel *The Gods Themselves* (1972) is an early depiction of a society based on the moon where there is no restriction on any forms of nudity or sexual experience. The Stonewall Riots was most recently made into a film,

Stonewall (2015), by the American director Roland Emmerich, which received widespread negative reception for its non-political story and lack of respect for people of colour who were important characters in the actual riots but were reduced to comic relief or minimal presence in the cinematic representation. In a scathing review, Mark Segal, a Stonewall veteran, said, '*Stonewall* is uninterested in any history that doesn't revolve around its white, male, stereotypically attractive protagonist. It almost entirely leaves out the women who participated in the riots and helped create the Gay Liberation Front, which included youth, trans people, lesbian separatists and people from all other parts of the spectrum of our community' (Web, n. p.).

These events were significant as they marked a turning point in the oppression faced by gays and lesbian in the United States. Historians such as Nicholas C. Edsall have compared it to the defiance displayed by Rosa Parks in her civil disobedience for refusing to give up her seat on a bus to a white customer. Given that the Stonewall Riots were very much a movement led by queers of colour, it is perhaps a fitting analogy to end this chapter:

> Stonewall has been compared to any number of acts of radical protest and defiance in American history from the Boston Tea Party on. But the best and certainly a more nearly contemporary analogy is with Rosa Parks' refusal to move to the back of the bus in Montgomery, Alabama, in December 1955, which sparked the modern civil rights movement. Within months after Stonewall radical gay liberation groups and newsletters sprang up in cities and on college campuses across America and then across all of northern Europe as well. (Edsall 333)

The Stonewall Inn Riots brought the 'homosexual' out of the closet on to the streets, and since then, through the 1970s and 80s, the American academia began to explore LGBT lives socially, culturally and philosophically. What emerged post-Stonewall was an identity-based politics, which, however, proved delimiting and constricting as the AIDS epidemic broke out in the 80s, taking the lives of hundreds of gay men. The AIDS epidemic spawned homophobia like never before, and LGBT activists had to find a way to combat this backlash. As Corber and Valocchi show, the inevitability of renouncing identity-based politics and embracing a 'queer' politics which, inspired by the works of Foucault, Lacan and Althusser, emphasised the performative nature of identity, was strongly felt. In the wake of the AIDS epidemic, when certain forms of gay male identities were being stigmatised and marked out as dangerous, AIDS activist organisations such as ACT UP contended that the focus must shift to types of sexual practices that expose people to HIV, from the people themselves who were perceived as engaging in these practices. Older ways of understanding the 'homosexual' as a distinct or deviant form of personhood, which was in vogue in the nineteenth and early twentieth centuries, were to be replaced. The need to re-locate sexualities in the realm of practices, and understanding it as concomitant with other aspects of subjectivity such as class, caste, race and location, was recognised, whereby the field of sexuality studies expanded infinitely. To address these multifarious dimensions of sexuality, its indeterminability, its endless possibilities, Queer Theory emerged, not to theorise sexuality per se but to underline the undesirability of essentialisation and normalisation in any form.

NOTES

[1] Anthony Burgess's *A Dead Man in Deptford* (1993), based on Marlowe's life, makes an interesting read with respect to retelling the history of the early modern theatre world. The novel is set in a fascinating underworld of thespians, spies, drunkards and other shady men, where male–male sexual intimacy was so commonplace that it did not stand out. The book narrated by an imaginary boy-actor, who had a sexual relationship with the promising Kit (as Marlowe was known in intimate circuits), dramatises Marlowe's life as a spy, interlaced with a troubling but erotic love affair with Thomas Walsingham. The Elizabethan theatrical world never stops surprising, for it reveals a whole range of 'un-parliamentary' activities, which mainstream English history has hesitated to record.

[2] This anachronism by the writer must be noted. In the eighteenth century, the term 'gay' meaning sodomites or sexually non-conforming men was not yet in circulation.

[3] W. H. Auden, fictionalised as Simon in Spender's *The Temple*, makes this observation.

[4] The anti-sodomy law

REFERENCES

Armstrong, Elizabeth A., and Suzanna M. Crage. 'Movements and Memory: The Making of the Stonewall Myth'. *American Sociological Review* 71.5 (2006): 724–51. Print.

Bray, Alan. 'Homosexuality and Signs of Male Friendship in Elizabethan England'. *Queering the Renaissance*. Ed. Jonathan Goldberg. Durham and London: Duke UP, 1994. 40–61. Print.

Burgess, Anthony. *A Dead Man in Deptford*. London: Hutchinson, 1993. Print.

Burton, Richard. 'Pederasty'. 1885–87. *Sexualities in Anthropology: A Reader*. Eds. Andrew P. Lyons and Harriet D. Lyons. Malden: Wiley-Blackwell, 2011. 103–05. Print.

Carpenter, Edward. 'Hermaphrodism Among Gods and Mortals'. 1919. *Sexualities in Anthropology: A Reader*. Eds. Andrew P. Lyons and Harriet D. Lyons. Malden: Wiley-Blackwell, 2011. 111–17. Print.

---. *The Intermediate Sex: A Study of More Transitional Types of Men and Women*. 1908. A Project Gutenberg of Australia eBook. Web. 27 September 2018. <http://gutenberg.net.au/ebooks04/0400391h.html>.

Carter, David. *Stonewall: The Riots that Sparked the Gay Revolution*. New York: St Martins Press, 2004. Print.

Corber, Robert J., and Stephen M. Valocchi. Introduction. *Queer Studies: An Interdisciplinary Reader*. Eds. Robert J. Corber and Stephen M. Valocchi. Malden: Blackwell, 2013. 1–17. Print.

Disney, John. *A View of Ancient Laws against Immorality and Profaneness.* Nottingham: Vicar at St. Mary's, 1729. Print.

Drescher, Jack. 'I'm Your Handyman: A History of Reparative Therapies'. *Journal of Gay and Lesbian Psychotherapy* 5:3–4 (2001): 5–24. Print.

Edsall, Nicholas C. *Toward Stonewall: Homosexuality and Society in the Modern Western World*. Charlottesville: U of Virginia P, 2003. Print.

Ehrenreich, Barbara, and Deidre English. *For Her Own Good: Two Centuries of Experts' Advice to Women*. 2nd edition. New York: Anchor Books, 2005. Print.

Ellis, Havelock. *Sexual Inversion. Studies in the Psychology of Sex. Vol. 2*. Philadelphia: F. A. Davis Company, 1908. Print.

Eng, David L. 'Freedom and the Racialization of Intimacy: Lawrence v. Texas and the Emergence of Queer Liberalism'. *A Companion to LGBTQ Studies*. Eds. G. E. Haggerty and M. McGarry. Malden: Blackwell, 2007. 38–59. Print.

Foucault, Michel. *History of Sexuality*. Vol. 1. 1976. Trans. Robert Hurley. Victoria: Penguin, 1984. Print.

Freud, Sigmund. *Letters of Sigmund Freud*. 1935. Ed. E. L. Freud. New York: Basic Books, 1960. Print.

hooks, bell. *Feminist Theory: From Margin to Centre*. Cambridge, MA: South End Press, 1984. Print.

Isherwood, Christopher. *Christopher and His Kind*. Intr. Gore Vidal. 1976. London: Vintage Books, 2012. Print.

Kuhn, Betsy. *Gay Power!: The Stonewall Riots and the Gay Rights Movement, 1969*. Minneapolis: 21st Century Books, 2011. Print.

Lyons, Andrew P., and Harriet D. Lyons, eds. *Sexualities in Anthropology: A Reader*. Malden: Wiley-Blackwell, 2011. Print.

Marhoefer, Laurie. *Sex and the Weimer Republic: German Homosexual Emancipation and the Rise of the Nazis*. Toronto: U of Toronto P, 2015. Print.

Mosse, George L. *The Image of Man: The Creation of Modern Masculinity*. Oxford: Oxford UP, 1996. Print.

Nandy, Ashis. *The Intimate Enemy*. 1983. *Exiled at Home*. New Delhi: Oxford UP, 1998. Print.

Norton, Rictor. *Homosexuality in Eighteenth Century England: A Sourcebook Compiled by Rictor Norton. Gay History and Literature: Essays by Rictor Norton*. Web. 12 April 2017. <http://rictornorton.co.uk/eighteen/>.

Parsons, E. C. 'The Zuñi La'mana'. 1916. *Sexualities in Anthropology: A Reader*. Eds. Andrew P. Lyons and Harriet D. Lyons. Malden: Wiley-Blackwell, 2011. 118–22. Print.

Ross, Alex. 'Berlin Story: How the Germans Invented Gay Rights – More than a Century Ago'. *The New Yorker*. 26 January 2015. Web. 14 May 2017. <https://www.newyorker.com/magazine/2015/01/26/berlin-story>.

Ruskin, John. 'Of Queen's Gardens'. 1864. Web. 1 August 2017. <https://openlibrary.org/books/OL7166081M/Of_queens'_gardens>.

Segal, Mark. 'I was at the Stonewall Riots. The Movie Stonewall Gets Everything Wrong'. *PBS Newhour*. 23 September 2015. Web. 28 September 2018. <https://www.pbs.org/newshour/arts/stonewall-movie>.

Spender, Stephen. *The Temple*. Intr. Stephen Spender. 1987. New York: Grove Press, 1988. Print.

Spurlock, John C. *Free Love Marriage and Middle-Class Radicalism in America*. New York: New York UP, 1988. Print.

Westermarck, Edward. 'Homosexual Love'. 1917. *Sexualities in Anthropology: A Reader*. Eds. Andrew P. Lyons and Harriet D. Lyons. Malden: Wiley-Blackwell, 2011. 106–11. Print.

Wright, Thomas. *The Life of Sir Richard Burton*. London: Everett, 1906. Print.

Young-Bruehl, Elisabeth. 'Are Human Beings "By Nature" Bisexual?' *Studies in Gender and Sexuality* 2.3 (2001): 179–213. Print.

CONTEMPORARY ISSUES IN QUEER STUDIES 1

Chapter Two

Queer Kinship, Dissident Citizenship and Homonationalism

The agendas of Queer Studies as a discipline and the LGBTQ movement across the globe have been multiplying and expanding steadily. It is no longer limited to the right to privacy or the right to life. The increasing polarisation of the LGBTQ movement along radical and assimilative coordinates, the convergence of issues of class, race, religion and migration with sexual identities, the capitalist co-optation of the potential queer consumer, increase in the number of HIV-AIDS–infected people, and the expansion of the movement beyond the geopolitical boundaries of Europe and North America into societies which have begun questioning the imperialism of Euro-American identitarian politics – all of these have spawned a nuanced polemic surrounding sexualities. In this chapter, we shall discuss three pressing issues of the moment: (1) the emergence of queer families, political and affective friendship networks, and reordering of traditional kinship patterns; (2) radical queer dissidence vis-à-vis assimilative agendas of a dominant homonormative movement, interpellated in capitalist discourses; and (3) most importantly, how homonormativity is extended to homonationalism – the white Euro-American strategy of using the excuse of protecting queer lives in order to promote Islamophobia, with the ulterior political motive of consolidating the image of the 'bad Muslim' Other. This, in turn, has brought in new challenges to the LGBTQ movement, which is now bifurcated into two streams – one that unquestioningly complies with the state's strategies of assimilating sexually non-conforming citizens, and another that resists such assimilation, further problematising the dissident citizenship status of queers.

QUEER COUPLEDOM, FRIENDSHIP AND FAMILIES OF CHOICE: FORGING QUEER RELATIONALITIES

All three components of the main title of this segment posit different challenges to, and provide various perspectives on, appreciating the necessity of queer kinship ties. Judith Halberstam, in a radical call for 'forgetting the family', summarises the various aspects of queer kinship which scholars and activists have promoted at various points in time:

> Queer interventions into kinship studies have taken many forms: some call for new models of family (Butler's Antigone as a substitute for Oedipus, Weston's chosen families as a substitute for blood bonds); others call for the recognition of friendship ties as kinship; and still other scholars ask that we recognize the difference that gay and lesbian parents make to the very meaning of family. But, few scholars call for a de-emphasis on family or a rejection of the family altogether. (317)

At the very outset, it is useful to admit that formulation of queer kinship – a real queering of kinship, so to speak – seems impossible. This is because imagining any form of kinship model beyond the Oedipal precedent is difficult. And, paradoxically, the extent of queerness of alternative models is always judged in terms of how far it has moved away from the Oedipal model, thereby reinstating the latter as the 'original' which can only be copied or not copied. In any case, emptying queer kinship models of heteronorms, especially within a capitalist imaginary of sustainable relationalities, is daunting and perhaps unachievable. As Freeman writes,

> When we imagine practitioners of non-reproductive sex extending their affinities over space, we tend to use the language of community or even nation, which does not distinguish the individual relationships within it. So, for instance, lesbians can be "married" just like their straight counterparts, with

> participating parties understanding themselves as spouses, husband and wife, or partners. (297)

To validate this statement, let us use three examples of non-Western kinship models, which though apparently opposed to the heteronormative biological family, fail to adequately queer its patterns of relationality, intimacy and generationality. Westermarck quotes a certain Dr Bogoraz who gave a fascinating account of how a young Siberian chukchi boy quite suddenly started feeling like a woman, began dressing like one, and also took a husband and performed all the work usually incumbent on the wife. Bogoraz saw this 'abnormal transformation' as 'abject immorality', which, however, was explained by the shamans as 'injunction of their individual deity'. The shamans themselves, as the myth went, could change their sex at will, a characteristic not only specific to the chukchi shamans, but was common to several tribes from the Siberian region. No matter how judgemental Dr Bogoraz was of this transformation, this provides an interesting example of an alternative kinship model in non-Western 'primitive' cultures. But, as it is not difficult to see, the model replicated is that of a hetero-patriarchal household. One may recall what Gayle Rubin says in connection to gender and kinship: the fact that trafficking of women through marriage is also a process of *enculturation* of women *as* women. What happens in this particular example of the chukchi lad's voluntary subjection to a husband is the enculturation of a biological man as a woman, in imitation of the Oedipal model. The only difference is that the chukchi boy did not relocate to the husband's house; rather the husband came over to stay in the *yurt* to which the 'lad' wife belonged. But, nonetheless, the hetero-patriarchal model remained intact.

Another interesting example is that of the *hijra* community of India. *Hijra* households or *kholi*s, which exist in abundance, exemplify a complex kinship structure, initiation into which takes place through rigorous rituals. Without elaborating on the contested identity of *hijra*s, often referred to as the 'third gender', let us examine whether the *kholi* effectively queers the Oedipal kinship model. A community of emasculated, transvestite men and hermaphrodites, *hijra*s, usually coming from economically deprived classes, reside together, abandoning their biological families. However, this household has an inviolable hierarchy – a *guru–chela* or mentor–disciple model – which also demands maintenance of an exacting code of conduct. Within this very rigid structure, younger *hijras* are expected to be deferential subordinates having economic and social obligations to the *gurus* (Reddy 156). The relationship is imitative of the normative mother–daughter relationship, reinforced symbolically through a ritualistic performance in which the younger *hijra* or the *dudh-beti* (milk daughter) is fed 'milk' by the 'mother' (*dudh-mata*) with drops of her own blood, establishing a lifelong blood-bond and also a symbolic bloodline through which cultural transmission from one generation to the next could be facilitated. The *hijra kholi* seems to be the site where two ideas of kinship – David Schneider's argument that kinship is a code of conduct and Pierre Bourdieu's notion of kinship as a form of shared substance between bodies contained within a *habitus* – converge, in both temporal and spatial sense. Freeman, who bases her thesis on 'queer belongings' on Schneider and Bourdieu's ideas, would find this performative transmission of bodily fluid, affect and culture, fitting well into what she says of the metonymic function of family photographs: 'This is a metonymic notion of reproduction that not only draws from the procreative register of meaning, but in some ways turns reflexively back upon it by insisting that all kinship may, indeed, be a matter of poses, gestures, performance' (307). Despite its apparent difference from the hetero-patriarchal family, the *hijra kholi* is, at best, a derivative of that architecture.

Don Kulick's work on Brazilian *travestis* or transgender prostitutes reveals another interesting kinship model, which, again, is apparently very queer but falls short of moving beyond the hetero-patriarchal imaginary of the family. Kulick, in this delightful ethnographic study of the *travesti*'s relationship with her numerous boyfriends, inaugurates an intriguing narrative of affection, sexuality and materiality that underwrites this contested relationship. *Travestis* are feminine men who 'remake' their bodies with the assistance of cosmetics, estrogen-based hormones and silicon: 'All travestis self-identify as homosexual. . . . They want to be feminine, they maintain, not female' (238). Kulick discovers that *marido*s, meaning husbands, are central to the life of a *travesti,* a 'kept' of sorts who the *travesti* 'maintains'. There is a fierce competition among *travesti*s for acquiring *marido*s from a limited supply of men in the locality, who are willing to forge relationships with them. Also, there are specific criteria that *marido*s should meet in order to be taken in: 'Travestis are drawn to men who are classically masculine [having] pronounced muscles and a big penis' (246). Additionally, he becomes even more attractive if he is known to have intercourse with women, but has never been penetrated himself or shown any interest in another man's penis. But what is perhaps troubling for radical queers to accept is that *travesti*s love imagining themselves as heterosexual women who also believe that they are *not* destined to be loved by men: '[A] male is a man *because* he desires a female; a travesti can feel like a woman *to the extent that* she desires a man and is desired, in return, by a man. It is this relationship between desire and the production of difference that excludes other homosexuals from consideration as partners for travestis' (249; emphasis in the original). The relationship is based on bestowing of material goods and money on the *marido* who is usually economically destitute. The *travesti* draws a sense of agency in being able to 'maintain' her *marido*, who she can throw out of the house at her will. While in a relationship, the *travesti* continues to work as a prostitute to which the 'kept' *marido* does not raise any objection, given that for his own sustenance he is dependent on the *travesti*'s income. This is a curious form of kinship which despite its remarkable difference from conventional families, somehow ends up mimicking heterosexual intimacies which are based on difference rather than sameness.

None of these extraordinary examples of kinship patterns are satisfactorily queer, underlining perhaps the impossibility of moving beyond the dominant model of the family, household and sexual intimacies. The more well-known same-sex families, common in most First World countries – which Kath Weston calls 'families we choose' – are more normative than disruptive, notwithstanding how far they strive to move away from the Oedipal model. We shall come back to this a little later.

It is important at this point to talk about queer friendships; for queer community formation across the globe, struggle for rights,

HIV-AIDS activism – all of these have been facilitated by bonds forged through the building of a sense of community. A now classical instance of how queer friendships could emerge is Adrienne Rich's much celebrated concept of the 'lesbian continuum' that included all women-identified experiences, whether sexual or intense non-sexual experiences such as 'bonding against male tyranny' (644). Challenging the perception that women have a natural and 'innate' sexual attraction for men, Rich raises the important issue that women's preference for women as passionate friends, partners, co-workers and lovers has been erased from history. Dismissing the idea that lesbianism is only a choice, Rich asks feminists who believe that social relations between the sexes handicap women, that if they 'dealt with lesbian existence as a reality and as a source of knowledge and power available to women' (632), they might end up questioning whether women would choose heterosexual relationships and marriage at all. In such a context, heterosexuality could be understood as a 'sexual preference' or choice, and not natural or given. Rich's revolt against 'compulsory heterosexuality' and her call for a 'lesbian continuum' is corroborated by Audre Lorde, who defines this continuum as all-pervading in 'the sharing of joy whether physical, emotional, psychic', and in the sharing of tasks – a political activism rooted in deep emotional and/or erotic ties. It is, according to Lorde, an empowerment which 'makes us less willing to accept powerlessness, or those other supplied states of being which are not *native* to me, such as, resignation, despair, self-effacement, depression, self-denial' (qtd. in Rich 53; emphasis added). This underscores a 'return to nature' as it were, when lesbianism is seen as authentic female existence. Rich's emphasis on the fact that lesbianism is *not* the same as male homosexuality, but is an exceptional female experience like motherhood, projects lesbianism as unrealisable if bracketed with other forms of oppressed sexualities. Rich's understanding of lesbianism as a political-emotional-erotic friendship, a return to an original state of female existence, was 'strategically useful to the women's movement because it promoted solidarity among women by minimizing differences that had the potential to divide them' (Corber and Valocchi 7).

If Rich's thesis on 'lesbian continuum' appears too radical a concept, it does make a case for queer friendships as the basis of community formation, real as well as virtual. Following Parmesh Shahani's argument that the virtual-versus-real debate is eventually unproductive, we agree that these queer communities are best defined by Benedict Anderson's understanding of communities – an imagined togetherness which exists because the members of the community believe that it exists. Queer communities are a form of kinship strengthened through exchanges and sharing of ideas, desires and emotions, without being judgemental. These communities provide a 'third place', as Oldenburg calls it, a space which is distinct from one's home or workplace, which, however, might not have a physical location. This may be understood if one briefly scrolls through Facebook pages devoted to the LGBTQ+ cause, pages where friendships are forged, 'coming out' is encouraged, and support systems are provided for those in need. In the context of Gay Bombay, an online–offline community, Shahani makes an important observation: for most gay men who are members of this community, the virtual or real space of Gay Bombay works like a secondary community of sorts – a place where it is not expected that every gay man will be friends with every other gay man, but there is certainly an imagined companionability, a sense of belonging, which gives members the freedom of being themselves without fear of discrimination. These communities are not just affective spaces, but also sites where political solidarities germinate. A recent volume, *Friendship as Social Justice Activism*, edited by a group of queer individuals who became friends through this sense of belonging to this imagined (global) community of queers, drives home this point:

> Friendship as social activism appears as an ethico-political relation with the self and with others through pleasure, affect, devastation, violence, support, loss . . . unclassifiable as a single state, except as a thing or a process. . . . Such ethico-political relations thrive within the realization of activist goals and through activist engagements helping to keep those bonds real . . . and provide a counter to capitalist modes of governance and coercion. (Banerjea et al. 5)

In fact, before same-sex marriage or civil union became an agendum on the LGBTQ wishlist, the movement drew strength from a politicisation of kinship, as Weston notes. In the 1980s, the focus shifted towards relationships, formation of families and living together in a civil union. While state-recognition of same-sex marriage or civil union is sometimes celebrated, as the LGBTQ movement's ultimate triumph, the radical queer position is vociferously against the idea of mimicking heterosexual families, a submissive act of homonormative appropriation of that model. This moment of triumph is also the triumph of the capitalist market's successful co-optation of the queer into its fold. Queerness and capitalism, as D'Emilio argues, have always shared an extremely ambiguous relationship: capitalism, while promoting the heterosexual family, has also brought in its wake greater freedom in expressing and pursuing individual choices, including sexual choices. One way of reconciling queerness to the family is to recognise the consumerist potential of the queer and assimilate them into the mainstream by promoting the queer family. As Eng writes,

> If the 1980s and 1990s witnessed the significant emergence of gay identity and visibility as a function of the free market, along with the development of a political movement for rights and recognition (especially in relation to the AIDS pandemic), it also marked the simultaneous consolidation of Right-wing ideologies under the sign of "family" and "family values". (40–41)

This neo-liberal, capitalist appropriation of the queer is the safest way to integrate them into the mainstream, given that the moral Right constantly harps on harnessing queer bodies into monogamous structures in order to reduce their vulnerability to stigmatised sexually transmitted diseases. This is unambiguously the intention in Justice Anthony Kennedy's (who authored the majority's opinion on legalising same-sex marriage in the United States in June 2015) endorsement of same-sex marriage:

> No union is more profound than marriage, for it embodies the highest ideals of love, fidelity, devotion, sacrifice, and family. . . . [The challengers] ask for equal dignity in the eyes

> of the law. The Constitution grants them that right. . . . The limitation of marriage to opposite-sex couples may long have seemed natural and just, but its inconsistency with the central meaning of the fundamental right to marry is now manifest. (qtd. in Imbert, Web, n. p.)

Such hegemonic (and populist) discourses of homonormativity which undermine queer radicalism constrict the social space available to the single queer person and those who are unwilling to marry. While many sexually non-conforming individuals happily embrace homonormativity, especially with the motive of enjoying state benefits extended to families, or because of emotional reasons, many find it incarcerating. The assimilation of queer individuals within homonormative structures severely silences the dissident voice of the queer (an issue we will take up in the next segment). The recognition of this radical queer voice is also extremely desirable in the time of homonationalist agendas.

DISSIDENT QUEERS IN THE TIME OF PRONOUNCED HOMONORMATIVITY AND HOMONATIONALISM

What is dissident citizenship? How does the nature of dissidence change when the state begins co-opting dissident citizens into its fold? The current status of queer dissidence provides an excellent example of how the nature of resistance, opposition and rebellion alters over time, contingent upon changing state policies, no matter how liberal democratic they may appear from a distance. In this context, the idea of a 'sexual citizen' (Weeks) also becomes a contested one, especially when, in the First World nations, considerable 'primacy has been [already] given to sexual subjectivity' (Weeks 35). It is important to note how the idea of citizenship – the notion of belonging to a state – and the idea of being queer – a radical, dissenting, individualistic position – are riddled with contradictions: the relationship is extremely volatile, with 'queer citizenship' posing an oxymoronic identity. Perhaps the queerness of queer citizenship is sustained in the citizen's constant revolt against the state, and a deeply disquieting feeling that despite the state's favourable policies of accommodating sexual minorities, the queer citizen is perpetually in a state of non-belonging. As Butler and Spivak discuss,

> The state is supposed to service the matrix for the obligations and prerogatives of citizenship. It is that which forms the conditions under which we are juridically bound. We might expect that the state presupposes modes of juridical belonging, at least minimally, but since the state can be precisely what expels and suspends modes of legal protection and obligation, the state can put us, some of us, in quite a state. It can signify the source of non-belonging, even produce that non-belonging as a quasi-permanent state. (3–4)

In what sense are sexual minorities dissident citizens? Sparks writes, '[D]issident democratic citizenship can usefully be conceptualized as the public contestation of prevailing arrangements of power by marginalized citizens through oppositional, democratic, noninstitutionalized practices that augment or replace institutionalized channels of democratic opposition when those channels are inadequate or unavailable' (83).

Sexual minorities, to start with, have used both institutionalised as well as non-institutionalised forms of dissent – forming organisations such as Queer Nation, or by peaceful demonstrations like the Pride Parade, in which any (dissident) individual could participate, whether or not the latter is affiliated to an organisation. The concept of sexual citizenship was first employed by David Evans in 1993 as a way of focusing attention on rights to a range of sexual identities and practices linked to the state. Weeks writes, 'The idea of sexual citizenship has many features in common with other claims to citizenship. It is about enfranchisement, about inclusion, about belonging, about equity and justice, about rights balanced by new responsibilities' (39).

It is different from other forms of citizenship precisely because it draws out into the public what so far was kept locked in private spaces: the body and its pleasures and socially rooted choices about identities and sexual experiences. This struggle for acquiring recognition as sexual citizens is still on in developing countries, one fitting example of which could be the debates surrounding the Transgender Persons (Protection of Rights) Bill, 2016, in India.

Turning to the West, if one considers granting of the rights to marry to sexually non-conforming citizens as a glorious moment of acquiring equity and justice, a teleological closure of sorts for the LGBTQ movement, one needs to pause and rethink, for by now another more radical form of dissidence has already emerged within the movement, the goal of which was never unitary to begin with. This moment, a political accomplishment of great value, is described by David L. Eng as a moment of 'queer liberalism', a product of a 'progressive' US' neoliberal understanding of freedom which could be made universal 'through liberal political enfranchisement and the rights of citizenship, and through the globalization of capitalism and the proliferation of "free" markets' (39). As explained above, for the radical queer, the homonormative appropriation of the movement was not the goal of the movement at all. Those who refuse to accept granting of marriage or civil union rights as a benevolent 'inclusive' gesture of the state are thrust into a precarious zone, in which their dissidence is even reproved by the members of the LGBTQ community. This group of radical queers can be best described as 'subaltern counterpublics' – 'parallel discursive arenas where members of subordinated social groups invent and circulate counterdiscourses to formulate oppositional interpretations of their identities, interests, and needs' (Fraser 123). The state-endorsed homonormativity has acquired a hegemonic status in First World countries, and those who are outside it are the new dissident citizens, subalterns within the community to which they thought they belonged. These subaltern queer counterpublics contest the established boundaries separating politics from economics and domestics, displacing hegemonic elements of the means of interpretation and communication; they keep inventing newer discourses to interpret and articulate their needs (see Fraser).

Let us take the intriguing case of the ally of America, its 'true friend', Israel – currently being hyped as a tourist destination particularly for well-off gays. The American media has been relentlessly promoting Tel Aviv, Israel's most hi-tech city, the 'party capital' of the Middle East, as the world's gayest city for a long time, particularly since 2011, when the White City, as it is popularly known, topped the list by defeating cities such as New York, Toronto and Sao Paulo in a poll conducted by GayCites.com and American Airlines. The Tel Aviv Pride Parade, since then, has become the most sought after world event among the queer population, with queer travellers flocking to the city in large numbers every June. What makes Tel Aviv worthy of the attention of the United States as the gay mecca is its geopolitical location – its closeness to Palestine – and its demography – a Jewish majority. Israel, as a Jewish state, has always been an ally of the United States, a relationship that goes back to the Cold War days and has been reinforced by their anti-Palestine stance. Currently the two countries have joined hands in their fight against Islamic terrorism and are developing sophisticated military technology together. Most importantly, as policy analysts Michael Eisenstadt and David Pollock point out: 'Israel remains a counterweight against radical forces in the Middle East, including political Islam and violent extremism. It has also prevented the further proliferation of weapons of mass destruction in the region by thwarting Iraq and Syria's nuclear programs' (Web, n. p.). All that sounds wonderful; but the deep politics in projecting Tel Aviv's queer liberalism is to show the rest of the Islam-dominated Middle East as homophobic by contrast. While many queers are in compliance with the United States, the dissident voice is being heard, stridently challenging the strategic ploy in entrenching Islamophobia by *using* queer lives. A remarkable example was set in the Toronto Pride of 2010. The Queers Against Israeli Apartheid succeeded in reversing the censorship of the term 'Israeli Apartheid' by the Pride organisers. Tim McCaskell, a member of Queers Against Israeli Apartheid, said, 'This is a victory for the Palestine solidarity movement, which has faced censorship and bullying tactics from the Israel lobby for far too long. The Israel lobby learned a tough lesson today about our community's proud history of standing up to censorship and human rights abuses' (Anon., Web, n. p.).

Something even more important had happened a year earlier in Tel Aviv. On 1 August 2009, a masked gunman entered a meeting of Aguda, Israel's oldest LGBTQ group, and shot down two members and severely injured twelve others. In a mass rally a week after this incident, even Right-wing politicians 'came out'. They so far had remained closeted fearing hostile reaction from their conservative constituency. Every single political party *used* this incident to further their own agendas, and a 'deal' was struck. What was this deal? As Gross writes,

> Its terms are that "we" will be good, normative and Zionist gays, who are willing to partake in the discourse of Israel as a liberal democracy and collaborate, directly and indirectly, in the state's use of gay rights as a fig leaf for Israeli democracy, and in return we will get sympathy and some support from the state. (Web, n. p.)

What was lost in the process of accepting this deal? Dissident queer voices were by implication expected to shut up, and the 'good gays' were expected to comply with the state, especially with Right-wing politicians, in advancing their oppressive policies towards Palestine as well as the migrants, if they did not want to lose state endorsement. However, the state's obnoxious political game was not too difficult to see through. The dissident retaliation was witnessed in the 2010 Tel Aviv Pride that used to be showcased as Israel's carnivalesque testimony of liberalism.

Queer radical activists announced an alternative parade a few days before the municipal-sponsored parade, criticising the state's co-optation of the LGBTQ movement and using it as a vehicle to further their oppressive schemes. A rainbow flag with the words 'We refuse to celebrate while others suffer' was unfurled as a slap on the state-interpellated queers celebrating Israel's cultivated performance of liberalism and democracy; and this marked an unambiguous splintering of the queer-bloc. But, as Gross reports, the conformist queers were even more disconcerted by a rumour that radical queer activists brandishing Turkish and Palestinian flags were to 'occupy' the parade. As the alarm rang through Tel Aviv of a possible intervention of the queer Left-wing activists, Israeli nationalist Right-wing groups arrived at the parade for the first time to distribute miniature national flags to the participants, while some participants wore stickers with messages such as 'I am a proud Zionist' and 'No to the occupation of the parade'. The fear of dissident voices overwhelmed the all-is-hunky-dory-in-Israel image projected by the Pride so far. Although the Turks and Palestinians did not eventually arrive, two parallel Prides made it clear that the state's colonisation of the LGBTQ movement was without consent from a significant number of queers. It remains doubtful whether Tel Aviv's topping the list of gay destinations of the world in 2011 was a genuine outcome of a democratic poll or it was another sly strategy to redeem Israel's image as a queer liberal state – an image which was remarkably tarnished the year before.

The Tel Aviv case presents an excellent example of what Jasbir Puar calls 'homonationalism'. In her path-breaking work, *Terrorist Assemblages: Homonationalism in Queer Times*, Puar examines how liberal politics incorporate certain queer subjects into the fold of the nation state through developments including the legal recognition through the overturning of anti-sodomy laws and the proliferation of mainstream representations. These incorporations have reallocated many queers from being figures of death (via the AIDS epidemic) to subjects endorsing life and productivity (gay marriage and reproductive kinship). Puar contends, however, that this tenuous inclusion of some queer subjects depends on the production of populations of Orientalised terrorist bodies. Heteronormative ideologies that the US nation state has long relied on are now accompanied by homonormative ideologies that replicate narrow racial, class, gender and national ideals. These 'homonationalisms' are deployed to distinguish upright 'properly hetero', and now 'properly homo', US patriots from perversely sexualised and racialised terrorist lookalikes – especially Sikhs, Muslims and Arabs – who are cordoned off for detention and deportation. Revisiting her thesis, Puar notes,

> Homonationalism . . . is not simply a synonym for gay racism, or another way to mark how gay and lesbian identities became available to conservative political imaginaries; it is not another identity politics, not another way of distinguishing good queers from bad queers, not an accusation, and not a position. It is rather a facet of modernity and a historical shift marked by the entrance of (some) homosexual bodies as worthy of protection by nation-states, a constitutive and fundamental reorientation of the relationship between the state, capitalism, and sexuality. To say that this historical moment is homonational, where homonationalism is understood as an analytics of power,

> then, means that one must engage it in the first place as the condition of possibility for national and transnational politics. ('Rethinking Homonationalism' 337)

However, homonationalism as a discourse did not originate in the United States, and it is not precisely a post–9/11 phenomenon. The first politician to argue on these lines was the Dutch activist Pim Fortuyn, an openly gay former sociology professor and a former Marxist who increasingly travelled Rightward. His core argument against Muslim immigration to the Netherlands was his contention that Islam posed a terrible threat to Western progressive values, especially its sympathy towards LGBTQ rights. 'In Holland, homosexuality is treated the same way as heterosexuality', he noted at one campaign event, 'In what Islamic country does that happen?' (qtd. in Erickson, Web, n. p.) Fortuyn's newly founded political party took second place in the 2002 Dutch elections, nine days after he was assassinated. This argument found enthusiastic supporters in the Euro-American world, especially after 9/11.

The Orlando shooting (12 June 2016), where a Muslim man gunned down 49 queer Americans, opened up an accidental political field in which the then Republican presidential candidate Donald Trump played a win-win game. He used this incident to project Hillary Clinton, his Democratic opponent, in poor light, by questioning her sympathies towards immigrants. In a dramatic speech made just after the incident, Trump said, 'Forty-nine wonderful Americans were savagely murdered by an Islamic terrorist. This time the terrorist targeted the LGBTQ community. No good, and we're gonna stop it. As your president, I will do everything in my power to protect LGBTQ citizens from the violence and oppression of a foreign hateful ideology'. He went on to add,

> The burden is on Hillary Clinton to tell us why we should admit anyone into our country who supports violence of any kind against gay and lesbian Americans. . . . Hillary Clinton can never claim to be a friend of the gay community as long as she continues to support immigration policies that bring Islamic extremists to our country who suppress women, gays

> and anyone who doesn't share their views or values. (qtd. in Graham, Web, n. p.)

While Trump was busy making a strong case for ousting and banning the Muslim Other, it was soon discovered that the gunman's religious affiliation had nothing to do with the killing. But by then, what had to be achieved was achieved. A solidarity rally that was taken out immediately after the incident at the Stonewall Inn in Greenwich Village, the queer-rights landmark in New York City, was rent with shouts of 'Muslims are the problem!' It was a moment of racist and xenophobic othering openly driving a wedge through an LGBTQ solidarity rally, collapsing its principles and ideologies. Even though there are many Muslim LGBTQ groups – like Muslims for Progressive Values, Muslim Alliance for Sexual and Gender Diversity, Al-Fatiha (named after the first chapter of Quran, which means 'The Opening') and Lavender Crescent – queer Muslims exist as a sort of ghost contingent (see Graham).

Dissident voices certainly exist, but a majority are sold out to the state's baits that are tactically hung in front of the dissenters, baits which are enticing enough to make them abandon their politics of dissent and willingly turn into law-abiding citizens, to settle down into familiar structures of homonormativity. Analysing the *Lawrence v. Texas* ruling as well as Massachusetts' legalising of same-sex marriage in 2003, Eng quotes Hannah Arendt who made the extremely valuable point that citizenship is nothing less than 'the right to have rights'. Eng elaborates,

> Seen from this perspective, queer liberalism's appeals to the state mark a significant moment in which the politics of "Queer Nation" and "US citizen" are no longer antithetical, a fact evident in the astonishing August 2004 coming-out statement (scripted with the assistance of the Human Rights Campaign) of former New Jersey Governor James McGreevy: "My truth is that I am a gay American". (41)

So, has the death knell of queer politics been clearly tolled in the First World nations? Yes and no. A certain group of citizens still willingly remains outside the fold, and protests against the state's strategies of blunting queer radicalism. What is scary is that the lure of homonormativity in a late capitalist society is so overwhelmingly irresistible that a new majority/minority discourse would further splinter the movement across the globe – even in countries where the struggle is still for legal recognition. The homonormative majority would in many ways dominate, marginalise and vilify those who would balk at joining their herd.

REFERENCES

Anon. 'Queers Against Israeli Apartheid'. 23 June 2010. Web. 13 June 2017. <https://queersagainstapartheid.org/2010/06/23/queers-against-israeli-apartheid-wins-battle-against-censorship/>.

Banerjea, Niharika, Debanuj Dasgupta, Rohit K. Dasgupta, and Jaime M. Grant, eds. *Friendship as Social Justice Activism: Critical Solidarities in a Global Perspective*. Chicago: U of Chicago P, 2016. Print.

Bourdieu, Pierre. *Outline of a Theory of Practice*. Trans. Richard Nice. New York: Cambridge UP, 1977. Print.

Corber, Robert J., and Stephen Valocchi. Introduction. *Queer Studies: An Interdisciplinary Reader*. Eds. Robert J. Corber and Stephen Valocchi. Malden: Blackwell, 2013. 1–17. Print.

D'Emilio, John. 'Capitalism and Gay Identity'. 1983. *The Lesbian and Gay Studies Reader*. Eds. Henry Abelove, Michele Aina Barale, and David M. Halperin. New York: Routledge, 1993.100–13. Print.

Eisenstadt, Michael, and David Pollock. 'Friends with Benefits: Why the U.S.–Israeli Alliance is Good for America'. *The Washington Institute: Policy Analysis*. 7 November 2012. Web. 11 January 2017. <http://www.washingtoninstitute.org/policy-analysis/view/friends-with-benefits-why-the-u.s.-israeli-alliance-is-good-for-america>.

Eng, David L. 'Freedom and the Racialization of Intimacy: *Lawrence v. Texas* and the Emergence of Queer Liberalism'. *A Companion to Lesbian, Gay, Bisexual, Transgender, and Queer Studies*. Eds. George E. Haggerty and Molly McGarry. Malden: Blackwell, 2007. 38–59. Print.

Erickson, Amanda. 'Trump's Support of Gays is Right out of the European Far-right Playbook'. *The Washington Post*. 1 February 2017. Web. 13 May 2017. <https://www.washingtonpost.com/news/worldviews/wp/2017/02/01/trumps-support-of-gays-is-right-out-of-the-european-far-right-playbook/?utm_term=.9f139cbf21ab/>.

Evans, David. *Sexual Citizenship: The Material Construction of Sexualities*. London: Routledge, 1993. Print.

Fraser, Nancy. 'Rethinking the Public Sphere: A Contribution to the Critique of Actually Existing Democracy'. *Habermas and the Public Sphere*. Ed. Craig J. Calhoun. MIT Press: 1992. 109–42. Print.

Freeman, Elizabeth. 'Queer Belongings: Kinship Theory and Queer Theory'. *A Companion to LGBTQ Studies*. Eds. G. E. Haggerty and M. McGarry. Malden: Blackwell, 2007. 295–315. Print.

Graham, David A. 'The Complicated Pain of America's Queer Muslims'. *The Atlantic*. 14 June 2016. Web. 17 August 2017. <https://www.theatlantic.com/politics/archive/2016/06/lgbt-muslims-orlando/486923/>.

Gross, Aeyal. 'Israeli GLBT Politics between Queerness and Homonationalism'. *Bully Bloggers*. 3 July 2010. Web. 18 October 2017. <https://bullybloggers.wordpress.com/2010/07/03/israeli-glbt-politics-between-queerness-and-homonationalism/>.

Halberstam, Judith. 'Forgetting Family: Queer Alternatives to Oedipal Relations'. *A Companion to LGBTQ Studies*. Eds. G. E. Haggerty and M. McGarry. Malden: Blackwell, 2007. 315–24. Print.

Imbert, Fred. 'Obama: Same-sex Marriage Decision will Strengthen our Communities'. *CNBC*. 26 June 2015. Web. 11 July 2015. <http://www.cnbc.com/id/102777294>.

Kulick, Don. 'A Man in the House: The Boyfriends of Brazilian *Travesti* Prostitutes'. 1997. *Queer Studies: An Interdisciplinary Reader*. Eds. R. J. Corber and Stephen Valocchi. Malden: Blackwell, 2013. 237–54. Print.

Oldenburg, Ray. *The Great Good Place: Cafés, Coffee Shops, Bookstores, Bars, Hair Salons and Other Hangouts at the Heart of a Community*. New York: Paragon House, 1989. Print.

Puar, Jasbir, K. *Terrorist Assemblages: Homonationalism in Queer Times*. Durham: Duke UP, 2007. Print.

---. 'Rethinking Homonationalism'. *International Journal of Middle Eastern Studies* 45 (2013): 336–39. Print.

Reddy, Gayatri. *With Respect to Sex: Negotiating Hijra Identity in South India*. Chicago: U of Chicago P, 2010. Print.

Rich, Adrienne. *Blood, Bread and Poetry: Selected Prose*. New York: W. W. Norton, 1986. Print.

---. 'Compulsory Heterosexuality and Lesbian Existence'. *Signs* 5.4 (Summer 1980): 631–60. Web. 12 January 2017. <https://www.jstor.org/stable/3173834>.

Schneider, David. *A Critique of the Study of Kinship*. Ann Arbor: U of Michigan P, 1984. Print.

Shahani, Parmesh. *Gay Bombay: Globalization, Love and (Be)longing in Contemporary India*. London: Sage, 2008. Print.

Sparks, Holloway. 'Dissident Citizenship: Democratic Theory, Political Courage, and Activist Women'. *Hypatia* 12.4 (Fall 1997): 74–110. Print.

Spivak, Gayatri, and Judith Butler. *Who Sings the Nation State?* Kolkata: Seagull, 2011. Print.

Weeks, Jeffrey. 'The Sexual Citizen'. *Theory Culture Society* 15.35 (1998): 35–52. Web. 24 October 2018. <http://tcs.sagepub.com/content/15/3/35>.

Westermarck, Edvard. 'Homosexual Love'. 1917. *Sexualities in Anthropology: A Reader*. Eds. A. P. Lyons and Harriet D. Lyons. Malden: Wiley-Blackwell, 2011. 106–11. Print.

Weston, Kath. *Families We Choose: Lesbians, Gays, Kinship*. New York: Columbia UP, 1997. Print.

Chapter Three

The Rural Queer: Moving Beyond the Metropolis

Studies on queer identities and queer spaces have had somewhat of an urban bias. From ethnographic work on queer lives in the West by scholars such as Sharif Mowlabocus to new and emerging work on queer lives in the Global South such as Elisabeth Engebretsen's *Queer Women in Urban China* and Naisargi Dave's *Queer Activism in India* provide fascinating accounts of queer lives in the city but neglect to discuss the queer experience in rural areas.

David Bell and Gill Valentine, in one of the early studies of rural lesbian and gay lives, argue that studies on ruralism whilst encompassing issues on gender, class and ethnicity, neglect discussing sexuality. In fact, when rural queers are discussed, their experiences are problematised as backward spaces of repression which need to be left behind for queer emancipation. But, as Bell and Valentine discuss in their article, there are lesbians and gay men who live in the countryside and there are those who visit rural areas to make use of the various resources these spaces have to offer. The rural offers an important perspective in addressing issues of queerness and sexuality that have not been fully explored. In this chapter we engage with a range of interdisciplinary scholarship and visual/literary texts on the rural queer from a global perspective to discuss how queerness and rurality are imagined, experienced and lived.

RURAL QUEER LIVES

Geographical identity clearly shapes the lived experiences of LGBTQ individuals, leading to migration, dislocation and 'sexual exiles'. Johnson, Gilley and Gray have argued that 'rural' does not necessarily mean isolation. In fact, they cite the American rural as an example where new communication technologies and transportation have radically transformed these spaces. However, Annes and Redlin, in their study of masculinity and gay men in rural France and the United States, argue that the lack of role models and visibility of homosexuality was a major factor for many gay men (279). Popular cultural artefacts such as television shows and movies became a source of information for many of these men; but rather than providing a source of information it caused more confusion as they did not recognise themselves in these discourses.

Rurality in the context of queer lives might be better understood not just as material space but also as symbolic imaginaries (Gorman-Murray et al). Scholars such as David Shuttleton have invoked the concept of the 'gay pastoral' to draw attention to the rural as a site of belonging. Discussing the British film *Beautiful Thing* (1995), Shuttleton argues that the woodland setting signifies the naturalness of same-sex love and an endorsement of its 'authenticity'. The rural in this context is not the one of the repressed closet but rather one of escape and retreat from the consumerist hypersexualised urban gay male culture. Shuttleton invokes Raymond Williams's classic *The Country and the City* (1973). Williams argues that British literary imagination depicts the city as a site of capitalist production and labour with loss of romanticism and by contrast, the countryside as natural, unadulterated and romantic. He rejects such a dualistic explanation and mythologisation of the city/countryside. Instead he argues that both are inextricably linked to cultural and romantic imaginaries. Moving to contemporary Britain, Browne and McGlynn, in their study of the equalities landscape in rural Sussex, illustrates the complexities of implementing LGBT equality legislation in the countryside. They question the narrative of progressive agenda only being enacted by 'liberal urban communities' and illustrate how hostile rural areas can also do the same. They both argue that whilst much of the earlier literature on rural sexualities has tended to focus on the recurring issues of availability of services for sexual minorities, recent scholarship such as theirs have gone about challenging this narrative of the 'intolerant' rural.

Queer lifeworlds are predicated upon rural-to-urban migration. As Weston has argued, the city is contrasted as a binary to rural queer existence where the urban space is represented as a 'beacon of tolerance'. Manalansan, writing about queer Filipino immigrants, argues that such movements across space is not simply a move from tradition to modernity – it should also be seen as a rewriting of the traditional and a contestation and reformation of identities rather than just assimilation (14). Mary Gray's study of rural lives in America suggests that discovering one's queer self requires three things – privacy, a visible social community and a safe space (5). For many queer people growing up in the countryside, the concept of privacy remains unachievable. Another factor that Bernadette Barton's study of the 'red states' in America found was the role of the Church around which communities have grown. Barton argues that as most of these Churches construct homosexuality as sinful, lesbians and gay men from the region must choose between staying in what she calls the 'toxic closet' or risk rejection and ostracism from the people who are supposed to care for them the most – their families, friends and neighbours (5). This leads to a lack of self-esteem, as Barton notes. Not only do these gay individuals have to hide their sexuality, but they also have to endure sitting through sermons calling them sinners and calling for their death in extreme cases. She notes that for many respondents this life of being 'othered' have given them a unique position, which her respondents describe as 'the view from the margins', and thus she argues that rural queer foster stronger friendships and kinship ties leading to 'enduring friendships and increased happiness' (237).

There are many complicated issues related to rural queer lives and the ethics of doing such research. The global push towards visibility politics which demands recognition and political currency related to being 'out and proud' comes with its own concerns about demands of safety and justification. As Bell and Valentine so eloquently asked in their essay, who does this kind of research benefit and who might it harm? (120)

RURAL QUEER SPACES

One of the consistent characteristics of the research into the rural queer is questioning the narrow definition of queer visibility/invisibility. What most of these studies demonstrate is that there are varying levels of visibility exhibited by rural queer men and women and an expectation to be 'functionally invisible' (Gray 96). The tensions around family expectations, religion and community shape public visibility in rural settings. The rural closet, as Schweighofer argues, depends not upon just identifying as gay but on gayness being a major factor of one's identity. It could be argued that visibility politics and queer urban liberalism have also led to feelings of incompatibility for many rural queers who prioritise other parts of their identity such as parenthood or professional roles. Weston's study found that large number of queer men and women from the countryside often returned to rural living as a result of feeling incompatible with urban queer cultures.

Gorman-Murray, Pini and Bryant have also noted another flow of queer migration where city-born queer people move to rural areas for personal and political reasons (5). The most well known of these are lesbian separatist groups in the United States, the United Kingdom and Australia who have formed lesbian communes along the lines of feminist and ecofeminist politics. The rural space is seen as an alternative to the consumerist capitalist society of the cities. The rural space, in this instance, also signifies a rejection of heteropatriarchal powers. Gorman-Murray, Pini and Bryant, citing David Bell's earlier work, also note that semi-separatist communities of gay men called 'radical faeries' have also sought to establish rural lives in a rejection of heteropatriarchal capitalism of the city.

Studies on rural/semi-urban queer spaces in India have thrown up some interesting examples as well. *Launda* dancers are a community of trans women who perform in the rural belt of Uttar Pradesh and Bihar in India. This community of poor dancers mostly migrate during the wedding season in spring and summer to perform.

As discussed elsewhere (Dasgupta, 'Launda Dancers: The Dancing Boys of India'), sexual exploitation by wedding bands who hire these dancers has become synonymous with the tradition of *launda* dancing, with many of the boys forced into prostitution. At the same time, however, ethnographic research among this community has brought up some interesting observations about kinship and friendship arrangements. Most of these young dancers have found village life isolating and at times violent, but the village is also a space where they have formed intimate bonds with one another and sympathetic individuals outside the community. In fact, many of the dancers have claimed that they preferred the strong friendship bonds they get to develop during these brief periods in rural India with other *laundas*, over the anonymity they face on a daily basis in the city. A similar study by Boyce and Dasgupta on small towns in India has called it a 'room to breathe' (220). Several gay men who were interviewed found the queer culture in the city 'excessive' with the constant media intrusion described as a panopticon (Foucault) where they felt under constant surveillance. For many of these individuals the small town of India offered greater anonymity and safety than the metropolitan cities.

Studies in rural southeastern China by scholars such as Friedman have also challenged the narrative of rural spaces as sexually repressive. Friedman argues that premarital socialising and even sexual activity is not completely unheard of. Her research shows that there has been a shift in perceptions from the dominant discourse of identifying sexuality primarily with reproduction and marriage to a more diverse range of sexual pleasures and identities.

John Howard's essay 'Homosexuals in Unexpected Places?' provides a strong critique of doing gender and sexuality research beyond the metropolis. Howard argues that whilst there is a fight to ensure that private spaces such as malls and superstores in small towns are made to respect freedom of speech, it is also imperative to pay attention to the ways in which gay men and women are re-appropriating the most conservative and unaccommodating spaces to assert their identity (67). Howard's critique situates itself within the scholarship emerging from the Global South which have argued that the rural needs to be re-imagined beyond the usual way of characterising it as a space of isolation and repression, and scholars need to recognise the many gay men and women who are carving out different ways of living, survival and celebration within that place.

THE UNSAFE RURAL?

In contesting the overall lens of queerness and rurality as an object of analysis and to understand the geographic politics of this space, it is important to also assert that discourses and practices of sexuality-based work undertaken by NGOs and CBOs have almost always viewed the rural space in the realm of inequality and neglect. There is an urgent need to challenge the normalisation of the metronormativity of queer research which is urban-centric (Halberstam). Gavin Brown uses the term 'ordinary city' to call for more engagement with cities and towns which are beyond the metropolis. Brown discusses that there are two main slippages in the focus of such research: there have been more studies on, first, the study of 'gay space within the city', and second, on commercial gay centres of production (by which he means gay districts and neighbourhoods clustered around the cities which support certain kinds of heteronormative identities and living). The imagination of the rural space as being hostile with issues around access makes this narrative even more recurring. However as a host of literature (Abelson; McGlynn) has demonstrated that this is far from true. There is very little engagement with some of the key issues around friendship, acceptance and simplicity which characterise the countryside and rural heartlands of many countries.

There has been an increase in the number of blogs and social media pages which have been set up to combat growing prejudice around the rural and queer lives there. Many people recount stories of feeling alone within their rural homes and deciding to migrate to larger cities, only to come back and discover a place different from the one they had left behind. This short extract from Rachel Garringer demonstrates this:

> I finally did move home in 2011 and I was really worried about it, I definitely didn't know what it was going to be like, I felt

> like I was going to be incredibly isolated, maybe not have community, would I ever be able to date here, what's it like to be here full-time. And I've largely found that there are rural queer folks all over the place who are not only surviving but thriving either in the communities where they came from or into chosen communities they've moved to, and I think there are unique challenges to being queer in rural places but I also feel like there are really unique joys to it. And I think for some queer folks who grow up in rural places, they care just as much or more about, for example, the mountains where they were raised, or the plains or whatever landscape it was or whatever traditions and histories around farming or different things that are happening in rural places, that as they do about their queerness. (Web, n. p.)

Several scholars (Kirkey and Forsyth; Soderstrom; Whittier) have now discussed how rural queers deploy discourses and construct their own rural identities which are in opposition to the commercialised urban gay identities of the larger cities. This re-imagining of the rural space as one of acceptance and tolerance offers a different narrative to the prevailing one. This productive re-imagining of rural sexualities is also useful because it shows the complicated ways through which queerness is constructed and that there is not just one way of 'being' or 'living' as queer people.

RURAL QUEER NARRATIVES

Fictional and narrative representations of queer identities have framed the urban as associated with being out and proud whilst the rural is seen as closeted and homophobic. Through the framing of the rural as incompatible with queer lifestyles, a binary division is created where queer visibility is seen as 'impossible' outside the metropole.

Radclyffe Hall's *Well of Loneliness* (1928) traced the story of its main protagonist Stephen Gordon's progress from isolationism in her country estate to finding 'community' and love in the urban queer community of Paris. The novel maps a pattern that is now recreated in most queer fiction – that the construction of lesbian and gay identities throughout the nineteenth and twentieth centuries required the abandonment of the rural/country home in order to find a community in the city or abroad. In the case of Stephen, not only is she forced to leave her country home but even the country to try and find happiness abroad which is later described as a 'queer revelation'. What is interesting in this novel is also the construction of the city as diverse and global. Stephen and her partner Mary revel in the anonymity of the city which is a far cry from the claustrophobic existence in their rural backgrounds. They befriend other queer couples from the Scottish Highlands and rural United States who have all made their way to urban Paris to experience freedom. In the English countryside Stephen thinks she is the only one of 'her own kind'; but with the journey to the city she realises that there are many more queer people like her who are all looking for community and kinship.

In sharp contrast to Hall's novel is the more recent collection of first-person accounts of gay men about living and working in American farms, collected by Will Fellows. Fellows' ethnographic collection about the lives of gay men growing up on farms during the twentieth century offers a different perspective to urban-centric gay narratives. Fellows argues that within the plain spoken narratives of these men one can find illuminating candour, insight and a sense of humour. As Fellows points out, popular culture in the United States as elsewhere has expanded with more varied perspectives and representations of gay men and women but it continues to neglect the rural queer who are made to believe that those rural roots are irrelevant and embarrassing. A similar book is Michael Riordon's *Out Our Way* (1996) which is based on interviews with over three hundred gay men and women in rural Canada. The sixty narratives collected here depict individual struggles to fit in and deal with a life that has often been imposed upon then and locate the harshness of isolated existence.

There are a variety of film and visual narratives about queer lives in the country. Annie Proulx's 'Brokeback Mountain' (1997) which was later adapted by Ang Lee as a neo-Western drama (2005) is perhaps one of the most well-known. It is a groundbreaking tale set in idyllic rural American Midwest where two cowboys find romance and sexual satisfaction only to be separated due to societal heteronorms. The film was a huge critical success with its fair share of controversies, but most importantly, it opened up a forum for discussing sexuality, homophobia and hate crimes in rural America. The publication of the book *Beyond Brokeback: The Impact of a Film* (2007) collected deeply moving stories of fear, aspiration and resilience of the rural queer community which was sparked by the film. Christopher Pullen, in his study of the web forums which were set up right after the film's release, tells us that whilst most of the discussions were around the film and the book, a curious undercurrent started to flow up where the discussions around the film died down with the personal stories coming to the forefront. He further argues that a need in the audience to find an outlet for their responses to the film was evident in the 50,000 to 100,000 users who visited the forums every month. These users were not only reading but also engaging with the contributions and using the film to explore their own issues of living as queer people in rural America.

Representations of the rural in queer narratives outside the United States remain quite limited. Many of the celebrated queer films from Britain – *Weekend* (2011), *My Beautiful Launderette* (1985) or the recent *My Brother the Devil* (2012) – have mostly dealt with queer politics, romance and coming out within the inner city estates of London or other big cities such as Manchester or Nottingham. A slightly different trajectory was followed in Stephen Beresford's historical drama *Pride* (2014) which tells the true story of lesbian and gay activists from London who organised to raise money for families affected by the British Miners' Strike. An unconventional friendship is struck between the organisers (who later went on to be called Lesbian and Gays Support the Miners – LGSM) and a small mining village called Onllwyn in Wales. The film shows the anxiety faced by the villagers about the lesbian and gay activists coming into their midst. Despite some early hostilities and anti-gay sentiments, the miners are convinced that the group genuinely care about building solidarities between two groups that are under attack from the government and the police. This was a politically significant moment as the 1985 Pride March in London honoured this alliance with the miners leading the march and the National

Union of Miners finally pressuring the Labour Party (which was in opposition during that time) to incorporate queer rights in their party programme. The film dispels the notion that the countryside is inherently homophobic or even heteronormative, and is a pivotal example of how commitment to queer social justice transcends the urban/rural divide.

There are some interesting rural queer narratives from the Global South. Apichatpong Weerasethakul's *Tropical Malady* (2004) tells the romantic story of a soldier and a country boy both of whom pay regular visits to a Thai jungle. Through its surreal storyline the film frames the countryside and the jungle as a queer space which protects their secret and allows their romance to blossom. Another very interesting film is Yudho Aditya's *Pria* (2016). *Pria* portrays the complexity of being a queer Muslim male in rural Indonesia. The film shows the remoteness of parochial isolation, as we watch a teenager's struggle with his Islamic duty to marry and his non-conformist sexual identity. India has also seen a growth of queer films in the last two decades, though almost all of them are set in the city. An exception to this is Sridhar Rangayan's *Yours Emotionally* (2007). The film starts in a village in India where Ravi, a young Indian man from England, heads to an all-night gay party. The film has a non-linear storyline with surreal sequences. The village seems to exist outside conventional Indian sociocultural norms, and through its magic realism, the film frames it as a queer Utopia with exalted scenes of defying tradition, acceptance and compassion.

These various queer narratives from rural areas and their representation on print and screen lend a voice to the different axes of recognition and being. Being queer is a fragmentary experience, and understanding and experiencing sexual citizenship needs to go beyond the urban/rural binary (Gorman-Murray, Pini and Bryant).

RURAL QUEER INDIA

As mentioned earlier, there is very little work on rural queer studies in India. Among a very small handful of such studies is Maya Sharma's work on lesbian women from the working class, *Loving Women: Being Lesbian in Unprivileged India*. It took great patience and determination to reach out to the various voices portrayed by Sharma in her book. These are women who navigate their subjectivity around compulsory marriage with little access to the metropolitan movements around gay rights that are now so popular and important in contemporary India (also see Dasgupta, *Digital Queer Cultures in India*; Dave). In these interviews, Sharma also demonstrates that the currency of a term like 'lesbian' means very little to her vernacular interlocutors. As Vimlesh, a factory worker, says, 'I do not know the word lesbian . . . why create such categories between male and female. We are all humans aren't we?' (61) It succinctly captures the neoliberal agenda of naming and visibility politics that have been critiqued by several scholars in both India and abroad. For Sharma, recovering these voices from obfuscation is a personal journey. The right to live openly as queer people has been discussed as 'privileged'. For these women, many of who come from small towns and villages, their very existence is based on navigating the strictures of domesticity and yet being able to express their same-sex love. It would be important to point out that whilst Sharma's interlocutors live in semi-urban and urban cities and are unprivileged, many of them are migrants who have moved from villages and small towns to seek better lives in the anonymous city.

Aniruddha Dutta argues that the formation of identities in postcolonial South Asia has developed within modern regimes of power based on social differences and rigid caste politics. Dutta's work with small-town queer and trans individuals in Berhampore and Ranaghat provides an objective study of how many queer/trans communities accommodate plurality and locally varied representations. Many of these groups, as Dutta argues, were set up in the mid-2000s by community members who formed CBOs to attract state funding and governmental support to expand networks of kinship and care through HIV-AIDS prevention services. Dutta's ethnography also provides a way of understanding the diversity of localised queer identities with local kinship structures and even language. She goes on to argue how these communities are often derided and shunned within elite gay organisations for being too loud or vulgar, based on class dynamics. A similar observation is also provided by scholars such as Ila Nagar. Nagar's work on janana communities in Lucknow discusses the consequences of illiteracy, class and non-metropole locations on queer lives in small towns. Nagar argues that whilst the media in India have a narrative which shows higher levels of acceptance and positive representations of queer people, these are all centred in urban areas, and these 'progress' figures fail to discuss the lives of those living in small towns and villages who remain 'digitally untouched' by the growing queer social media. She argues that the many jananas living in small towns desire invisibility and a different mode of living. This hardly 'fits' the neoliberal regimes of visibility politics of post-377 India and thus local cultures such as these are not included within the queer narrative in India.

Boyce and Dasgupta's work also attests to this. They argue that a prevailing narrative of queer life-trajectories, in India and elsewhere, has been oriented around escape from small towns to larger and potentially more anonymous cities where a sense of freedom from heteronormative social mores and familial obligations may be imagined and experienced. In these terms, migration to big cities has been imagined both geographically and temporally – cosmopolitan centres offering not only anonymity and potential social venues for queer subjects, but also a seemingly more modern outlook and attitude wherein same-sex desires might more readily find context and expression. They further argue that the relationship between modernity, queer desires and the Indian state is marked primarily through the fight for securing sexual rights which does not take into account the multiplicity that exists within queer lives in small-town India. The prevailing narrative within the imaginaries of queer lives in small towns are seen as sites that need to be left in order for fully realised sensibilities to take shape.

It would also be worthwhile to point out that class and caste can often be important factors to take into account when discussing rurality in India. As discussed by Boyce and Dasgupta, the stratified existence of queer people on class lines in urban towns provides a significant point of contention to the commonality of queer communities. Similarly in 2015, when the First Telangana Pride Swabhiman Walk was organised by the Bahujan activist Kancha Ilaiah Shepherd, a larger discussion was initiated on Dalit identities in queer spaces. Caste and class intersections in relation to small-town/rural queer spaces was also discussed in several other contexts such as in January 2016 when a public dialogue titled 'Transfeminisms and the Intersectionality of Oppressions' was organised by Sambhabona Trust in West Bengal. Access to spaces and the choice of voices that get represented is also a direct factor related to caste/class and region which often sees urban upper-class/upper-caste voices always being presented over those from rural/semi-urban lower classes/castes.

****

A review of the available literature on rural sexualities has shown a remarkable shift over the years – from the exploration of the troubled and closeted lives of rural gay men and women to a focus on how the rural itself has been fundamental in the development of gay and lesbian identities. The overarching narratives surrounding isolation, safety and tolerance are now also giving way to newer research which point to positive experiences of sexual minorities in rural spaces. Whilst queer visibility plays an important role in political activism, the strategic representational politics of queer people living in the countryside offers new ways of reimagining how one can bring about social and political progress – one that is not tied to neoliberal visibility politics.

REFERENCES

Abelson, Miriam J. '"You aren't from around here": Race, Masculinity, and Rural Transgender Men'. *Gender Place and Culture* 23.11 (2016): 1535–46. Print.

Annes, Alexis, and Meredith Redlin. 'The Careful Balance of Gender and Sexuality: Rural Gay Men, the Heterosexual Matrix, and Effeminophobia'. *Journal of Homosexuality* 59.2 (2012): 256–88. Print.

Barton, Bernadette. *Pray the Gay Away: The Extraordinary Lives of Bible Belt Gays*. New York: New York UP, 2012. Print.

Bell, David, and Gill Valentine. 'Queer Country: Rural Lesbian and Gay Lives'. *Journal of Rural Studies* 11.2 (1995): 113–22. Print.

Boyce, Paul, and Rohit K. Dasgupta. 'Utopia Or Elsewhere: Queer Modernities in Small Town Bengal'. *Urban Utopias: Excess and Expulsion in Neoliberal South Asia*. Eds. T. Kuldova and M. Varghese. London: Palgrave Macmillan, 2017. 209–25. Print.

Brown, Gavin. 'Urban (Homo)sexualities: Ordinary Cities and Ordinary Sexualities'. *Geography Compass* 2.4 (2008): 1215–31. Print.

Browne, Kath, and Nick McGlynn. 'Rural Lesbian, Gay, Bisexual, and Trans Equalities: English Legislative Equalities in an Era of Austerity'. *Sexuality, Rurality, and Geography*. Eds. A. Gorman-Murray, B. Pini and L. Bryant. Maryland: Lexington Books, 2012. 35–50. Print.

Dasgupta, Rohit K. *Digital Queer Cultures in India: Politics, Intimacies and Belonging*. London: Routledge, 2017. Print.

---. 'Launda Dancers: The Dancing Boys of India'. *Asian Affairs: Journal of the Royal Society for Asian Affairs* 44.3 (2013): 442–48. Print.

Dave, Naisargi. *Queer Activism in India: A Story in the Anthropology of Ethics*. Durham: Duke UP, 2012. Print.

Dutta, Aniruddha. 'Legible Identities and Legitimate Citizens: The Globalization of Transgender and Subjects of HIV-AIDS Prevention in Eastern India'. *International Journal of Feminist Politics* 15.4 (2013): 494–514. Print.

Engebretsen, Elisabeth. *Queer Women in Urban China*. London: Routledge, 2015. Print.

Fellows, Will, ed. *Farm Boys: Lives of Gay Men from the Rural Midwest*. Madison: U of Wisconsin P, 1996. Print.

Foucault, Michel. *The History of Sexuality Vol. 1*. Vancouver: Vintage Books, 1990. Print.

Friedman, Sarah. 'Spoken Pleasures and Dangerous Desires: Sexuality, Marriage, and the State in Rural Southeastern China'. *East Asia* 18.4 (2000): 13–39. Print.

Garringer, Rachel. '"We Need to Change that Idea that Rural Areas are Unsafe because It's Not True"'. *I'm From Driftwood: The LGBTQ Story Archive*. Web. 3 November 2018. < https://imfromdriftwood.com/rachel_garringer/>.

Gorman-Murray, Andrew, Barbara Pini, and Lia Bryant. Introduction. *Sexuality, Rurality, and Geography*. Eds. A. Gorman-Murray, B. Pini and L. Bryant. Maryland: Lexington Books, 2012. 1–20. Print.

Gray, Mary. *Out in the Country: Youth, Media, and Queer Visibility in Rural America*. New York: New York UP, 2010. Print.

Halberstam, Jack. *In a Queer Time and Place: Transgender Bodies, Subcultural Lives*. New York: New York UP, 2005. Print.

Hall, Radclyffe. *The Well of Loneliness*. London: Jonathan Cape, 1928. Print.

Howard, John. 'Homosexuals in Unexpected Places?: A Comment'. *American Studies* 48.2 (2007): 61–68. Print.

Johnson, Colin, Brian Gilley, and Mary Gray. 'Introduction'. *Queering the Countryside: New Frontiers in Rural Queer Studies*. Eds. Colin Johnson, Brian Gilley, and Mary Gray. New York: New York UP, 2016. 1–21. Print.

Kirkey, Kenneth, and Ann Forsyth. 'Men in the Valley: Gay Male Life on the Suburban-rural Fringe'. *Journal of Rural Studies* 17 (2001): 421–41. Print.

Manalansan, Martin. *Global Divas: Filipino Gay Men in the Diaspora*. Ann Arbor: Duke UP, 2003. Print.

McGlynn, Nick. 'Slippery Geographies of the Urban and the Rural: Public Sector LGBT Equalities Work in the Shadow of the "Gay Capital"'. *Journal of Rural Studies* 57 (2017): 65–77. Print.

Mowlabocus, Sharif. *Gaydar Culture: Gay Men, Technology and Embodiment in the Digital Age*. Farnham: Ashgate, 2010. Print.

Nagar, Ila. 'Digitally Untouched: Janana (In)Visibility and the Digital Divide'. *Queering Digital India: Activisms, Identities, Subjectivities*. Eds. R. K. Dasgupta, and D. Dasgupta. Edinburgh: Edinburgh UP, 2017. 97–111. Print.

Pullen, Christopher. *Gay Identity, New Storytelling and the Media*. London: Palgrave Macmillan, 2009. Print.

Riordon, Michael. *Out Our Way: Gay and Lesbian Life in the Country*. Toronto: Between The Lines, 1996. Print.

Schweighofer, Katherine. 'Rethinking the Closet: Queer Life in Rural Geographies'. *Queering the Countryside: New Frontiers in Rural Queer Studies*. Eds. M. Gray, C. Johnson and B. Gilley. New York: New York UP, 2016. 223–43. Print.

Sharma, Maya. *Loving Women: Being Lesbian in Unprivileged India*. New Delhi: Yoda Press, 2007. Print.

Shuttleton, David. 'The Queer Politics of Gay Pastoral'. *De-Centring Sexualities: Politics and Representation Beyond the Metropolis*. Eds. D. Shuttleton, D. Watt, and R. Phillips. London: Routledge, 2000. 125–46. Print.

Soderstrom, Mark. 'A Single Queer Voice with Polyphonic Overtones: Elise Matthesen and the Politics of Subjectivity in the Twin Cities'. *Queer Twin Cities*. Twin Cities GLBT Oral History Project. Minneapolis: U of Minnesota P, 2010. Print.

Weston, Kath. *Families We Choose: Lesbians, Gays, Kinship*. New York: Columbia UP, 1995. Print.

Whittier, D. K. 'Social Conflict among "Gay" Men in a Small(er) Southern Town'. *Rural Gays and Lesbians – Building on the Strengths of Communities*. Eds. J. D. Smith, and R. J. Mancoske. New York: Haworth Press, 1997. 53–72. Print.

Williams, Raymond. *The Country and the City*. New York: Oxford UP, 1973. Print

Chapter Four

Queer Area Studies: Malaysia and China in Focus

Over the last few years there has been a growing body of scholarship on Queer Studies emerging from the Global South. These have ranged from studies on queer arts and practices, and queer identity formation, to activisms and protest movements. This chapter will focus on two Southeast Asian countries for a comparative study. Geopolitical formations are important for Queer Studies as discourses of sexuality need to be studied through the lens of colonialism, transnationalism and the national/regional. Through a queer and feminist grounding we analyse the sociopolitical, literary and cinematic landscape of two countries – Malaysia and China. This kind of cross-cultural comparison and study offer new insights for queer scholarship. As Anjali Arondekar has argued, 'the project of geopolitics in all its avatars has emerged to play a similarly redemptive role in the new formations of queer scholarship' (237). Whilst doing this, we are attentive to the fact that contemporary scholarship on queer globalisations and studies on transnational level often imbalance national contexts. As Cakirlar has argued, these studies are often partial when informing about lived sexualities. Regionality as a concept within queer studies, borrowing Gayatri Gopinath's work, is useful in exploring the particularities of sexual lives that cut across complex national, global and regional processes. She argues that the concept of queer region invokes an 'alternative mapping of sexual geographies that links disparate transnational locations' (343).

Chiang and Wong further argue, 'Queer regionalism reckons with the vertical logics of Euro-American empire, but at the same time a queer regional model signals greater attention to less orderly bilateral and horizontal intraregional traffics of queerness across different countries and regions in Asia' (1645).

The two case studies discussed here explore the ways in which the complex national/regional formations of queerness emerge as objects of inquiry. We use a transnational (Liu and Rofel) and regionalist (Chiang and Wong) approach to open up a new analytical framework to productively study queer sexualities and its circulation across Southeast Asia. The analysis of these two examples strategically revisit scalar and regional discourses on queer area studies.

CASE STUDY 1: MALAYSIA

Malaysia provides an interesting terrain in the study of queer identities. While queer scholarship on Malaysia is sparse, these are significant interventions in understanding how queerness is articulated in Malaysia. This case study is divided in four sections. The first section discusses the sociocultural background of same-sex sexualities in the country. The second section covers *Body 2 Body*, a significant and pathbreaking anthology of queer writings from Malaysia. The third section examines queer representations in Malaysian cinema. The fourth and final section looks at the impact of the Internet and new media on queer lives in Malaysia.

Sociocultural Considerations

Malaysia is a constitutional monarchy with a predominant Muslim population; but it also includes Buddhists, Christians and Hindus. As a former colony of the British Empire, its laws were shaped by colonial-era stipulations, which is true for many former colonies in Asia and Africa. Postcolonial Malaysia is framed by a tension between religion and traditionalism. Same-sex sexual activity in Malaysia is punishable by twenty years in prison and further corporal punishment. The criminal ban on non-procreative sex (anal and oral) also covers heterosexuals, though it is used almost exclusively against queer people. Malaysia's Penal Code (Section 377), it may be noted, also includes flogging. Convicts are flogged with a bamboo cane. Furthermore, Sections 337 and 337a prevent any homosexual man from escaping conviction and covers all forms of 'gross indecency'. Such a vague wording allows the prosecution to often discriminate against queer people. The Malaysian government, in particular, has over the years tried to silence any kind of discussion on same-sex rights, and none of the political parties express any proposals for LGBTQ rights.

Despite these legal restrictions, scholars such as Sharon Bong have chronicled numerous instances of same-sex Malaysian couples living together in an arrangement culturally similar to marriage, if not legally so. While some of them encounter resistance, for many acceptance of their same-sex marriage by their families offers a mode of resilience. Some of the narratives collected by Bong with the help of her participants are testaments to the struggle that gay men and lesbians face. In a particular instance, Bong narrates the story of Dave, who came out to his parents only to face hate speech and domestic violence. Dave's experience of being criminalised by the state and infantilised by his family is not atypical in a country where unmarried men are not seen as adults. The tyranny of the family that is hostile to queerness can also be traced back to the patriarchal system and construction of masculinity (see also Mellström). When families do demonstrate support for their relatives' same-sex relationships, the family home can become a space for same-sex couples to affirm their relationship in a ceremony or receive counselling.

Religion is another important aspect through which gender and sexual identity in Malaysia is policed. A report from Human Rights Watch (2015) pointed out how Sharia (Islamic law) was invoked to prohibit trans women from cross-dressing and to subject them to assault and extortion. One of the most prominent cases of homophobia and a national-level discussion on homosexuality took place with the 1998 arrest of a policeman, Anwar Ibrahim, when he was accused of corruption and sodomy. Despite his claims of innocence, Ibrahim was jailed. The former Prime Minister Mahathir

Mohamad responded that homosexuals should not hold public office in Malaysia (Advocate, Web, n. p.). As with many other Asian countries, grassroots-level organising around sexual health advocacy allows conversation and advocacy work. The PT Foundation is one of the leading organisations in this regard, organising regular events for queer people in Malaysia.

Literary Considerations

Moving on from the sociocultural considerations, this section will focus on the queer literary output from Malaysia. One of the most notable is the pioneering anthology of fiction and non-fiction, *Body 2 Body*, edited by Jerome Kugan and Pang Khee Teik. The collection includes twenty-three chapters and an introduction by the editors. This rich and varied representation of queer life in Malaysia is the first of its kind. The collection is divided into two sections: 'narratives of difference' and 'strategies of desire' most of which are autobiographical in tone. Kugan and Teik begin their introduction by recounting how the Ministry of National Unity and Social Development, while visiting a university in 2003, declared that universities were being run by 'soft men' and highlighted the need for toughening up the effeminate boys of Malaysia. Ultimately, in response, some universities implemented boot camps run by army men, after which many boys 'threw fabulous parties in camouflage drag' (2). The rest of the book follows this kind of humour and pathos as the authors describe their daily struggle of being queer in a society that is homophobic. Themes include coming out to family, being trapped in oppressive community structures, and escaping violence and stigma.

Brian Gomez's 'What Do Gay People Eat?' (15–25), the first story in the collection, is a humorous account of a father who is waiting to welcome his son's boyfriend and does not know how to entertain him. Written in a humorous style, it brings up many issues around 'naming' and recognition. The father recounts how hearing the phrase 'Prasad and his boyfriend' still makes him feel strange (18). Over the course of the story, the father's ignorance turns to acceptance and even resilience when he confronts a homophobic man in a barber shop. Another notable story is Zed Adam's 'The

Old Fig Council' (141–51), which is a surreal tale involving animals and humans. It starts with the death of a man in a pink shirt in the forest and the council swinging into action to see that the guilty is punished. It is an allegorical tale of homophobia and redemption.

Most of the stories deal with middle-class English-speaking characters, and the perspective of the editors is notably urban-centric. The characters are mostly young and work in white-collar jobs or go to college. The language employed and the occasional use of Malaysian colloquialism (such as the use of *lah* and *appa*) situate the collection very much within Malaysia, giving it a national authenticity. Despite the urbanity and affluence of the characters, the stories deal with issues of state repression, violence and struggles with community intolerance. The stories also celebrate love and eroticism. As the first and pioneering queer collection, *Body 2 Body* provides an important addition to the narrative of same-sex sexualities in Malaysia.

Queer Cinema

Cinema plays an important role in social activism by representing sociocultural realities of the contemporary moment, to imagine new possibilities of living. Through a subversion of heteronormativity it provides a 'queer' way of experiencing popular culture. Cinema in Malaysia, as in other countries of the Global South, is a site where the boundary between tradition and modernity is contested. There are numerous films being produced in Malaysia where representation of queerness is being offered as a form of resistance, provocation and possibilities. Khir Rahman's *Dalam Botol* (2011; In a bottle) is hailed as one of Malaysia's first queer feature films that, despite its queer aesthetics and support for non-heteronormative lives, became a box-office success. The film tells the story of a gay couple, Ruby and Ghaus, whose relationship begins to falter after Ruby undergoes a sex reassignment surgery. The rejection by her lover, followed by a personal tragedy, sets Ruby off on a path of self-discovery. As Joe Yan argues, despite its sometimes misinformed and unrealistic treatment of the trans characters, the film was a significant moment in Malaysian cinema. Prior to this, filmic representations of gay and trans characters had been limited to supporting characters or those offering some kind of comic relief. With this film, queer characters moved from the periphery to the centre stage. The film is credited with 'normalising' queerness in its representation of the trans and homosexual as being as viable as the heterosexual. Alicia Izharuddin, however, is a bit more critical of the film. According to her, the film perpetuates the conflation between being gay and trans, where sex reassignment surgery is seen as the ultimate goal. She argues that the film has been used by a homophobic media as a cautionary tale. According to Izharuddin, compared to feature films such as *Dalam Botol,* independent films being made in Malaysia are engaging much more positively with LGBTQ issues ('Dalam Botol, Malaysia's First "Gay" Film').

There are also a few other films that have been significant in this nascent queer cinema movement in Malaysia. Osman Ali's documentary *Bukak Api* (2000), which tells the story of *mak nyahs* (Malaysian male-to-female transsexuals), was banned soon after its release due to its sympathetic portrayal of sex workers and trans people. Ng Hock Soon argues that the film challenges the national construction of identities by directly and indirectly attacking the country's endeavour to modernise and erase 'what it deems vulgar and anomalous' (119). The film uses re-enactment as a way of telling its story, to achieve its authenticity. Ng Hock Soon argues that, while compromising the 'truth value' (125), this was essential in order to capture the voices of disenfranchised groups who are under constant policing and surveillance.

Mien Ly is another important figure in Malaysian video art whose work is hailed by scholars such as Izharuddin ('The Short Films of Mien Ly and an Articulation of Feminist Queer Theory in Malaysia') for responding to the patriarchal and heteronormative society in Malaysia. In addition to her work as a filmmaker, Ly is also an activist who has set up a filmmaking cooperative and organised a sexuality arts and rights festival. She is a regular speaker at international queer and lesbian feminist conferences and film festivals. Two of her films, *My Confession Diary* (2005) and *2 Boys, 2 Girls and a Beat Up Car* (2009), are hailed as landmark films whose themes around female sexuality and cultural transgressions have contributed to the dialogue on decolonisation and a feminist articulation of queer theory in Malaysia. Izharuddin argues that these films have an ethnographic quality that subverts the normative paradigm of First World feminists and male ethnographers speaking for the subalterns.

The films discussed here offer a political dialogue on how queerness gets treated within Malaysian culture and society. At the same time, they also allow a radical approach to the ways in which survival and protest strategies are being rethought through popular culture and art by the country's queer communities. Notwithstanding some of the criticisms around these films and their representational politics, it is important to understand the radical nature inherent both in the making of these films and the actual viewing by the general public in the context of the increased surveillance of queer bodies by Malaysian state authorities. In that regard, it allows these works to offer a critical discourse around queerness and also demands multiple interpretations.

Influence of the Internet

To conclude, it would be essential to mention the growth of virtual communities around Malaysia, especially in places like Kuala Lumpur. The role of new media and information technology has been immense in the growth of queer communities and queer socialisation, and the case of Malaysia is no different. The lack of public spaces that are open and friendly for LGBTQ people has prompted an increase in websites/webzines and social media spaces for community building and consciousness-raising. Yunmei Wong argues that while the growth of information technologies in Malaysia has allowed certain social processes to accelerate for forum and community building, it has also led to the rise of Islamic fundamentalism through the policing of these digital spaces. Nationalism and religion are important aspects of identity and belonging in Malaysia. The struggles of LGBTQ people to be recognised as citizens of the country are ongoing. In addition to political and civil lobbying, art and public culture has started to play an important role in offering that critical discourse and dialogue.

CASE STUDY 2: CHINA

There has been a growing scholarship on Chinese queer cultural studies in the last few years – these include studies on media (Berry, Martin and Yue), ethnographic interventions (Engebretsen), activism (Engebretsen, Schroeder and Bao), historiography (Chiang), and so on. This area thus requires renewed attention from scholars of queer studies. This case study is divided into four sections. The first section provides a sociocultural background, followed by discussions on queer Chinese literatures and queer Chinese visual texts, and finally the role of the Internet in Chinese queer activism and identity formation.

Sociocultural Considerations

Elisabeth Engbretsen's ethnography on queer women in China, based on two years of fieldwork, examines the ways in which Chinese *lalas* (female bisexuals, lesbians and trans women) live and negotiate daily existence within the heteronormative mainstream of Chinese culture. Engebretsen argues that whilst China is undergoing rapid changes brought about through globalisation and neoliberalism, attitudes towards queerness remain muted. China has seen a tremendous growth in its trade and economy with a strong migration from rural areas to cities and speedy urbanisation leading to formation of new communities, but this has also broken down older forms of civic life. One of Engbretsen's primary questions is whether queerness in China is transgressive and disruptive of heteronorms or whether it co-opts itself within normativity. Kang argues that ancient Chinese political ideologies, religion and cultural norms regarded homosexuality as 'normal' and in some cases literature of that period, such as from the Ming dynasty, even promoted it. Scholars such as Hinsch state that opposition to homosexuality can be traced to the influence of Christianity and Islam on Chinese culture during the medieval period with the first statute banning same-sex intercourse carried out in the fourteenth century during the Jiajing era.

Engbretsen interrogates what 'normative' and 'normalcy' actually mean to queer Chinese people. She argues that the co-option of kinship values and familial ideals should not be seen as a failure of queer identity politics but should rather be contextualised within the ways in which these are reconfigured by queer people within the politically oppressive regime of China. This logic of normalisation is one of the various mechanisms through which queer people in China cope with the oppressive regime. Through a positive construction of their sexuality (monogamous, family-oriented), it represents the self by balancing 'the personal desire for happiness and the social norm of respectability' (Engebretsen 57).

Jeffreys and Yu point out that since the 1980s there has been a growth of a queer underground subculture in China with cruising zones in restaurants, bars and hotels. This can be traced to the rapid urbanisation as well as a mainstream media which has signalled recognition, if not acceptance, despite the strict censorship laws of the country. They further argue that same-sex activity and identity should not be conflated and many individuals do not identify themselves as gay, homosexual or *tongzhi* (a term used to refer to sexual minorities in Taiwan, Hong Kong and mainstream China). One such group is the 'Money Boys' – men who have sex with men for commercial reasons but do not identify as queer. In such contexts, cultural and social circumstances also determine acceptance and hence the need for many queer individuals to aspire for respectability.

In comparison to some of its Southeast Asian neighbours, the legal scenario in China for LGBTQ individuals are somewhat liberal. Consensual sex amongst adults has been legal since 1997 when the national penal code was amended; and since 2001 homosexuality is no longer treated as a mental illness. However, despite this, the cultural and social scenario remains fraught with queer individuals often facing police harassment and social denouncement. There are many ways in which they cope with these issues. Engebretsen notes that some queer individuals develop a cooperative strategy by which they date an individual of the opposite sex whilst continuing to privately date, or have sex with, other queer individuals. For women though, Engebretsen argues, marriage could be liberating as it allows them an opportunity to leave their controlling parents for independence and freedom. Marriage is an important issue within Chinese culture and many queer individuals either end up having symbolic same-sex marriages or cooperative marriages which is a form of contract marriage that gives social legitimacy. Through these strategies queer individuals find new ways of being included within the kinship structure and the 'respectable' mainstream.

Literary Considerations

The first two queer novels in Chinese come from Taiwan – Pai Hsien-Yung's *Nièzǐ* (1983; translated as *Crystal Boys* into English in 1989) and Chen Ruoxi's *Zhihun* (1986; translated into English as *Paper Marriage*). Liu, in 'Why does Queer Theory Need China?, argues that whilst Hsien-Yung's novel received much critical attention from scholars, such attention was not paid to Ruoxi's novel. Both novels are transnational tales which problematise Chinese identity and what it means to be Chinese. Writing about the latter novel, Liu argues, 'Chen's queer novel thus shows that the geopolitical identity and future of China is not contingently related to sexuality' (292). *Crystal Boys* is set in 1960s Taipei and follows the life of a young man – Li Qing. After his expulsion from school for his homosexuality, Qing is also thrown out of his home by his father. He starts frequenting a popular cruising park for other gay men and much of the novel deals with his interactions and meetings with these other characters. Fran Martin, in *Situating Sexualities*, argues that there are various interpretations of the novel. *Crystal Boys*, whose Chinese title *Nièzǐ* translates as 'bad sons', is also seen as an allegory of the unrelenting father figure of China and the bad son/province of Taiwan. In *Queer Marxism in Two Chinas*, Liu also argues that the emergence of Chinese queer novels is not just about the arrival of a self-identity politics but rather a development that is shaped by the geopolitics of the Cold War and Chinese Marxism.

There is also a close relationship between films and literature in China. The film *Lan Yu* (2001), based on the queer novel *A Story from Beijing* which has been circulating anonymously on the Web since the mid-1990s, is a case in point. The story is about a young village boy, Lan Yu, who goes to university in Beijing. In the city he has sex with other men for money. He meets Handong, a wealthy businessman and his first customer, and falls in love with him. Their relationship goes through several ups and downs and Handong at one point breaks Lan Yu's heart by saying that he would get married to a woman. Finally, when Handong realises his mistake and acknowledges his love for Lan Yu, the latter dies in a tragic car accident. Many of the novels of this era often portrayed such catastrophic endings of same-sex relationships. The idealised and often imaginary queer Utopias created in these novels appealed to queer readers; and they let readers imagine what living openly could feel like (see Christini). This genre of literature, called 'comrade literature', is exclusively available online and emerged in the late 1990s. It exists primarily as an informal discursive practice where Chinese netizens write and post stories on the discussion boards of popular *tongzhi* websites. There are now hundreds and thousands of such novels and short stories designated as 'comrade stories' (see Leng).

Queer Cinema

The first Chinese gay and lesbian film festival was held at Beijing University in November 2001. It lasted only for a day before it was shut down by the government. Since then the queer cinema movement has grown in mainland China with a range of films celebrating queer lives, documenting queer activism and raging against sociopolitical censorship. As Spencer states, despite the government banning such films and imposing strict censorship, many of these films are now available on the Internet or 'can be purchased from boxes under the counter in DVD shops' (374).

The spectrum of queer cinema emerging from China is fascinatingly diverse. They span a range of genres and styles and include low-budget underground films, highly commercialised films and art house films. Leung argues that there has been a growth of new queer Chinese cinema since 2002. These films are 'queer' not just because they represent LGBT lives, but for the various ways through which they challenge and reconceptualise parameters of heterosexuality. The aesthetic conventions used in many of these films unsettle normativity and celebrate resistance.

One of the most celebrated queer Chinese films comes from Hong Kong – Wong Kar Wai's *Happy Together* (1997) which won the best director award at the Cannes film festival. The film's plot revolves around a couple – Ho and Lai – who are in a destructive relationship where they constantly break up and reconcile with each other. Whilst Lai is the more stable of the two, we see how Ho manipulates and uses Lai. The film deals with a variety of issues – from sexual promiscuity to emotional kinships and familial ties. The film has also been criticised for the way in which it marginalises the two characters – the film ends with Ho as a solitary man and Lai still trying to come to terms with his past trauma. Yue strongly contends, 'As a film which the Asian and gay communities have taken pride in, the discourse of homophobia appears to have undermined the emergence of an Asian queer spectatorship. In *Happy Together*, the homophobic erasure of gay visibility has revealed the straight morality of its discourse through the oppressive force of its narrative . . .' (256).

In contrast, a new generation of art films such as *Fish and Elephant* (2003) emerging from mainland China provides a stronger political and social content representing queer lives in China. *Fish and Elephant* follows Xiaoqun, an elephant keeper in a Chinese Zoo, and Xialing, her girlfriend. Their relationship is tested when Xiaoqun's mother comes to visit her in an attempt to set her up in a marriage. Xiaoqun is also followed by an ex-lover, Junjun, who is fleeing from the police on account of having murdered her father. The film was well received in several international film festivals though it had a tough time trying to be screened in China. Fran Martin, discussing female homoerotic representation in Chinese cultures in *Backward Glances*, argues that there is a complex representational politics at play which is both a social commentary on cultural life as well as a political critique of heteronormativity.

There have also been some very interesting documentaries that have been made in recent times documenting queer lives and queer families. Fan Popo's *Mama Rainbow* (2012) and *Papa Rainbow* (2016) document the ways in which Chinese families step up and support their queer children. The documentaries include interviews with mothers and fathers of young Chinese queers from different classes and regions of China, and they reflect on their parental roles, their changing attitudes towards homosexuality and how they have taken leadership roles within the LGBTQ+ equality movement in China. Spencer argues that many of these 'underground films' will soon fade away and disappear as state-sponsored film archives and museums in China do not preserve alternative histories. There is thus a need for further engagement and memorialisation of these visual texts which are a major contribution to our understanding of queer lives and queer representation in China.

Influence of the Internet

This section looks at the growth of new media technologies and how it has changed Chinese queer lives in recent years. Tang, writing about queer spaces in Hong Kong, laments that the non-existence of anti-discrimination laws, conservative family values and a somewhat homophobic media make it difficult for queer communities to cope even in contemporary times. She argues that privacy and same-sex intimacies are difficult to negotiate and risky hiding strategies are often critical for many queer individuals. Tang does not categorically call all living spaces as oppressive, but rather shows the ways in which these negotiations take place. The growth of new media and social media sites has in recent years provided a different avenue for sexual exploration and production of queer spatiality in China.

In their pioneering collection, *Mobile Cultures: New Media in Queer Asia*, Berry, Martin and Yue assert that 'in the past five years the Internet has done to Asia's gay and lesbian communities what Stonewall enabled in the West over the past twenty-five years' (2). The advent of camera-equipped smart phones has massively changed the landscape of communication and social interaction, affording queer citizens of China opportunities for discussion, socialising and accessing media that was previously unavailable to them due to strict censorship laws. Shaw and Zhang have argued that censorship laws in China make it difficult for many queer Chinese filmmakers to make their films available to the domestic audiences; however, through video sharing platforms and Internet-based distribution channels they have found new ways of distributing their content and also interacting with domestic audiences. Chinese webcast series such as *Queer Comrades* (*Tongzhi as Folks*) and

Gay Lab Show are pioneering series promoting queer activism, alliances and entertainment which has led to considerable social impact in informing the general public about queer issues.

Microblogs such as *SinaWeibo* are particularly significant as they show how queer individuals are interacting with one another and promoting awareness of queer rights and representational politics. Engebretsen and Schroeder, writing about queer activism in China, say that Chinese queer people are negotiating queer social spaces which, instead of being confrontational, use specific strategies and priorities. The Western-style politics of 'out and proud' in this context can both liberate and limit the development of queer politics in China.

REFERENCES

Advocate. 'Former PM Says Gays should not Rule Mostly Muslim Malaysia'. *Advocate.* 9 November 2007. Web. 7 November 2018. <http://www.advocate.com/news_detail_ ektid40937.asp>.

Arondekar, Anjali. 'Geopolitics Alert!' *GLQ: A Journal of Lesbian and Gay Studies* 10.2 (2004): 236–40. Print.

Berry, Chris, Fran Martin, and Audrey Yue, eds. *Mobile Cultures: New Media in Queer Asia.* Durham: Duke UP, 2003. Print.

Bong, Sharon. 'Negotiating Resistance/Resilience through the Nexus of Spirituality–Sexuality of Same Sex Partnerships in Malaysia and Singapore'. *Marriage and Family Review* 47.8 (2011): 648–65. Print.

Cakirlar, Cuneyt. 'Introduction to Queer/ing Regions'. *Gender Place and Culture* 23.11 (2016): 1615–18. Print.

Chiang, Howard. *Sexuality in China: Histories of Power and Pleasure.* Seattle: U of Washington P, 2018. Print.

Chiang, Howard, and Alvin Wong. 'Queering the Transnational Turn: Regionalism and Queer Asias'. *Gender Place and Culture* 23.11 (2016): 1643–56. Print.

Christini, Remy. *The Rise of Comrade Literature: Development and Significance of a New Chinese Genre.* MA Diss. Leiden University, 2005. Print.

Engebretsen, Elisabeth. *Queer Women in Urban China: An Ethnography.* Abingdon: Routledge, 2014. Print.

Engebretsen, Elisabeth, William Schroeder, and Hongwei Bao, eds. *Queer/Tongzhi China: New Perspectives on Research, Activism and Media Cultures*. Copenhagen: Nordic Institute of Asian Studies Press, 2015. Print.

Gopinath, Gayatri. 'Queer Region: Locating Lesbians in Sancharam'. *A Companion to Lesbian, Gay, Bisexual, Transgender and Queer Studies*. Eds. G. Haggerty, and M. McGarry. Malden: Blackwell, 2007. 341–54. Print.

Hinsch, Bret. *Passions of the Cut Sleeve: The Male Homosexual Tradition in China*. Berkeley: U of California P, 1992. Print.

Hock Soon Ng, Andrew. 'The Politics of Reclaiming Identity: Representing the Mak Nyahs in Bukak Api'. *LGBT Transnational Identities*. Ed. Christopher Pullen. London: Palgrave, 2012. 114–29. Print.

Human Rights Watch. *World Report 2015: Malaysia*. Web. 6 November 2018. <https://www.hrw.org/world-report/2015/country-chapters/malaysia>.

Izharuddin, Alicia. '*Dalam Botol*, Malaysia's First "Gay" Film: Two Steps Forward, One Step Back'. *LSE: Equity, Diversity and Inclusion*. Web. 6 November 2018. <http://blogs.lse.ac.uk/equityDiversityInclusion/2011/04/dalam-botol-malaysias-first-gay-film-two-steps-forward-one-step-back/>.

---. 'The Short Films of Mien Ly and an Articulation of Feminist Queer Theory in Malaysia'. *Intersections: Gender and Sexuality in Asia and the Pacific* 38 (2015). Web. 6 November 2018. <http://intersections.anu.edu.au/issue38/izharuddin.html>.

Jeffreys, Elaine, and Haiqing Yu. *Sex in China (China Today)*. Cambridge: Polity Press, 2015. Print.

Kang, Wenqing. *Obsession: Male Same Sex Relations in China, 1900–1950*. Hong Kong: Hong Kong UP, 2009. Print.

Kugan, Jerome, and Pang Khee Teik, eds. *Body 2 Body: A Malaysian Queer Anthology*. Petaling: Matahari Books, 2009. Print.

Leng, Rachel. *Chinese Comrade Literature, Queer Political Reality and the Tongzhi Movement in the People's Republic of China*. Durham: Dukespace Publications, 2012. Print.

Leung, Helen. 'Homosexuality and Queer Aesthetics'. *A Companion to Chinese Cinema*. Ed. Y. Zhang. Malden: Blackwell, 2012. 518–34. Print.

Liu, Petrus. *Queer Marxism in Two Chinas*. Durham: Duke UP, 2015. Print.

---. 'Why does Queer Theory Need China?' *Positions: East Asia Cultures Critique* 18.2 (2010): 291–320. Print.

Liu, Petrus, and Lisa Rofel. 'Beyond the Straight(s): Transnationalism and Queer Chinese Politics'. *Positions: East Asia Cultures Critique* 18.2 (2010): 281–89. Print.

Martin, Fran. *Backward Glances: Contemporary Chinese Cultures and Female Homoerotic Imaginary*. Durham: Duke UP, 2010. Print.

---. *Situating Sexualities: Queer Representation in Taiwanese Fiction, Film and Public Culture.* Hong Kong; Hong Kong UP, 2003. Print.

Mellström, Ulf. *Masculinity, Power and Technology: A Malaysian Ethnography*. London: Routledge, 2003. Print.

Shaw, Gareth, and Xialong Zhang. 'Cyberspace and Gay Rights in Digital China: Queer Documentary Filmmaking under State Censorship'. *China Information*. Web. 7 November 2018. <https://doi.org/10.1177/0920203X17734134>.

Spencer, Norman A. 'Ten Years of Queer Cinema in China'. *positions* 20.1 (2012): 373–83. Print.

Tang, Denise. *Conditional Spaces: Hong Kong Lesbian Desires and Everyday Life*. New York: Columbia UP, 2011. Print.

Williams, Walter. 'Islam and the Politics of Homophobia: The Persecution of Homosexuals in Islamic Malaysia Compared to Secular China'. *Islam and Homosexuality*. Ed. S. Habib. Santa Barbara: Praeger, 2007. 1–22. Print.

Wong, Yunmei. 'Queer Travels: Networked Society, Digitizing Queerness and Political Surveillance'. *AOIR: Selected Papers of Internet Research* 14 (2013). Web. 6 November 2018. <https://spir.aoir.org/index.php/spir/article/view/856/pdf>.

Yan, Joe. Y. 'Necessary Facets: Queer Representation in Malaysia'. *Conference Proceedings of the 3rd International Conference on Performing Arts as Creative Industries in Asia*. Sabah: U of Malaysia Sabah, 2013. 142–54. Print.

Yue, Audrey. 'What's So Queer about *Happy Together*? a.k.a. Queer (N) Asian: Interface, Community, Belonging'. *Inter-Asia Cultural Studies* 1.2 (2000): 251–264. Print.

Chapter Five

Reading Queerly

Queer theory enables deconstructive, often disruptive, reading of canonical texts so far not perceived as queer. 'Reading queerly' unravels power structures and disciplinary mechanisms which have 'commonsensically' persisted for years, and that nobody thought of questioning. As Teresa de Lauretis points out, 'Queer theory conveys a double emphasis—on the conceptual and speculative work involved in discourse production, and on the necessary critical work of deconstructing our own discourses and their constructed silences' (iv). The 'Q' in LGBTQ+ often connotes 'questioning'. 'Queer' and 'questioning' can be used alternatively in the sense that it implies a political position, an oppositional reading tactic that relentlessly subverts and dismantles any form of normative interpretation. The disruptive power of 'queer' is succinctly articulated in a tweet by the iconic Colin Self, 'a trans-disciplinary, post-riot *grrl* diva': 'If you are not queer, you are not paying attention' (qtd. in Duncan, Web, n. p.). Reading queerly demands this scrupulous attention which brings about the insight to dissemble what has so far appeared commonsensical, located within heteronormative registers of knowledge. When read queerly, symbols, images and words seem to yield themselves to a deconstructive interpretation whereby new meanings surface, which were always there but had remained unseen. Since the popularisation of queer theory within the academia, scholars have often revisited canonical texts to *dis*-cover in them undercurrents of unspoken desires, resistances to normativity, rupturing of binaries and ambiguous sexualities:

Geoffrey Chaucer, William Shakespeare, Mary Shelley and Thomas Gray to Bankim Chandra Chattopadhyay, Rabindranath Tagore, Harper Lee or Sa'adat Hasan Manto, just to name a few, have all been queerly read and to fascinating outcomes. Glenn Burger, in his queer 'rethinking' of Chaucer and *The Canterbury Tales*, makes this interesting point, which, in our opinion, creditably sums up the theoretical disposition of the queer literary critic:

> We do not want to be "gay" or "lesbian" (to the extent that such terms, however intentionally resistant, reinscribe modern identity systems as inherent and natural), the queer theorist would say, and, more importantly, we have never been heterosexual (to adapt Bruno Latour's formulation). That is, although we live within the inheritance of the modern West's formulation of sexuality (described so forcefully in Foucault's *History of Sexuality*) and the interiorized selves and liberal subjects it subtends, this inheritance remains haunted by the past it has sought to leave behind and remains unable to secure the future it so phantasmatically insists upon. To the extent that queer theory asks us to imagine outside the box of modern sexual identity politics and regimes of sexuality, then, it also asks us to rethink our relationships with temporality and the work of historicization. (xvii–xviii)

In connection to this extract from Burger, let us take a look at the Jataka tales, dealing with the previous births of Gautama Buddha in both human and animal form. John Garrett Jones was the first to point out the unmistakably homoerotic nature of these stories, in which compared to the wife of the Bodhisattva, his friend, often named Ananda ('pure joy'), shows more fidelity, consistency and devotion in loving and accompanying him. Several tales narrate how male friends grow impatient, anguished and tend to lose their health on being separated; heterosexual marriage is consistently belittled; and relationship with the opposite sex is generally discouraged. Same-sex love is often justified in terms of rebirth: a divine intervention to reunite (heterosexual) lovers separated in a previous birth. The erotic energy undercutting these tales of intimate friendship can be partly justified by the commonplaceness of same-sex love within Buddhist monastic cultures, which many experts in Buddhist Studies have shown. Zwilling writes, 'That a certain laxity toward homosexuality has existed at times among Buddhist monastics is confirmed by such phenomena as the *dob dob* of Tibet, a semi-military monastic fraternity who openly engaged in pederasty, as well as by the Mongolian monks reported by Owen Lattimore to have justified their homosexual relationships on "theological grounds"' (209–10). Using terms such as 'pederasty' and 'homosexuality' to describe these sexual intimacies is anachronistic, no doubt, but, for a modern readership, these terms are used for convenience. Jones's and Zwilling's readings, informed by the 'historicizing impulse in queer theory itself' (Burger x), reinforce each other. (However, Jones's work was produced much before Queer Studies had emerged as a discipline.) On the other hand, revisiting religious discourses in search of queer-affirmative narratives, as exemplified by the works of Zwilling, helps buttress a historically testified resistance to worldwide religious denigration of homosexuality as a repugnant, cardinal sin.

Another important strand of queer criticism of literary texts involve revisiting authors whose sexuality remained unknown to the general reading public for the greater part of their literary career or was only revealed after their death. But there was, in the West, a clandestine practice of sharing literary works among readers who belonged to the homosexual subculture. In the introduction to an anthology with a self-explanatory title, *Pages Passed from Hand to Hand: The Hidden Tradition of Homosexual Literature in English from 1748 to 1914*, Mitchell and Leavitt write that 'men who were sexually attracted to other men' formed a 'distinct and numerous reading class', who belonged to a network which helped them 'locate' homosexuality in literature, which they 'passed on to one another. Word of mouth dissemination: *read this*' (xiv; emphasis in the original). Again, there are several examples of writers holding back their explicitly 'homosexual' books for a long time before they eventually 'came out' in print. Christopher Isherwood was one such writer whose later works – such as *Christopher and His Kind* (1976) in which the writer looked back on his formative, youthful Berlin years – filled up the gaps and elisions in his previous writings. Gore Vidal, while introducing the book, wrote, 'Art and sex . . .

intertwine in Isherwood's memoirs'; his earlier memoirs are fiercely 'reticent' about his sexuality, until in *Christopher and His Kind*, he chose to break the silence so much so that Vidal compared him, along with W. H. Auden, to Marlowe: '. . . each might have echoed Marlowe's mighty line: I have found that those who do not like tobacco and boys are fools' (xvii). By this time, it was 'safer' to be homosexual and 'out', given that the buggery laws of England and Wales were repealed in 1967. Even so, E. M. Forster did not bring out *Maurice*, which was nearly complete in 1914 – it was published posthumously in 1971. Yet Forster, who was well-acquainted with the homosexual subculture of England, is known to have risen in defence of Radclyffe Hall's path-breaking 'lesbian' novel, *The Well of Loneliness* (1928), with several other gay men. But surprisingly, not until his death did people know about Forster's homosexuality: not even his biographer Lionel Trilling was aware of it (Leavitt xiii). There are several such writers whose sexuality when discovered by the world attracted renewed critical attention. Forster's widely circulated novels, *A Passage to India* (1924) and *Howards End* (1910), for instance, have been queerly deconstructed to rediscover in them a tactically hidden queer narrative voice, which struggled to be heard against constricting heteronormative barriers. Commenting on the elusiveness that lies at the heart of *Howards End*, P. B. Armstrong writes,

> [Forster] invokes the powers of narrative authority even as he undercuts them, he offers definitive wisdom even as he exposes its partiality, and he pretends to mediate oppositions even as he demonstrates the ineluctability of difference. These contradictions convert the double structure of the *closeted secret* into a way of playing with the reader's assumptions about normative beliefs and normative relations. . . . (307; emphasis added)

But it is done so ingeniously and inconspicuously that it goes unobserved, and is often interpreted as a failure in narrative structure.

Forster's refusal to publish *Maurice* in his lifetime probably arose from a constant fear of censorship, of public shaming and of being branded as obscene. An interesting story is told by Stephen

Spender when he rediscovered a 'draft' of his novel *The Temple* (1929) in a rare book section of an American university library, and sat down to rewrite it much later. An extremely 'frank' account of a hedonistic summer spent with his closest of friends, Isherwood and Auden, Spender did not dare publish *The Temple* for a wider readership, for its (homo)sexual explicitness. Yet he had to write this novel, an act of iconoclasm as it were, for one result of stringent censorship in Britain was 'to make us wish to write precisely about those subjects which were most likely to result in our books being banned' (Spender x). It can be assumed that this novel, like *Maurice*, must have been circulated clandestinely from 'hand to hand' among like-minded readers. But it remained unknown to the public until it was republished in 1988, when Spender was 79. By the time Spender published *The Temple*, a separate category called 'gay and lesbian literature' had begun to appear in bookstores and library catalogues. A self-consciously queer literature had begun to proliferate like never before, especially after the Stonewall Inn Riots in 1969 and most significantly, after the AIDS alarm began to ring loud in Western societies. Writers whose sexuality was not known or were not read queerly during their lifetime also came to be included in queer literature syllabi and library catalogues, along with the contemporary writers of both Western and non-Western origin.

In the following two segments, we shall deal with two texts – one from the English canon and the other from the canon of Bangla literature – which do not have any overt markers of queerness; but, when read queerly, these texts reveal hidden desires, fantasies, resistances and misgivings which could be metaphorical of queerness.

A QUEER READING OF MAUGHAM'S 'THE LOTUS EATER'

The short story 'The Lotus Eater' (1935; pub. 1940), by Somerset Maugham (1874–1965), has been part of the English literature curriculum for decades. Written in the backdrop of World War I, the story about a man's decision to retire from the monotonous life of a bank manager in London and to spend a life of leisure in Capri, a place he madly fell in love with, has been read as a philosophical take on industry versus indolence, and the price one might have to pay for choosing the latter over the former. Wilson's grand plan of ending his life exactly after twenty-five years, the time till which his annuity would financially support him, his unsuccessful attempt at committing suicide when that time arrived, and his eventual degeneration into a pitiable, partially insane man who hides 'like a hunted animal' (Maugham 87) at the sight of humans approaching him, have been interpreted as a commentary on the existential nature of life – one's helplessness in the larger cosmic design of things which is beyond his comprehension and control, and one's inevitable failure in endeavouring to take 'the course of his life into his own hands' (87). Now it is public knowledge, thanks to Maugham's biographer Ted Morgan, that the story is based on Maugham's close friend and sexual partner John Ellingham Brooks (1863–1929), a pianist and a classical scholar who had escaped to Capri, along with numerous other homosexual Englishmen, following the trial of Oscar Wilde in 1895. The story itself has barely any resemblance to that of Brooks who Maugham often visited. However, even if this extra-textual knowledge was not available, 'The Lotus Eater', the title of which speaks back to the *Odyssey* and Tennyson's 'The Lotos-Eaters', reinforcing the metaphor of indolence and its many evils, could reveal unmistakable markers of queerness, when located in history vis-à-vis the cultural referents in the text.

The possibility of reading 'The Lotus Eater' as a queer text is enabled by the writing of the history of homosexuality in England and Western Europe which could be brought upon to dwell on the text, without the particular biographical information mentioned above. The first-person narrator invites the reader into the text with the lure of revealing to them the life of a man whose uniqueness, or rather queerness, lies in refusing to live a life that 'circumstances have thrust' upon him (73). Maugham's Wilson is freed of a family – his wife and son have died. The loss of the family, on which the narrator scarcely dwells, does not become an occasion for mourning; rather, it is an opportunity for escaping the 'selfsame rails' (73) to which the responsibility of looking after a family constricts one.

Except towards the end of the story, when Wilson is infantilised after his unsuccessful attempt at committing suicide, and the absence of a family to take him back is reflected upon briefly, for the greater part of the story, during the twenty-five happy years Wilson spends in Capri, there is not a single moment in which the unavailability of a family is mourned. Rather, the impression the narrator gives is that Wilson has completely given himself up to the indolent life of Capri – its stunning beaches, exquisite liquors, extraordinary flora and fauna, and general hedonism – soaking in all its pleasures and congratulating himself on being able to take that unusual leap of voluntarily retiring from service and choosing to relocate to Capri. Even though Wilson's sexuality is kept elusive in the text, the way the narrator portrays him – an aesthete drunk on Capri's unnerving beauty – is indicative enough of his queerness, given his location in history. Significantly enough, Wilson himself draws attention to this: 'When you live in a place like this, with all its associations, it seems to make history so actual. You might almost be living in historical times yourself' (77).

What associations and historical times is Wilson referring to here? Certainly, Capri's Roman past – particularly, Tiberias and his sybaritic palace, Villa Jovis, which Suetonius had described as a place given to wild debauchery. But through Wilson, Maugham was also pointing towards a more contemporary time. The story was written at a time when the homosexual subculture in the Weimar Republic was in full swing, greatly inconveniencing the Nazis, who would later put an end to it on coming to power. Western and Southern Europe had become a favourite haunt for English and American intellectuals, homosexual or not, who constantly escaped to Europe from strictures on any kind of sexual excess. Anybody who is aware of Capri's reputation as a haunt of homosexual men and women would immediately recognise the queer drift in Maugham's story, without even having access to the author's biography. Rilke and Norman Douglas were in love with Capri; so were Oscar Wilde, Henry James, Truman Capote, Tennessee Williams, Christopher Isherwood, Gore Vidal and Graham Greene, to name a few. It was a regular getaway for lesbians as well. As Stephen Spender says in his introduction to *The Temple*, one great attraction of Europe to the

British and American men was the availability of sex, not to mention high-quality liquor (Spender x). Capri had turned into a homosexual paradise, owing to the efforts of the German industrialist Friedrich Alfred Krupp and the French poet and real-estate heir Jacques d'Adelswärd-Fersen, both millionaires. Notably, the latter built a palace next to the ruined palace of Tiberius. In the hyper-luxury of the palace, d'Adelswärd-Fersen invited innumerable lads from outside and often indulged in elaborate orgies (see Hone).

Maugham's text dwells for a while on the ruins of Tiberius's palace, about which Wilson seems to have done considerable research. But, notably, it was not just Tiberius, or the disarmingly beautiful Capri locales, that provoked Wilson to give up on his job. He tells the narrator how he chanced upon a 'fest' at the Punta di Timberio – the Catholic Church's feast of the Assumption – only a garb behind which the hedonistic pagan feast of Venus was celebrated (Maugham 80). Anyone familiar with the seventeenth-century painting *The Feast of Venus* by Rubens would know what the feast entails – unharnessed sexual energy, mirthful drinking, and a grand festival of erotic love, involving unclothed nymphs and winged cupids. This feast of Venus, followed by a breathtaking view of the moonlit Faraglioni, decided for Wilson what he was so far considering as a possible option. This is conclusive evidence of Wilson's sexuality. However, one more aspect of the text which has often gone unnoticed can actually seal the text's unambiguous queerness.

It is interesting to note how the narrator positions himself with respect to Wilson and his friend in the text. The narrator is a major character, and it is through him that the reader is introduced to Wilson. He is judgemental, but he also maintains a curious detachment, enabling the reader to form her own opinion about Wilson. But what appears fascinating is the 'all-male' camaraderie the text exhibits: the three men – Wilson, the narrator and his friend (who could be based upon Maugham's novelist friend E. F. Benson in whose villa Brooks resided in Capri) – share moments of pleasure, be it in swimming in the emerald waters of the sea, getting sunburnt on the beach, or in the cafe, 'gossiping' about scandals which are aplenty in Capri, or in getting drunk together in a beautiful moonlit night. Though no sexual overtones underlie the descriptions of these moments of togetherness, it is not difficult to spot the homoerotic energy in them. What Maugham paints here is a common sight in Capri, of small groups of men hanging out together, indulging in sexual excesses.

To reiterate, a queer reading of 'The Lotus Eater' does not require the information that Maugham was homosexual, that he was considerably uncomfortable about it (see Morgan), and that he had an erotic friendship with Brooks. The queer reading is facilitated only when the informed reader, well-versed in the history of the emergence of homosexual subcultures in the West, approaches the text as a product of a particular time, and located in a particular place whose reputation as a homosexual elysium (even asylum) has gone down in the collective memory of the queer community.

Unfortunately, in undergraduate classes in South Asia, the queerness of the text is rarely reflected upon. One example is the book *Narrative and Narration: A Study of the Modern Short Story* (2008) which was written as a study guide for the English Honours students of the University of Calcutta. In this book, a group of teachers from the erstwhile Presidency College (now a university) then affiliated to the University of Calcutta, comment on and annotate five English short stories which were part of the undergraduate syllabus. (Some of these stories are still part of the syllabus, though 'The Lotus Eater' has been removed.) In this volume, 'The Lotus Eater' is subjected to a hackneyed reading, as a narrative about the modern man's dilemma and his existentialist crisis, when the commentator mentions in passing the probable similarity between the characters of Wilson and Brooks almost perfunctorily, citing Morgan (Gupta 44). To further 'invisibilise' the text's queerness, the commentator seems to speculate on several aspects of the narrative – such as whether it was the death of his wife and child that provoked Wilson into this self-imposed exile. This appears misplaced when one recalls Wilson's own dismissive attitude towards his family, and his general disapproval of his wife who was always concerned about what other people would say and, unlike him, was averse to travelling and exploring (see Maugham 81). Such reductive readings are unsurprising since it is a practice among traditionalists to warily expunge even obvious signs of queerness from texts they consider sanctified in the canon. The power of compulsory heterosexuality is such that it can readily subsume and eliminate all markers of queerness in an urgency to reestablish and safeguard its own inviolability.

A QUEER READING OF TAGORE'S *CHOKHER BALI*

In this segment we shall discuss another canonical text – Rabindranath Tagore's Bangla novel *Chokher bali* (The Grain of Sand, 1902), a product of colonial modernity in South Asia. Inspired by Bankim Chandra Chattopadhyay's *Bishbriksha* (The Poison Tree, 1872), Tagore wrote a complex novel, breaking significant taboos, unravelling the forbidden passions of a widow who was expected to desist from all forms of corporeal pleasures. While Tagore's Binodini scandalised puritans by articulating her desires and questioning patriarchal norms that imposed on widows a life of stringent abstinence, the novel's queer currency was also channelised through the friendship between Mahendra and Bihari, the two male protagonists, though in an understated way. In 2002 (revised in 2009), Tapabrata Ghosh brought out a path-breaking book, *Gora ar Binoy* (Gora and Binoy), named after the two male protagonists and intimate friends of Tagore's *Gora* (*The Fire-Faced*, 1910), a politically volatile novel set against the backdrop of the nationalist movement. Ghosh begins by observing that the public sphere of the nineteenth- and early-twentieth-century Kolkata was dominated by men, and a peculiarly intimate friendship – emotional or political – existed among them, which had unmistakable 'queer signs'. But, these signs were usually glossed over, since there was no 'culture of [queer] perception' at that time that could enable one to decode the homoerotic over/undertone of these friendships or examples of *maitri-rati* (which can be roughly translated as 'erotics of friendship'). But Tagore was an exception, and he often returned to portraying this special male–male bonding in his novels and plays (Ghosh 10). *Chokher bali* was followed by several other novels, such as *Ghare baire* (*The Home and the World*, 1916), *Gora* and *Chaar adhyay*

(*Four Chapters*, 1934), in which the trope of male–male friendship formed the central element of the plot.

Ghosh argues that Tagore's interest in male–male friendship could be inspired by the writings of Walt Whitman and Edward Carpenter, whom Tagore had met once. Tagore's deep appreciation of *Leaves of Grass* and *Towards Democracy*, in which both Whitman and Carpenter talk about a comradeship based on a deep erotic 'adhesiveness', could have been symptomatic of his interest in male–male bonding, which was also an 'adhesive' force in nation-building, best exemplified by Bankim Chandra Chattopadhyay's *Anandamath* (1882) which was translated into English by J. S. Lipner with the suggestive title, *A Sacred Brotherhood* (2005). Notably, Tagore, in his essay *Jatharthodosor* ('The Right Companion'), had translated parts of *Symposium*, especially Aristophanes's theory of the conjoined bodies (male–male, female–female, male–female) separated by Zeus. This indicates that Tagore seems to be well-versed in Western discourses of homosexuality (Ghosh 35).

However, what escapes Ghosh's attention is a curious coincidence. In 1902, the very year Tagore published *Chokher bali*, Edward Carpenter brought out *Ioläus: An Anthology of Friendship*, which many identify as the first English-language book on a homosexually themed 'reading', as Mitchell and Leavitt observe (xiii). This book is a detailed cultural anthropological account of same-sex friendships across civilisations and times – a friendship which in modern parlance can be read as 'homosexual'. There was, as one realises today, an effort on Carpenter's part to engage in painstaking research to excavate lost signs of homoeroticism which when rediscovered could provide a historical justification for his own relationship with George Merrill. It is unknown whether Tagore knew of this book, but his acquaintance with *Towards Democracy* is well-established. Tagore had certainly read the lines quoted below, and many other similar lines:

> O joy divine of friends!
> To hold within the circle of one's arms
> More than the universe holds:
> So sweet, so rare, so precious beyond words,
> The god so tenderly mortal!

> Not kisses only or embraces,
> Nor the sweet pain and passion of the flesh alone;
> But more, far more,
> To feel (ah joy!) the creature deep within
> Touch on its mate, unite, and lie entranced
> There, ages down, and ages long, in light,
> Suffused, divine – where all these other pleasures
> Fade but to symbols of that perfect union! (Carpenter, 'Towards Democracy', Web, n. p.)

However, Tagore had his restrictions of belonging to a largely homophobic society, and he did not go beyond a certain limit in portraying male–male friendship. Moreover, he was writing at a time when nationalist discourses were bent on constructing a virile image of the Bengali male who could take on the oppressive British Raj and eradicate forever the disparaging label, 'effete', given to him by the coloniser. Yet, as testified by *Ghare baire*, Tagore was deeply critical of the nationalist celebration of virility, violence and the uncontrolled audacity of going to any extent on the pretext of achieving independence. In any case, all his aforementioned novels were successful in addressing the homoerotic undercurrent in male–male bonding. But, as we shall show, Tagore's women are not mere passive actors in this drama of homosocial/homoerotic male bonding. This in turn makes his novels remarkably modern and contemporary.

Chokher bali defies norms in many ways, the foremost being Tagore's unpretentious representation of female sexuality. However, the Mahendra–Bihari bonding, which is one of the prime movers of the plot, is rather complex. Bihari has a loving dependency on Mahendra/Mahin-da, despite his strong personality and self-assertiveness. Mahendra, who shares an overtly Oedipal bond with his mother Rajlakshmi, makes unjust demands on Bihari, almost like a child, as if Bihari were his property. Bihari relents most of the time so as not to hurt his Mahin-da, even to the extent of giving up Ashalata, for Mahin-da, so far obdurately opposed to marriage, falls in love with her. At the beginning of the novel, Rajlakshmi identifies Bihari's unwavering fidelity to Mahendra. After considering whether she should speak to Bihari about marrying her friend's daughter, she abandons the idea, wondering – 'Bihari and marriage? He is preoccupied with Mahin only. He has never thought of bringing a wife' (Tagore 10). Mahendra, on the other hand, maintains a fierce 'monogamy' when it comes to Bihari, and is proud of it: 'He was fastidious in the matters of love, and was very pure, on which he used to pride himself. In fact, because he had befriended Bihari, he did not want to accept anybody else's friendship. Even if anyone showed interest in him, he used to make special efforts in avoiding him' (45). Such 'pure' friendship, secured with fidelity and monogamy, is put to test, first when Asha comes into Mahendra's life as his wife, followed by the extremely attractive and intelligent Binodini, whom both friends find difficult to ignore. Although Bihari gives up his love for Ashalata for his Mahin-da, he does not mind Mahin-da's undivided attention towards her, even when Rajlakshmi, distraught by such unabashed show of marital bliss, complains to him. But when he discovers that Binodini is gradually replacing Ashalata in Mahin-da's affection, and he anticipates disaster, he does make it clear that he is averse to Mahin-da's adulterous fondness for Binodini. Bihari almost behaves like Mahendra's mother, trying to save a philandering son. He constantly admonishes Ashalata who, being naive and unassuming, misses his warning: '*Bouthan*, it is better to take precaution against a disease than to cure it through medical treatment' (55). Mahendra's abandoning himself to Binodini's charm inconveniences Bihari long before Ashalata could gauge her husband's shifting allegiance. The Oedipal tension between mother and son on the entry of the wife in the earlier part of the novel is replicated in Bihari's desperation to protect Mahendra from the 'seductress'.

However, the novel takes a more intricate turn when Binodini seduces Bihari, having conquered Mahendra and also developed a condescension for his spinelessness. For the first time, Bihari and Mahendra confront each other when Mahendra is surprised by Bihari's self-assertion, his brazen declaration that Binodini has willingly abandoned Mahendra and has come to him, and is therefore *his*. Bihari's fidelity towards Mahendra collapses and Mahendra is taken aback by his betrayal. Binodini eventually does not marry either Mahendra or Bihari, and leaves for Kashi, repentant but successful in driving an irreparable wedge in their relationship.

Tapabrata Ghosh observes that in Tagore's novels, this male–male friendship (*maitri*) is usually driven into a terrible crisis on the arrival of a heterosexual love interest (*priti*). What Tagore does may not appear unique, for examples of such contestation between homoerotic bonding and heterosexual desire is commonplace in fiction. Although Ghosh does not acknowledge this anywhere, his theoretical framework is to some extent informed by Eve K. Sedgwick's seminal book, *Between Men: English Literature and Male Homosocial Desire* (1985/1992), particularly her reading of 'erotic triangles' in European fiction. Sedgwick's argument draws heavily from René Girard's *Deceit, Desire, and the Novel* (1971) and Gayle Rubin's 'The Traffic in Women: Notes toward a Political Economy of Sex' (1975), both influenced by the works of Freud and Lacan, and also Lévi-Strauss (particularly in the case of Rubin). As Girard observes, in love triangles in which two men desire a single woman, the female love interest is usually determined by her already being the choice of the person who has been chosen as a rival. Rubin, on the other hand, echoing Heidi Hartmann's definition of patriarchy in terms of 'relationships between men', observes that 'patriarchal heterosexuality can best be discussed in terms of one or another form of the traffic in women: it is the use of women as exchangeable, perhaps symbolic, property for the primary purpose of cementing the bonds of men with men' (qtd. in Sedgwick 26). Both these analyses apply to Tagore's *Chokher bali* where women are a 'conduit' in a relationship in which the primary partners are men, as Lévi-Strauss has pointed out (*The Elementary Structures of Kinship*). Rubin finds this an 'extraordinary statement', but reproves Lévi-Strauss, questioning his celebration of this statement: 'Why is he not, at this point, denouncing what kinship systems do to women, instead of presenting one of the greatest rip-offs of all time as the root of romance?' (201)

Although Tapabrata Ghosh does not address this at all in his analysis, Tagore indeed answers this question (which is further problematised by Rituparno Ghosh's adaptation of the novel in 2003) and herein lies his uniqueness. Tagore's Binodini wields an extraordinary agency in ruining the partnership between the two male friends, by asserting her sexuality, and by exhibiting outstanding wit and audacity in moving from one man to the other, separating them in the process and mocking the fidelity and monogamy that defined the relationship between them earlier. In his adaptation of the narrative, Rituparno Ghosh, a queer filmmaker, changes the ending of Tagore's novel, attributing to Binodini a greater agency. While in Tagore's novel, Binodini rejects Bihari's proposal for marriage and settles for a life of exile and penitence in Kashi, in Ghosh's film, Binodini is impenitent. She rejects both Bihari and Mahendra, and joins the nationalist movement, explaining her move to Ashalata in a letter that cements a deep bonding between the two women. This is extraordinary in the sense that Ghosh seems to propose female bonding as counteractive to male bonding that defines, reinforces, and sustains patriarchy.

Notably, Tagore's *Chokher bali* is not a love triangle, but a quadrilateral one in which two overlapping erotic triangles exist: Mahendra–Asha–Bihari and Mahendra–Binodini–Bihari. If Asha conforms to the Lévi-Straussian notion of the woman as a conduit to buttress patriarchal, homosocial bonds between men, Tagore introduces Binodini as a foil to Asha, who completely topples this male homosocial conspiracy of repeatedly using women as a passive object in their project of reinforcing their friendship. The ending of Tagore's novel, where Binodini apologises, can be looked upon as an unfortunate compromise on the part of the author; or else, his novel would not have found any takers in the early twentieth century. Rituparno Ghosh's film, returning to the novel after a hundred years, redeems Binodini, bringing to the fore the original text's queer-feminist currency (Bakshi). In this sense, the film is an answer to Tapabrata Ghosh's observation that in Tagore's times there was no 'culture of [queer] perception' – it was certainly there by the time the film *Chokher bali* was made. Instead of highlighting the homoerotic bonding between Mahendra and Bihari, Rituparno Ghosh empowers Binodini in a remarkable way, whereby the hegemony of male–male friendship to which women have always played a subordinate, passive role, is seriously challenged. Undoubtedly, Tagore had already prepared the ground for Ghosh's postmodern queer-feminist vision.

REFERENCES

Armstrong, P. B. 'The Narrator in the Closet: The Ambiguous Narrative Voice in *Howards End*'. *MFS Modern Fiction Studies* 47.2 (2001): 306–28. Print.

Bakshi, Kaustav. '*Chokher Bali*: Unleashing Forbidden Passions'. *Silhouette: A Discourse on Cinema* 9.3 (2011). Web. 11 December 2017. <https://learningandcreativity.com/silhouette/chokher-bali-unleashing-forbidden-passions/>.

Burger, Glenn. *Chaucer's Queer Nation*. Minneapolis and London: U of Minnesota P, 2003. Print. Medieval Cultures Series.

Carpenter, Edward. *Ioläus: An Anthology of Friendship*. 1902. New York: Mitchell Kennerley MCMXVII, 1917. Print.

---. 'Towards Democracy'. *The Edward Carpenter Archive*. Simon Dawson, n.d. Web. 11 January 2018. <http://www.edwardcarpenter.net/ectd1.htm>.

de Lauretis, Teresa 'Queer Theory: Lesbian and Gay Sexualities'. *differences* 3 (1991): iii–xviii. Special issue. Print.

Duncan, Fiona. 'Colin Self is the Embodiment of Queer Theory'. *Vice*. 21 March 2014. Web. 11 June 2014. <https://www.vice.com/en_us/article/kwpzbm/colin-self-is-the-embodiment-of-queer-theory>.

Ghosh, Rituparno, dir. *Chokher Bali: A Passion Play*. Shree Venkatesh Films, 2003. DVD.

Ghosh, Tapabrata. *Gora ar Binoy* [Gora and Binoy]. Rev. Edition. Kolkata: Ababhash, 2009. Print.

Girard, René. *Deceit, Desire, and the Novel: Self and Other in Literary Structure*. Trs. Yvonne Freccero. Baltimore: Johns Hopkins UP, 1972. Print.

Gupta, Jayati, ed. *Narrative and Narration: A Study of the Modern Short Story*. New Delhi: Anthem Press, 2008. Print.

Hone, Michael. *Capri: A Homosexual Paradise*. Create Space Independent Publishing Platform, 2016. Print.

Jones, John Garrett. *Tales and Teaching of Buddha: The Jataka Stories in Relation to the Pali Canon*. London: George Allen & Unwin, 1979. Print.

Leavitt, David. Introduction. *Maurice*. By E. M. Forster. 1971. London: Penguin Books, 2005. xi–xxxvi. Print.

Lévi-Strauss, Claude. *The Elementary Structures of Kinship*. Boston: Beacon Press, 1969. Print.

Lipner, J. S. *Anandamath or A Sacred Brotherhood*. Oxford: Oxford UP, 2005. Print.

Maugham, Somerset. 'The Lotus Eater'. *Modern Prose: Stories, Essays and Sketches*. Ed. Michael Thrope. Delhi: Oxford UP, 1973. 72–87. Print.

Mitchell, Mark, and David Leavitt, eds. *Pages Passed from Hand to Hand: The Hidden Tradition of Homosexual Literature in English from 1748 to 1914*. London: Vintage, 1997. Print.

Morgan, Ted. *Somerset Maugham*. New York: Simon and Schuster, 1980. Print.

Rubin, Gayle. 'The Traffic in Women: Notes Toward a Political Economy of Sex'. *Toward an Anthropology of Women*. Ed. Rayna Reiter. New York: Monthly Review Press, 1975. 157–210. Print.

Sedgwick, Eve K. *Between Men: English Literature and Male Homosocial Desire*. 1985. New York: Columbia UP, 1992. Print.

Spender, Stephen. Introduction. *The Temple*. By Stephen Spender. New York: Grove Press, 1988. ix–xiii. Print.

Tagore, Rabindranath. *Chokher bali* [The Grain of Sand]. Kolkata: Biswa-Bharati, 1902. Print. Translation of quotations from the text is by Kaustav Bakshi.

Vidal, Gore. Introduction. 1976. *Christopher and His Kind*. By Christopher Isherwood. London: Vintage Books, 2012. ix–xii. Print.

Zwilling, Leonard. 'Homosexuality as Seen in Indian Buddhist Texts'. *Buddhism, Sexuality and Gender*. Ed. Jose Ignacio Cabezón. Delhi: Satguru Publications, 1992. 203–14. Print.

Chapter Six

Seeing Queerly

The history of queer cinema stretches far back and is almost as old as the invention of cinema itself. Whilst cinema has numerous examples of the camp figure or the sissy, the dragged up hero, these have mostly been used to provide comic relief or at the most to offer a narrative of comparative criticism. As Demory and Pullen have argued, the foundational premise of classical Hollywood is based on the overused formula of the chivalric romance, bourgeois novel and the American melodrama. There has been little engagement with queer consciousness other than the occasional slippages (see White, for instance) or sub-textual hints. In this chapter, we explore contemporary scholarship on film and visual criticism that have taken the figure of the queer further, offering critical approaches to address the production and reception of queer characters. The chapter is divided into three parts. In the first part we discuss 'new queer cinema' followed by a discussion of queer Hollywood which offers progressive pathways to extend the reading of queer characters in film and television, and we conclude pointing to emerging work on global queer cinemas.

NEW QUEER CINEMA

Queer cinema in the West has evolved along two trajectories. The first trajectory follows a recuperative logic. Contrasting the negative/ limiting portrayal of homosexuals in mainstream films, it tries to revive this image and incorporate it within mainstream cinema. Most of the films along this trajectory attempt to create an alternate space for the queer within the mainstream genre. Many of them are strongly invested in history, attempting thus to intervene and 'queerise' certain moments in history, or to claim certain figures as queer heroes/martyrs. The other trajectory, however, rejects altogether the representative possibilities of the mainstream genre. According to Stacey, this strain of films 'reject[s] cinema as either a re-assuring space of positivity or a potential route through which to win the acceptance of wider audiences' (2). Employing avant-garde techniques, these films celebrate difference and sexual leeway and resist reduction to a normative coding, thereby questioning the paradigm of normativity itself. These films even problematise the notion of the positive image of the queer (an attempt that marks the more mainstream recuperative agenda), and some of them explore notions of pederasty, vampirism, homicide and sexual abuse, reading into all of this a defiant logic.

An inaugural moment in this latter trajectory was B. Ruby Rich's 1992 essay on 'new queer cinema'. A well-known figure to scholars of queer cinema, Rich's essay, 'The New Queer Cinema', coined the term to identify a group of films that use techniques of avant-garde social constructionism, of creating socially constructed reality to rework histories. Her exploration of the ever-changing contours of queer cinema attest to the many ways in which queerness is represented, performed and critiqued on the screen. At the very outset, Rich states that these films are strongly influenced by art, activism and 'recoded aesthetics' (xv) linking the independent movement to the avant-garde.

A question that naturally arises is regarding the origins of this cinema – what gave rise to this new queer cinema (NQC hereafter)? How did it start at all? Rich identifies four elements that gave rise to NQC: 'the arrival of AIDS, Reagan, camcorder and cheap rent' (xvi). Of these four, the rise of the camcorder has surely been one of the most interesting and important facets. Recent films screened at the London Lesbian and Gay Film Festival chronicling the rise of AIDS activism in the United States – *How to Survive a Plague* (David France, 2012) and *United in Anger: A History of Act Up* (Jim Hubbard, 2012), for instance – have also documented the power of the image, especially for queer activism, made possible through the invention of this little device which enabled 'the easy production of electronic media at the personal level' (Rich xvii) by recording these tumultuous times for posterity.

Derek Jarman (1942–94) and John Waters (b. 1946) are two towering figures of queer cinema. Jarman used his films to speak for gay rights and to portray his personal struggle with AIDS, and ushered in a new form of queer aesthetics. As Rich writes of Jarman, 'imagine a cross between Andy Warhol and Keith Haring, but somebody alive and kicking, warm and generous, irreverent and uncompromising' (49). Rich points out the postmodern importance of Jarman's work and the space he commanded within British media (which was not always favourable). Jarman's funding woes can be attributed to the fact that he worked in Thatcherite Britain and a film fraternity which worked strongly against his work. He made some exciting films like *Jubilee* (1978), *Caravaggio* (1986), *The Last of England* (1987) and *Edward II* (1991), which critiqued social injustice, homophobia and the state. *Edward II* was one of his finest critiques of the ways in which compulsory heterosexuality and institutional homophobia has repressed queer people in English history.

John Waters, in a similar vein, is known for his transgressive cult films in the United States. From *Mondo Trasho* (1969) and *Pink Flamingos* (1972) to *Hairspray* (1988), Waters has celebrated the outrageous and created an entire countercultural movement around his films. Waters's films were widely celebrated by the queer community. For instance, *Pink Flamingos* is famous for nudity, voyeurism and masturbation, and has been termed by scholars such as Kutzbach and Mueller as an early example of 'abject art' which aestheticises the un-aesthetic through an experience of disgust. Later on in *Hairspray*, Waters would use a subtler form of nostalgic filmmaking to narrate the story of the American civil rights movement and the collective triumphs of the Black community in Baltimore and the NAACP (National Association for the Advancement of Colored People). About him Rich writes, 'Waters predates the New Queer Cinema history by decades, he's a creature of the hippie past, the countercultural revolution, a pre-Stonewall era of shock and awe. He's an indelible part of NQC prehistory, a patron saint presiding over its doings, chuckling at its follies, applauding its successes' (6).

Rich argues that NQC was a cultural response to the troubled times of the noughties and emerged as an aesthetic reaction to it. She looks beyond the 'texts' of the films themselves by also interrogating the relationship between gay and lesbian film festivals and their audiences. Rich argues that such festivals were a space where many of these films were either embraced or rejected by their intended public. However, as a critic, Rich is troubled by the boundaries imposed by the demands of the communities and the limits of tolerance displayed when confronted with uncomfortable ideas and representations. She notes, 'Queer audiences see themselves as complicit in these representations, as if they are compromised or validated by them' (38).

What is important to remember here is also the contribution of scholars such as B. Ruby Rich to the NQC movement. Her writing during this phase makes an important contribution in getting enough people to the theatres and ensuring the survival of the movement and keeping the conversation going.

Another stream of films which came out during this time was the avenging lesbian genre which glamorised the killing of men by women. In the essay 'Lethal Lesbians', Rich examines a sudden popular interest in a group of films that were being made by heterosexual men in which 'lesbians teamed up to commit murder as a way of sealing their bond' (xxv). Rich's essay looks at the intention of the filmmakers as well as the reception of the films themselves. She is not entirely dismissive of these films but rather notes that in these films 'the haunting figure of the pathological lesbian killer has been rescued from historical neglect and social isolation, given a partner and even celebration' (117). It is not entirely made clear what gave rise to this genre and why these films were made during that period. Rich however agrees that this genre elicited both progressive and regressive responses from the public sphere. At the same time, she adds a cautionary note in pointing out that these films, in most cases, reverse/subvert the power dynamics by which 'lesbians are more likely to be murdered than be murderous' (118).

The area of homophobic violence and transnational responses has been explored more recently by Pullen, and Herek and Berrill.

It is also important to remember that the NQC movement is not confined to the United States but also comes from places such as Latin America where they intersect with the larger queer political movements. Rich is particularly fascinated by Cuba. She points out the contradictions which exist, positing Cuba as an extremely homophobic country with a rich LGBTQ subculture. In her analysis of *Fresa y Chocolate* (1994), she argues that the film was fundamentally meant for Cuba and Cubans, and not for an international queer public, which in itself was evidence of the changing attitudes in the country. She further notes that the film was suffused with sympathetic characters that invite both empathy and identification.

QUEER HOLLYWOOD

It is also important to study and understand how popular culture and mainstream Hollywood have dealt with queerness. Benshoff and Griffin have argued that it is within the sphere of popular culture that many people probably learn what they do know about sex and sexuality. Alexander Doty, in the landmark book *Making Things Perfectly Queer*, uses this approach to find new ways of reading mainstream television and popular cinema. Borrowing from audience and reception theory, Doty argues that the audience is an active participant within mass culture, suggesting that the queerness of mass culture develops in three areas: influences during the production of texts; historically specific cultural readings and uses of texts by self-identified gays, lesbians, bisexuals and queers; and adopting reception positions that can be considered 'queer' in some way, regardless of a person's declared sexual and gender allegiances (xi). Benshoff and Griffin, in their study of queer American films, argue that images are important and images matter as they are always political. They go on to suggest that a history of these films show the history of queer struggles and the 'future course of queer American cultures' (17). The film *Milk*, which was made by Gus Van Sant in 2008 based on the life of Harvey Milk, the first openly gay person to be elected to the San Francisco Board of Supervisors, is a good example of this. Harvey's activism and subsequent assassination had been the subject of a 1984 documentary, *The Life and Times of Harvey Milk*, directed by Rob Epstein. Gus Van Sant's film, however, has a distinctly recuperative agenda in mind. The film is structured in a way that it projects the martyrdom of its protagonist (brilliantly portrayed by Sean Penn). It begins with Harvey sitting at a recording machine the night before his assassination and looking back on his years of political activism. Thus, from the very beginning, we anticipate the assassination that will close the film. In a brilliant meta-narrative move, Harvey attempts, like the director, to narrativise his story right at the onset. This clearly spells out the film's agenda. In a style typical of biography filmmaking, Van Sant shows Harvey's life progressively in flashbacks. Harvey grows into his political persona, politicises the private, loses his boyfriend Scott and ultimately, after several failed attempts, is elected to public office – the San Francisco Board of Supervisors. Rich argues that films like *Milk* have contributed not only to a new form of gay male representation but have also drawn new LGBT audiences in small towns and rural areas, thus opening up new spaces for discussion and dialogue on the struggles of queer people (257). Henderson is critical of the distorted ways in which American media represents queer cultures and identity, and seeks to study the difference that social class makes on queer subjectivity and representation. Queer cultural production is quite uneven, operating within a mainstream mantle of production as well as taking place outside the 'norm'. According to Henderson, queer cultural products are sometimes highly conventional and institutional, or at other times more ephemeral or community based (4).

Consider for example television shows such as *Queer as Folk* (Ron Cowen and Daniel Lipman, 2000–05), *Will and Grace* (James Burrows, 1998–2006) and *The L Word* (Ilene Chaiken, 2004–09). Contrary to popular television depiction, not all queer people in America (and by extension in the rest of the world) are rich, white or professionals. Henderson argues that whilst working-class people are the majority of the US population, they are also the most demeaned; they are 'physically just too much: too messy, too ill, too angry, too needy, too out of control, too unrestrained and, critically too sexual' (35). This representation of the working class as the unrestrained can be traced back to the colonial imagination of assigning hyper-degenerate sexuality to labouring non-intellectual classes and hyper-effeminacy to the intellectual non-labouring class. As true with many such cultural impositions, television networks and movie distributors have been careful to represent queer sex in such a way that guards 'the presumed modesties and class aspirations of their straight audiences' (36). Films like *Milk* and Ang Lee's *Brokeback Mountain* (discussed in chapter 3) both challenge, and assimilate to, the social class biases within mainstream Hollywood. Mathew Bolton, writing about *Brokeback Mountain*, argues how the film adaptation effectively queers its audiences: '*Brokeback Mountain*'s audience is one that recognises not only universal human experiences of love and desire but also the profound differences produced by culture that too often values one kind of love over another' (266).

Another interesting example is the classic Hollywood film *Boys Don't Cry* (Kimberley Pierce, 1999). The film is based on the real life events which led to the transphobic murder of Brandon Teena. Whilst earlier analyses of the film have ranged from an archival reading of gender ambiguity and studies on spectatorship to desires of young people (Halberstam; Pidduck), Henderson addresses it as a 'class text'. She reads it as a narrative of rural white working-class youth in America. She examines how this working-class abjection structures transgender representation especially within a space where class and gender variance is rooted in exclusion and within a hierarchy. She argues, 'In *Boys Don't Cry*, class marks gender trauma and gender variance is both the hope and denial of class transcendence' (14). She further points out that by 'reading queerness for class and class for queerness, exposes the availability and malleability of shaming and excess in pathologising queer and class others' (30).

Another interesting film to contemplate is Miranda July's feature film *Me and You and Everyone We Know* (2005), a representation of a 'world of people socially and culturally at risk' (Henderson 60). July's work is not obviously queer in the usual sense, and it does not work within the parameters of same-sex eroticism or gender variance. Its disruption of normative categories of recognition therefore makes it a text worth considering. Henderson analyses the film to bring up the frayed and insecure conditions of working-class life. Her response is not to romanticise this deprivation but to use it as a 'new way of thinking about relations among cultures, feeling and social possibility, about cultural forms as affective resources in the project of queer class solidarity' (17).

Demory and Pullen state that love is the foundational premise on which Hollywood, especially queer Hollywood, narratives depend. Romance is central not only to the romantic genre but it also characterises the subplots of various other genre films and television programmes. Demory and Pullen also identify the success of *Brokeback Mountain* as a film as marking the evolution of public attitudes towards queer love/same-sex romance (3). In effect, this film signalled the mainstream acceptance of queer films which was already underway in the art house films and the NQC movement that we discussed previously.

When discussing love and romance within queer Hollywood, *I Love you Phillip Morris* (Glenn Ficarra and John Requa, 2009) is a good example. Chan identifies the 'negative' representations within the film as offering a critical step towards a negotiated and more accommodating politics of consuming Hollywood's gay romances. Chan contends that by infusing romantic love with negativity, the film forces the viewers to rethink stereotypical gay clichés and the ideological flawlessness of Hollywood's heteronormative romantic narratives with their happy endings (24).

In sharp contrast, Demory, in her analysis of the television show *Queer as Folk,* one of the best-known queer shows to have a mainstream fan base, reads it as a melodramatic text. She shows how it uses contradiction and the de-stability associated with the genre (melodrama), instead of realism, to 'queer' the show. Instead of moving towards a final resolution, the show, with its seemingly unsatisfactory ending, addresses the myth of 'happy queer love' in contemporary America.

Marriage and family are also important tropes through which some queer films in Hollywood subvert heteronormative romantic conventions. Julia Erhart, for instance, examines the narrative of the 'donor conception' in lesbian and non-lesbian films. She looks at how issues such as queerness are managed and what kind of perspective is actually represented within them. She identifies the film *The Kids are Alright* (Lisa Cholodenko, 2010) as showing the perspective of donors and children, which earlier films such as *The Switch* (Josh Gordon and Will Speck, 2010) excluded. The film's interest in the world of donor conception and the lesbian-headed family make it quite unique (91), significantly disrupting the world of normative parenting that mainstream media glorifies. Thus, because of its 'engagement with the queer practice of family construction' (92), the film makes a contribution to the theme of queer love without any significant precedent.

We would like to suggest that the subversive and transgressive illustrations of queer love can also be found within marginalised groups such as transgenders, porn stars and drag queens, and through 'marginal' forms such as punk films and pornography. Intersections exist between heteronormative forms of love and the erotically marginal. Curran Nault's investigation into Bruce LaBruce's punk film *No Skin Off My Ass* (1993) sees the film as a conflation of romance and unsimulated sex scenes, and through that it effectively challenges both romance and punk conventions. As Nault notes, 'At first glance, *No Skin* may be just another fine gay romance, but on further inspection the film is quintessentially queercore in its opposition to status quo articulations of sexuality, punk and love' (176).

Demory and Pullen question 'what happens when stories of queer love are adapted from one medium to another' (7), thus suggesting that there may indeed be something queer in the very act of adapting. Pullen, writing about Tom Ford's *A Single Man* (2009) which was adapted from Christopher Isherwood's novel, considers how such recordings and representations explore the aesthetics of the discursive body, thus offering the potential for queer love being actually enhanced. He looks at the film as a dual text where the viewer's knowledge about Isherwood and the original source forms a dialectic, extending the body of Isherwood as a catalyst for new imaginings (242).

It is worth noting that the key and recent scholarship on queer cinema that we have discussed in this chapter is mostly Western in their focus and origin. This is due to the fact that scholarship on non-Western queer cinema has emerged much more recently and is still at a nascent stage as we write. Schoonover and Galt pay critical attention to queer cinema's place in the world asking, what might or could the world mean to queers, and what does queer cinema mean for the world? (4) By bringing the reader to the intersection of queer politics and world cinema, it asks both how queer films construct ways of being in the world and what is the political value of the worlds that queer cinema creates. In terms of scholarship from India, readers might want to look at Bakshi and Sen's work on the relationship between queer cinema and Section 377; Rajinder Kumar Dudrah's work on queer Bollywood; and Datta, Bakshi and Dasgupta's work on queer Bengali cinema. We have also analysed queer cinema in India at length in chapter 8 of this book. There are also other works on queer cinema that have emerged from Mexico (Smith), Israel (Yosef), Latin America (Foster), South Asian queer diasporas (Gopinath) and broadly Asia (Grossman), to name a few.

REFERENCES

Bakshi, Kaustav, and Parjanya Sen. 'India's Queer Expressions On-screen: The Aftermath of the Reading Down of Section 377 of the Indian Penal Code'. *New Cinemas* 10.2–3 (2012): 167–83. Print.

Benshoff, Harry M., and Sean Griffin. *Queer Images: A History of Gay and Lesbian Film in America*. Lanham: Lexington Books, 2006. Print.

Bolton, Mathew. 'The Ethics of Alterity: Adapting Queerness in *Brokeback Mountain*'. *Queer Love in Film and Television*. Eds. P. Demory and C. Pullen. London: Palgrave Macmillan, 2013. 257–68. Print.

Chan, Kenneth. 'Bad Boys Need to Love too: The Cinematic Negativity of Gay Romance in *I Love you Phillip Morris*'. *Queer Love in Film and Television*. Eds. P. Demory and C. Pullen. London: Palgrave Macmillan, 2013. 23–32. Print.

Datta, Sangeeta, Kaustav Bakshi, and Rohit K. Dasgupta, eds. *Rituparno Ghosh: Cinema, Gender and Art*. London: Routledge, 2015. Print.

Demory, Pamela. 'True Love Queered: Sex, Melodrama and Romance in *Queer as Folk*'. *Queer Love in Film and Television*. Eds. P. Demory and C. Pullen. London: Palgrave Macmillan, 2013. 69–82. Print.

Demory, Pamela, and Christopher Pullen. Introduction. *Queer Love in Film and Television*. Eds. P. Demory and C. Pullen. London: Palgrave Macmillan, 2013. 1–12. Print.

Doty, Alexander. *Making Things Perfectly Queer: Interpreting Mass Culture*. Minneapolis: U of Minnesota P, 1993. Print.

Dudrah, Rajinder Kumar. *Bollywood Travels: Culture, Diaspora and Border Crossings in Popular Hindi Cinema*. London: Routledge, 2012. Print.

Erhart, Julia. 'Donor Conception in Lesbian and Non-lesbian Television Film and Families'. *Queer Love in Film and Television*. Eds. P. Demory and C. Pullen. London: Palgrave Macmillan, 2013. 83–94. Print.

Foster, David. *Queer Issues in Contemporary Latin American Cinema*. Austin: U of Texas P, 2004. Print.

Gopinath, Gayatri. *Impossible Desires: Queer Diasporas and South Asian Public Cultures*. Durham: Duke UP, 2005. Print.

Grossman, Andrew, ed. *Queer Asian Cinema: Shadows in the Shade*. London: Routledge, 2000. Print.

Halberstam, Jack. *In a Queer Time and Place: Transgender Bodies, Subcultural Lives*. New York: New York UP, 2005. Print.

Henderson, Lisa. *Love and Money: Queers, Class and Cultural Production*. New York: New York UP, 2013. Print.

Herek, Gregory M., and Kevin Berrill, eds. *Hate Crimes: Confronting Violence against Lesbians and Gay Men*. Thousand Oaks: Sage, 1992. Print.

Kutzbach, Konstanze, and Monika Mueller, eds. *The Abject of Desire: The Aestheticization of the Unaesthetic in Contemporary Literature and Culture*. Amsterdam: Rodopi, 2007. Print.

Nault, Curran. '*No Skin Off My Ass*: Bruce LaBruce and the Curious Case of Queer Punk Love'. *Queer Love in Film and Television*. Eds. P. Demory and C. Pullen. London: Palgrave Macmillan, 2013. 181–92. Print.

Pidduck, Julianne. 'The *Boys Don't Cry* Debate: Risk and Queer Spectatorship'. *Screen* 42.1 (2001): 97–102. Print.

Pullen, Christopher. 'Ford's *A Single Man* and Bachardy's *Chris and Don*: The Aesthetic and Domestic Body of Isherwood'. *Queer Love in Film and Television*. Eds. P. Demory and C. Pullen. London: Palgrave Macmillan, 2013. 233–44. Print.

---, ed. *LGBT Transnational Identity and Media*. Basingstoke: Palgrave Macmillan, 2012. Print.

Rich, B. Ruby. *New Queer Cinema: The Director's Cut*. Durham: Duke UP, 2013. Print.

Schoonover, Karl, and Rosalind Galt. *Queer Cinema in the World*. Durham: Duke UP, 2016. Print.

Smith, Paul Julian. *Queer Mexico: Cinema and Television Since 2000*. Detroit: Wayne State UP, 2017. Print.

Stacey, Jackie. 'Introduction: Queering Screen'. *Queer Screen: A Screen Reader*. Eds. Jackie Stacey and Sarah Street. Oxon: Routledge, 2007. 2. Print.

White, Patricia. *UnInvited: Classical Hollywood Cinema and Lesbian Representability*. Indiana: Indiana UP, 1999. Print.

Yosef, Raz. *Beyond Flesh: Queer Masculinities and Nationalism in Israeli Cinema*. Detroit: Wayne State UP, 2004. Print.

QUEERING CULTURAL STUDIES 3

Chapter Seven

Queer of Colour Critique

Queer Theory has had a long engagement with scholars of colour writing about the relationship between race, gender, sexuality and the nation state (Anzaldúa). In recent times, the field has seen the development of a 'queer of color critique'. Moraga and Anzaldúa's coedited *The Bridge Called My Back* (1981) marks the beginning of queer Latina scholarship in a field that has mostly been dominated by white scholars. The book centred on the experiences of women of colour emphasising the intersectional feminist sisterhoods. The editors of the volume did not want to think of this as a 'definitive' study of non-white feminism in the United States, rather, as Moraga and Anzaldúa explained, they expected it to become a catalyst around which more discussions could take place over time. Teresa de Lauretis argued that this volume was responsible for an important shift in feminist consciousness, noting that it made 'available to all feminists the feelings, the analyses, and the political positions of feminists of color, and their critiques of white or mainstream feminism' (221). Moraga and Anazaldúa explain that one of the biggest sources of separation amongst feminists of colour is homophobia:

> This fear that we (whatever our sexuality) breathe in every day in our communities never fully allows us to feel invulnerable to attack on our own streets, and sometimes even in the homes we grew up in (let alone in the white man's world). So often it is the fear of lesbianism which causes many of us to feel our politics and passion are being ignored or discounted by other Third World people. (105–06)

Several of the pieces in the collection by authors such as Barbara Smith and Cheryl Clarke respond to it, claiming 'lesbianism as an act of resistance' (an idea that occurred as the title of Clarke's popular essay).

There are several other important scholars whose work marks the broad theoretical trends in the journeys of queer of colour(s) and critical theory. Queerness has been named as sexualised 'surplus population' (Ferguson), 'racialized remainder' (Reddy), racialised hailing and subjectivity (Rodríguez), and as an 'assemblage which is spatially and temporally contingent' (Puar 204). These scholars have, over time, helped shape and reshape the field.

The term 'queer of color critique' was first coined by Roderick Ferguson in his *Aberrations in Black: Toward a Queer of Color Critique* (2003), which is now considered a canonical text in the field. Ferguson's queer of colour critique re-reads Marxian theories of alienation in order to situate the intersections of race, class, gender and sexuality. According to him, figures such as that of the Black drag queen and Mexican housemaid predicate the formation of US capitalism. Ferguson operates within, and yet disidentifies with, the overdeterministic approaches of historical materialism. He identifies culture as the terrain in which seemingly disparate formations such as Marxism, revolutionary nationalism and liberal humanism converge through their 'identifications with gender and sexual norms as ideals' (3). Ferguson notes, 'As queer of color critique challenges ideologies of discreteness, it attempts to disturb the idea that racial and national formations are obviously disconnected' (4).

Ferguson critically interrogates the urban commodity culture in the United States in order to situate the figure of the (Black) drag queen as a permanent fixture within commodity capitalism. In his approach to intersectionality Ferguson uses the commodification of queer subjects to engage with issues such as citizenship, nationalism and class. Ferguson's move allows one to rethink commodification as a racialised and sexualised process. He attends to 'women of colour coalitional politics' as 'a globally defined field of possibilities' (132) which allow contestation of the US normative culture and logics of capital. As Sharon Holland reminds us, 'Black lesbian subjects and their women-of-color allies have always haunted feminism's attempt to articulate itself, putting themselves in the position of challenging the racial inclusiveness of feminist theory and practice and at the same time pushing a developing lesbian/gay studies to describe the face of its constituency' (145–46).

In the context of queer Latinidad studies Rodríguez's work is important. She notes that identity is always in some kind of a flux and one that establishes relationship with the other: 'Identity is about situatedness in motion: embodiment and spatiality. It is about a self that is constituted through and against other selves in contexts that serve to establish the relationship between the self and the other' (4). Rodríguez also challenges the many ways in which 'queer' has, over time, become an umbrella term rather than a conceptual framework for challenging heteronormativity. She argues that the various spaces that we inhabit as queer people leave a mark on our lives and identities. For her, identity is not simply a list of categories but also a mode of being which is constructed, reconstructed and destroyed. She offers a rhizomatic reading which sees identity as having several directions, diversions and contradictions:

> Identity is more than a list of categories that name our sexuality, gender, HIV status, nation, age, ethnicity, ability, class, language, citizenship status, and religion. Even if we expand the list to include all the other significant features of ourselves, what do these attributes actually explain about our lives? What aspects of identity exceed the categories we have created to define our places in the world? How do memories of desire and violence mark us in ways that are similar and different from the ways we have been marked by color and gender? How do street corners and kitchen tables, friends and lovers, lullabies and taunts, private violations and public betrayals leave traces on our lives? How do the many moments of our daily existence determine how we view ourselves and the world around us? (22)

Queer Black and Brown bodies are subjugated, in order to maintain a regulated and hegemonic order of race, gender and sexual identity that marginalises and maintains them as the 'other'.

DISIDENTIFICATION AND COUNTERPUBLICS

The questions posed by Rodríguez are also reflected in Muñoz's work where he offers the concept of 'disidentification' as a way of understanding minoritarian sexual subjects. Muñoz's theory of disidentification builds on earlier work and argues that for those whose identities render them a minority, especially for queers of colour, identity negotiation takes place through a form of 'otherisation' where the majoritarian worldview punishes them for not being the normative subject model of a white heterosexual middle-class male. Muñoz argues that this takes place through an erasure of identities which are not considered heteronormative. He also notes how queer people of colour, as a result of the effects of colonialism, have been placed outside dominant racial and sexual ideology and heteronormativity. Muñoz notes that 'disidentification is about managing and negotiating historical trauma and systemic violence' (161). The subjects in this case, according to Muñoz, do not assimilate themselves within the mainstream heterosexual culture, and neither do they completely reject it; rather, they employ a strategy of being tactical and work with and against a cultural form.

Muñoz also calls disidentification as a form of survival strategy – through the process of disidentification, the queer subject reworks the cultural codes to place itself within the mainstream by both subverting the mainstream narrative and being included within it. He argues that through this process, different kinds of 'counterpublics' are being created. The idea of 'publics'/'counterpublics' is a direct response to the work of Jürgen Habermas, a German philosopher and sociologist who worked on the concepts of the public and the public sphere. Within the context of queer studies these were used by other queer scholars such as Michael Warner. Warner explores the concepts of 'publicity' and 'publicness', and meditates on how to make oneself 'public' without necessarily aligning with subaltern politics. He emphasises the agency of culture in the forms of art, public speaking, media and performance, and looks at how people can use culture to create a space for themselves in the social world. In other words, Warner does not address the intersection of 'publics' and 'politics', but rather how people express themselves as individuals and groups through participation in alternative subcultures. Habermas perceived the public sphere as a liberal democratic Utopia where continuous debate would ensure equal citizenship. Warner, however, believes that the public is not a cohesive entity, but actually comprise multiple reflexive counterpublics that respond to the Habermasian public that excludes the interests of potential participants. Muñoz defines counterpublics as communities and relational chains of resistance that contest the dominant public sphere. Counterpublics have the capacity of 'world-making' through a series of cultural performances that disidentify with the normative scripts of whiteness, heteronormativity and misogyny. Muñoz suggests that such work is vital for queer people of colour for survival and for affirming possibilities of another world. Muñoz's theory on disidentification and counterpublics is foundational to understandings of queer of colour performance art and has proved indispensable across a wide variety of disciplines.

QUEER OF COLOUR PERFORMANCE

There is a growing body of work on performances by queers of colour. We would like to briefly discuss the South Asian queer performer Kareem Khubchandani who is based in the United States. Khubchandani is an academic and queer performance scholar who is also a drag performer. He first came to prominence with his video, *Shit Gay Desi Boys Say*, on YouTube. This was followed quickly by several other videos with *Mere Angne Mein* and *Sari* being quite popular. *Sari*, which is set to Justin Bieber's tune from *Sorry*, is a reimagined video of a *desi* aunt who is emancipated, audacious and sexually flamboyant. In a piece discussing his queer performance, Khubchandani argues that the figure of the Asian 'aunty' was quite liberatory for him. She is a repository of culture and can see what is right or wrong, and she opens up a valuable space for queerness. The drag figure of Khubchandani is temporally and spatially situated as a hyphenated in-between within the global diaspora where South Asian-ness is celebratory as well as contradictory. As Khubchandani notes in one of his essays ('Snakes on the Dance Floor'), most Queer Studies critiques on Indian popular cinema have concentrated on the homosocial space or on representation politics. Very rarely do they look at how gay men in South Asia and the diaspora often mimic screen divas adopting effeminate gestures, leading to both praise and discipline. Through ethnography conducted on South Asian gay nightlife, Khubchandani reflects on his own performance of divas such as Rekha and Madhuri Dixit, and how these figures become icons of celebration and resistance for South Asian queers in the diaspora. He notes poignantly that queer gestures and Bollywood dance challenge the ways in which gay clubs often discipline us into gender:

> Queer gestures in the gay *desi* club remember the diva citizenship that has been quelled by neoliberal Bollywood. These bold enactments of aggressive femininity appear outdated because they recall a less "sophisticated" (read "capitalist" and/or "respectable") moment of Indian film choreography, but in these moments of queer sharing, they are revitalized through earnest and tributary reperformance. These gestures bring queerness into visibility through a sincere execution of anachronistic, animalistic, vulgar, foreign dance. The contagious nature of such queer gestures—the eruption of snakes on the dance floor—is a sharing of subaltern affects, bound simultaneously to pleasure and shame, a sharing that enables the possibility of a "we". (83)

Khubchandani's drag performance in *Sari* and *Mere Angne Mein* offer visibility to a kind of queer femininity that has often been sidelined on queer social media spaces. At the same time, the popularity of these videos are also testament to how digital media is being harnessed to offer an effective space for South Asian queer drag performance. These parodic performances should not be seen as 'mimicry', to borrow Bhabha's term, but rather as a way in which gender and queerness provide resistance to hegemonic frameworks of queer of colour performance. Queer art as performance can be a transformative experience, as queer of colour scholars such as Jin Haritaworn and Sara Ahmed have noted. Ahmed suggests that in performing dominant notions of happiness we cannot escape aligning ourselves with the 'good subject', one characterised as heteronormative and white, and that happiness is a privilege that they can experience happiness (11). Ahmed is not saying that as minoritised subjects we cannot pursue happiness. In fact, many queer activists talk about self-care to sustain their movements. Ahmed asks us to be critical of how dominant notions of happiness position 'good subjects' as those who are able to represent nationalism and colonial violence. Haritaworn also describes the birth of the 'hateful other'. Haritaworn argues that hate has an individualised and depoliticising tendency by sticking to racialised bodies that do not fit neoliberal subjectivity (141). Haritaworn points out that whilst trans people are claimed the 'innocent others' of homonationalism, the queer community is still unwilling to consider racialised trans lives as vulnerable or queer people of colour as 'coalition partners' (133).

Khubchandani's use of sari represents the knowledge and liberatory mode of South Asian activism that he learnt from his female relatives while growing up in Ghana. The sari is used by Indian women to represent both chastity and culture, and eroticism and mysticism (Banerjee and Miller; Begum and Dasgupta). As a cultural object, it also finds its place within queer/trans spaces across South Asia. Brockenbrough argues that the dual focus on the reproduction of, and resistance against, queer of colour marginality makes queer of colour critique a unique site for transformative knowledge production by, about and for queers of colour. Performance artists, such as Kareem Khubchandani, challenge the dominant whitewashing of performance cultures in the West. His performance breaks the white queer archive that is both oppressive and deeply colonial. Performances such as *Sari* act as archives storing the liberatory potential of South Asian feminisms and queer transformation.

NEOLIBERALISM, IMMIGRATION AND GLOBAL CAPITALISM

Chandan Reddy provides a critique of queer entanglements with global neoliberalism. Reddy points out the limits of the right-based approach within LGBTQ politics, by showing how law in its claim to neutrality actually produces conditions for racialised inequities.

He draws our attention to the increasingly contractarian nature of the US state, which operates through legal battles mediated by the judicial branch of the state. The state is judged by 'its ability to achieve fairness and neutrality in its engagement with social relations' (144). Reddy situates liberal rights discourses on the gay marriage movement in order to claim that 'race and gender are the critical cultural remainders of a modernity forcibly made ambiguous and temporarily resolved through the substantive subsumption of marriage into a right' (186). He re-reads US immigration (asylum) laws as an archive for the sighting of a racialised sexuality and as 'one site where the nation's official records are maintained and reproduced, giving those who seek identity through the law an identity of their kin' (165).

Eithne Luibhéid's work on US immigration and asylum also reads some of these important issues. Luibhéid argues that nation states decide whether to admit or refuse entry to migrants based on sexual considerations that crosscut racial, gender, class and geopolitical calculations: for instance, legal admission often depends on fitting into normative definitions of family, kinship or marriage, or claiming fear of persecution that takes a sexualised form or is based on sexuality. Conversely, migrants are often denied legal status when they cannot fit into normative definitions of family, or are believed to present sexual danger (for example, as supposed carriers of sexual diseases, or loose women, or men who might sexually prey on others, or sexual 'perverts'). Migrants continue to be governed in sexual terms after entering the nation state, especially through their interactions with economic, health, welfare and education systems. Moreover, citizens perceive migrants through a sexualised lens, often seeing them as exotic, sexually backward/traditional/repressed, highly fertile, bearers of perversion and disease, or as models of sexual and moral values that the citizenry should emulate. Through these processes, binaries such as us/them, citizen/migrant, and normal/deviant, are expressed, mapped onto bodies and places, and struggled over. Puar and Rai have written that the construct of the 'terrorist' relies on the knowledge of sexual perversity (failed heterosexuality, Western notions of the psyche, and a certain queer monstrosity). In *Terrorist Assemblages*, Puar argues that this displacement has occasioned the eruption of a new mainstream gay and lesbian politics that she terms 'homonationalism', in which gay and lesbian organisations increasingly advocate for assimilationist heteronormative rights such as marriage and adoption, and being part of the nation state (through military service or political office) (xxv).

An aspect of this kind of migration policy and narrative is centred on Muslims. As Haritaworn explains, earlier, migrants, and especially Muslim migrants, have been constructed as the new bogeyman. An example of queer of colour critique in practice can be seen in the analysis of queer Muslims in Europe by Fatima El-Tayeb, which touches on the larger themes explored in queer theory. El-Tayeb critiques some of the neoliberal constructions of what it means to be gay. As she points out, coming out is discussed as the 'acceptable face' (80) of being a liberal queer, and being in the closet is seen as backward. This of course does not in any way challenge the many other forms of religious and racial oppression that queer Muslims face or the intersectional oppressions faced by gay Muslims within white queer spaces or Brown heteronormative spaces. The ideas of migration and 'home' are also critiqued in that the ethnic migrant labourer lives amongst an 'increasingly segregated, criminalized and policed multi-ethnic population of color' (88). These queer diasporic and queer of colour critiques therefore act as a lens through which to view homonormativity and the various facets through which is functions. Those people of colour who are queer and undocumented experience individual and institutional discrimination based on their sexual identity and lack of Western citizenship.

Terms of transgression and their relation to politics of sexual alternatives can be especially complex. This can be mapped across the politics of remembrance – what we remember and what we deny in any given political movement; and what kind of alternative realities we may construct in the process, in relation to who is included in a movement and in what frame of reference. Queer politics in India has been criticised by several people for its lack of intersectionality in such terms – for example, with respect to issues pertaining to caste, class and gender-based exclusions (Dutta, *Kon rooper ontor*).

Activists in India have argued that cosmopolitan queer politics ends up denying sexual- and gender-dissident subjects whose appearance and social status might mark them as unsuitably modern. This has also been seen in the case of those from lower castes or classes, those from rural contexts, and/or those whose performance of gender might evoke overly effeminate forms of an otherwise 'male' embodiment, which may not readily reconcile with a 'gay' cosmopolitan subjectivity (Dutta, 'An Epistemology of Collusion'; Dutta, *Kon rooper ontor*; Boyce). As queer theorist Halberstam has argued, the ethics of complicity and the ways in which a 'politically pure history' (171) may be written might cast away the classed, racist (and casteist in the case of India) nature of some queer formations. Claims made for the necessary recognition of queer citizen subjects might thus be taken as a signifier for a progressive Indian polity. Yet, the integration of such politics with the politics of caste, class and gender-based exclusion remains unresolved in many instances.

To take an instructive comparative example, Gloria Wekker's work on 'homonostalgia' (cited in Haritaworn) explores ways in which the Netherlands is imagined as progressive in the context of proactive legislation for queer rights and gay marriage. Against this background, racial and racist anxieties in the Netherlands are often conceived around the figure of the Muslim (migrant), who is typically constructed as a figure whose social integration might drag these rights back. A similar sentiment is also being expressed by some in queer movements in India where Muslims and migrants are being constructed as the new 'degenerative other', threatening 'our' mode of being (Haritaworn). A queer of colour critique requires paying attention to these fissures, taking sexuality as a point of intersectionality, and pitching our tent with other minorities across on-going diversities and contestations.

Gayatri Gopinath, while writing about the queer diaspora, argues, 'While both queer of color and queer diasporic analysis are part of a collective endeavor to reshape queer studies through a thorough engagement with questions of race, nationalism, and transnationalism, it may also be useful to explore some of the points at which the interventions and emphases of each project both intersect and diverge' ('Bollywood Spectacles' 158). Rodríguez's and Gopinath's move away from the analytical traditions in continental philosophy towards the hermeneutic tradition provides direction for understanding how queer subjects of colour such as the gay asylum seeker (Rodríguez) and diasporic female queer subjects (Gopinath, *Impossible Desires*) navigate structural constraints in order to forge transnational diasporic coalitions. In this regard, it is pertinent to look back at Sara Ahmed's 2004 article that speaks about the role of emotions in the formation of white supremacy as well as subjects of colour. Building upon the works of Maurice Merleau-Ponty, Ahmed urges us to consider what emotions do. For Ahmed, emotions forge racialised collectives. She returns to Audre Lorde's *Sister Outsider* to show how bodies press upon each other in cramped public transportation in order to mark skin and space through racialised encounters. Ahmed's mobilisation of Sartre, Merleau-Ponty and Butler can show how queer of colour theorists have consistently mobilised women of colour thinkers in order to name how feelings, desires and emotions are racialised processes that ultimately work to (de)stabilise whiteness. Queer of colour scholarship can help us understand how racialisation, sexualisation and recent geopolitical trends such as the Syrian war, Brexit and the move towards conservative politics globally, converge and constitute one another.

Queer of colour critique is now a formidable interdisciplinary body of work that draws from the disciplines of history, literary studies, performance, anthropology and sociology. It seeks to destabilise relationships between sexual, racial and class-based oppression, whilst challenging mainstream discourses which take for granted notions of queer identity that may not necessarily be useful for people of colour. Thus, a queer of colour critique offers a specific kind of anti-racist, anti-capitalist queer scholarship.

REFERENCES

Ahmed, Sara. 'Collective Feelings Or, the Impressions Left by Others'. *Theory, Culture and Society* 21.2 (2004): 25–42. Print.

---. *The Promise of Happiness*. Durham: Duke UP, 2010. Print.

Anzaldúa, Gloria. *The Gloria Anzaldúa Reader.* Ed. A. Keating. Durham: Duke UP, 2009. Print.

Banerjee, Mukulika, and Daniel Miller. *The Sari.* London: Berg Publishers, 2003. Print.

Begum, Lipi, and Rohit K. Dasgupta. 'Contemporary South Asian Youth Cultures and the Fashion Landscape'. *International Journal of Fashion Studies* 2.1 (2015): 133–45. Print.

Boyce, Paul. 'The Object of Attention: Same-sex Sexualities in Small-town India and the Contemporary Sexual Subject'. *Sexuality Studies*. Ed. S. Srivastava. Delhi: Oxford UP, 2013. 183–202. Print.

Brockenbrough, Edward. 'Queer of Colour Critique'. *Critical Concepts in Queer Studies and Education: An International Guide for the Twenty-First Century.* Eds. N. Rodriguez, W. Martino, J. Ingrey, and E. Brockenbrough. London: Palgrave Macmillan, 2016. 285–98. Print.

de Lauretis, Teresa. 'The Technology of Gender'. *Feminist Communication Theory: Selections in Context.* Eds. L. Rakow, L. Wackwitz. New York: Sage Publications, 1987. Print.

Dutta, Aniruddha. 'An Epistemology of Collusion: Hijra, Kothi and the Historical (Dis)continuity of Gender/Sexual Identities in Eastern India'. *Gender & History* 24.3 (2012): 825–49. Print.

---. *Kon rooper ontor: 'Transgender' o 'Rupantarkami' poirchoy borgo o kichhu lingo-prantik manusher atmoprokasher bhasha* [Trans of Which Gender? 'Transgender' and 'Rupantarkami' Identity Categories and the Self-narratives of a few Gender-Marginalised Persons]. *Swikriti Patrika* 10 (2012). Print.

El-Tayeb, Fatima. '"Gays Who Cannot Properly Be Gay": Queer Muslims in the Neoliberal European City'. *European Journal of Women's Studies* 19.1 (2012): 79–95. Print.

Ferguson, Roderick. *Aberrations in Black: Toward a Queer of Color Critique*. Minneapolis: U of Minnesota P, 2003. Print.

Gopinath, Gayatri. 'Bollywood Spectacles: Queer Diasporic Critique in the Aftermath of 9/11'. *Social Text* 23.84–85 (2005): 157–69. Print.

---. *Impossible Desires: Queer Diasporas and South Asian Public Cultures.* Durham: Duke UP, 2005. Print.

Halberstam, Jack. *The Queer Art of Failure.* Durham: Duke UP, 2011. Print.

Haritaworn, Jin. *Queer Lovers and Hateful Others: Regenerating Violent Times and Places.* London: Pluto, 2016. Print.

Holland, Sharon. *Raising the Dead: Readings of Death and (Black) Subjectivity*. Durham: Duke UP, 2000. Print.

Khubchandani, Kareem. 'Snakes on the Dance Floor: Bollywood, Gesture and Gender'. *Velvet Light Trap* 77 (Spring 2016): 69–85. Print.

Luibhéid, Eithne. *Entry Denied: Controlling Sexuality at the Border.* Minneapolis: U of Minnesota P, 2002. Print.

Moraga, Cherríe, and Gloria Anzaldúa, eds. *This Bridge Called My Back: Writings by Radical Women of Color.* New York: Kitchen Table, Women of Colour Press, 1981. Print.

Muñoz, José Esteban. *Disidentifications: Queers of Color and the Performance of Politics.* Durham: Duke UP, 1999. Print.

Puar, Jasbir K. *Terrorist Assemblages: Homonationalism in Queer Times.* Durham: Duke UP, 2007. Print.

Puar, Jasbir K., and Amit S. Rai. 'Monster, Terrorist, Fag: The War on Terrorism and the Production of Docile Patriots'. *Social Text* 20.3 (2002): 117–48. Print.

Reddy, Chandan. *Freedom with Violence: Race, Sexuality, and the US State.* Durham: Duke UP, 2011. Print.

Rodríguez, Juana María. *Queer Latinidad: Identity Practices, Discursive Spaces*. New York: New York UP, 2003. Print. Sexual Cultures.

Warner, Michael. *Publics and Counterpublics*. Cambridge: MIT Press, 2002. Print.

Chapter Eight

Queer Studies in the Indian Academia

POSSIBILITIES AND RESISTANCES

THE GENESIS OF QUEER STUDIES IN THE WEST

Queer Studies began to be institutionalised widely around the time Teresa de Lauretis's special issue of *differences* (1991) was published, although Gay and Lesbian Studies had already entered First World university curricula after the Stonewall Inn revolution in 1969. The first undergraduate course on LGBT Studies was introduced in the University of California, Berkeley, in the spring of 1970. Soon after, Southern Illinois University Edwardsville and the University of Nebraska–Lincoln (UNL) began offering similar courses. However, campuses in the United States remained overtly homophobic for a long time, compelling teachers and students to hide behind straight masks.

Toni A. H. McNaron's semi-autobiographical *Poisoned Ivy: Lesbian and Gay Academics Confronting Homophobia* (1997) begins with a 'dismal and frightening' picture of the University of Minnesota campus in the early 1960s, when it was impossible for gay or lesbian academicians to 'come out' and declare their sexualities. Although a few campuses in California or New York City were comparatively more 'queer-friendly', in the 'overwhelming majority of cases, however, such faculty were silent, reluctant to risk credibility and jobs by announcing their sexual identities' (1). McNaron cites several instances, including her own experiences, to bring home the pathologised status of gay or lesbian academics who were always under the judgemental gaze of homophobes. For McNaron, the early days in Minnesota was akin to belonging to the inmate cells of a panopticon, unsure of who was keeping watch and waiting for a vulnerable moment 'to catch me in some glaring mistake' (5). The fear of being found out was so overwhelming that McNaron willingly subscribed to the imperative of self-surveillance by consciously quarantining her feelings and desires.

McNaron's inability to bring her sexual subjectivity into her lectures and writings was encountered by many across the United States, and it is a problem which many South Asian academics have to deal with even today. For a long time, even after institutionalisation of Queer Studies in the West, several Indian universities and colleges either kept explicitly queer texts out of their syllabus, or taught such texts with a lot of trepidation, often at the expense of providing reductive readings to students. One may cite the example of the early-modern play *Edward II* (1594) by Christopher Marlowe, which has been on the English literature syllabuses of several Indian universities for decades. In many Indian classrooms, the homoerotic relationship between Edward II and Gaveston, which flouts class hierarchy and causes Edward's eventual downfall, has often been cautiously glossed over as a 'decadent' friendship rooted in improvident pleasures, without explicitly discussing the sexual underpinnings of the relationship. The current scenario in India remains unfavourable for Queer Studies. Apart from a few postgraduate programmes in literature, sociology, gender or women's studies in a few metropolitan universities, Queer Studies is still largely non-existent. A large number of students graduating with English Honours/Major still remain ignorant of the queer dynamics in several canonical or contemporary texts or the sexualities of some of the celebrated authors they study.

Returning to the early days of the introduction of LGBT Studies into university curricula, one may cite the case of Louis Crompton, a professor at the University of Nebraska–Lincoln (UNL), who did not anticipate the severe state resistance a course on 'Homophile Studies' (1970) would spawn. Crompton later recalled what he had to deal with after introducing the course. State Senator Terry Carpenter ganged up with Robert Prokop who made a political issue out of the course, vilified it and broadcast it in the media, claiming that 'a subject like this should not be an elective course for students unless they are studying in the medical field' (qtd. in McNoran 170). A public hearing was scheduled a few days before the elections in which Prokop was seeking a seat in the university's Board of Regents. Carpenter, in his support for Prokop, made the statement: 'A nationwide movement is underway to make abnormal forms of behavior acceptable' (qtd. in McNoran 170). Henry Pederson of Omaha, Chair of the Legislative Health Committee, with whom Carpenter shared the interrogator's role, went to the extent of demanding that the objective of the course be altered. He argued that rather than showing homosexuals in a positive light, the course should be a vehicle for promoting homophobia: 'I hope this course teaches that homosexuality is abnormal conduct and should be avoided' (qtd. in McNoran 171).

The 'Homophile Studies' course was eventually withdrawn, although James Cole, a professor of psychology at UNL, offered a course on same-sex desires the same year. The garb of psychology, perhaps, acted as a protective armour against detractors. Crompton could not repeat his course; in 1973, he began offering another course on homosexuality in literature, which ran successfully for fifteen years without much resistance. Today there are more than forty courses in LGBT/Queer Studies being offered in various universities in the United States.

QUEERING THE INDIAN ACADEMIA

Writing about the colonial appropriation of attitudes to homosexuality in Indian literatures produced in the early twentieth century, Ruth Vanita observed in 2000: 'The homophobic attitudes evident in fiction find their counterpart in the studied silence maintained by the Indian academy on the subject of homosexuality. While picking up other kinds of critical theory generated in the Western academy, such as Marxism, feminism, deconstruction, and postcolonial theory, the Indian academy has by and large avoided lesbian and gay studies' (233). She maintained this view even in the 2008 revised edition of *Same-Sex Love in India*. Notwithstanding how some universities have begun including Gay and Lesbian Studies in their curricula, Vanita is absolutely right. Using a pseudonym, Tarun, an undergraduate student of a law school, wrote in *Sexualities* (2007), edited by Nivedita Menon:

> The absolutely uncritical manner of pedagogy in school does not allow any space for alternative ideas to be expressed. In the absence of any dialogue on sexuality, the only learning is from the images provided by the books and the teachers who are invariably heteropatriarchal. The story is not very different in most colleges either. However, what is different is the availability of space outside the curriculum for student activism. (128)

While even humanities and social sciences courses across India are largely imbricated in heteronormativity and continue to reinforce its legitimacy, there are not many Indian universities which have a queer or sexuality studies course on their curriculum. Homophobia prevails on campuses across India, and little or no organised attempts to combat it have been made, although, as Tarun observes, queer-friendly spaces have gradually begun to open up in some metropolitan universities. The few university teachers who pioneered the official introduction of LGBTQ Studies into the Indian academia have interesting – upsetting as well as funny – anecdotes to share – anecdotes which hint at the difficulties and resistances they had to encounter in their attempts to include sexuality studies in the syllabi. We shall return to these later. But first, it is important to examine what aided the emergence of Queer Studies in the academia in India. One must remember that in this particular case, it is impossible not to acknowledge the role of LGBTQ activism. Apart from that, there are several publications, conferences and seminars, films, documentaries and other cultural expressions that enabled the discipline to take root, notwithstanding how feebly or negligibly.

The 80s and the 90s: Emergence of a Discourse of Dissident Sexualities

In 1994, Ashok Row Kavi organised a conference where Subhash Salunkhe, the then Director of the Department of Health, Bombay, said in his opening address, '. . . it is wrong to say that "homosexuality" is only a western phenomenon which many of our conservative interests claim it to be . . .' (qtd. in Majumdar and Basu 279). Interestingly, this conference was reported against by the National Federation of Indian Women (NFIW, an affiliate of the Communist Party of India) which appealed to the Prime Minister of India to put a stop to it, for they thought that this conference purported to promote sexual permissiveness among the Indian youth who had, in any case, been exposed to the 'immoralities' of Western culture (Joseph 24).

This was not surprising, for several feminists were either opposed to acknowledging the existence of homosexuality or maintained a studied silence when it came to endorsing it. Feminist politics in India could still afford to keep the queer at bay, while the West had already seen a groundbreaking poststructuralist turn in feminist thought. A sex-positive feminism, including lesbian feminists, feminists of colour and feminists challenging the anti-pornography brigade, had begun to emerge from the late 1970s. Rebecca Walker, a twenty-three-year-old bisexual African-American woman born in Jackson, Mississippi, coined the term 'third-wave feminism' in 1992, to mark feminism's next significant leap – its bid to include queers and women of colour. However, Indian feminists languished in the ripples of the second wave which would take time to fizzle out completely. It has not yet, although the revolution in information technology that eliminated the culture lag in which South Asia was caught in the pre-Internet era, facilitated a progressive union of feminists and queers.

The stance taken by the NFIW revealed a deep-seated homophobia, a re-enactment of which was seen in the same year at the National Conference on Women's Movement in India, held in Tirupati. The participants conferred on the necessity of creating space for lesbian women within the women's movement. The proposal, predictably, met with belligerent opposition from a section of women activists who believed lesbianism was a psychological disorder. But the proposal was nonetheless included in the list of resolutions taken. The note of dissent against this proposal later claimed that the resolutions were rehashed to include the proposal, and that it was not taken during the conference (Menon 298–300).

Two years later, in 1996, Stree Sangam organised the First National Gathering of Women Who Love Women, in Bombay (Mumbai). In the same year, in August, Janaki Nair and Mary E. John organised a workshop to mark the silver jubilee year of the Interdisciplinary Research Methodology Workshop, the proceedings of which was published as *A Question of Silence?: The Sexual Economies of Modern India* (1998). Establishing the relevance of sexuality as a field of serious research, the workshop (and later the book) challenged the 'conspiracy of silence regarding sexuality in India, whether within political and social movements or in scholarship . . .' (John and Nair 1). Pointing out how sexuality is omnipresent in every conceivable social and cultural sphere, the workshop remarkably politicised discussions on sexuality, opening up under-researched areas cutting across several states of India: birth-control debates in Tamil Nadu, the legacy of Chalam in Andhra Pradesh, gender and violence in North India, celibacy, masculinity and discourses of nationalism, etc. Bringing together a number of progressive feminist thinkers, the workshop and the book problematised the notion of sexuality by linking it with modernism, nationalism, legal discourses and policies. It was one of the first books to talk about 'alternative sexualities' in its introduction, with references to the works of Giti Thadani and contemporary popular culture, among others. The section on 'alternative sexualities' ended with Nivedita Menon's cautionary note: 'to consider homosexuality as an alternative lifestyle is to leave unquestioned heterosexuality as the norm' (qtd. in John and Nair 36). Contemporary queer scholarship is particularly opposed to the term 'alternative sexualities', much on the same grounds as Menon dismisses it. The book's recognition of that in 1998 is worth mentioning.

While these events were taking place in India, the Indian queer diaspora in First World nations constantly fought for their rights, formed organisations, wrote books, made films, and conferred on the hostile atmosphere at home when it came to recognising queer rights. All these incidents, events and achievements were regularly reported in the Indian media, especially in the English language press, conjuring up a comparatively favourable environment for an academic discipline to emerge. At the same time, an alarming rise of right wing politics in India (signalled by the demolition of the Babri Masjid in 1992 and the resultant communal riots in various parts of the country) made it clear that possibilities of legalising homosexuality were to shrink in the near future. The need to contest the hostile stance of the state in this matter began to be felt with a deeper urgency.

The late 1980s and the early 1990s saw a proliferation of books and articles on dissident sexualities, which became ready reference material for academic courses. *A Lotus of a Different Colour: An Unfolding of the South Asian Gay and Lesbian Experience* (1993), edited by Rakesh Ratti, was one of the first anthologies to delve into South Asian queer diasporic experiences. Around this time, mathematician Shakuntala Devi's extremely sensitive *The World of Homosexuals* (1977), which had not found much attention earlier, got a new lease of life. R. Raj Rao's collection of short stories, *One Day I Locked My Flat in Soul City* (1995), unapologetically revealed the agony and anguish of being queer in India. Hoshang Merchant's *Yaraana: Gay Writing from South Asia* (1999) anthologised several genres of queer writings from India, with an excellent introduction that cast a critical glance on India's past, revealing a continuum of same-sex friendships in literature and culture of all religions and communities. *Facing the Mirror: Lesbian Writing from India*, edited by Ashwini Sukthankar and published in the same year as *Yaraana*, brought together insightful essays, confessions and fictional pieces. Giti Thadani, founder of the first lesbian organisation in India, Sakhi Collective (established in 1990), wrote *Sakhiyani: Lesbian Desire in Ancient and Modern India* (1996), constructing an intriguing narrative of ancient 'autonomous gynefocal cosmological traditions' (100) centred on female homoeroticism in India. Deepa Mehta's controversial film, *Fire*, released within two years of the publication of this book, further paved the path for talking about female homoeroticism. *Fire*, which was widely written about by academicians and journalists[1] based in India and the West, became an iconic cultural text which pushed open the door that had so far closeted the Indian lesbian, while ruffling fundamentalist feathers.

While queer texts were finding publishers as well as readers, spaces outside the universities, but not totally delinked from the academia, were opening up in the 1990s, which allowed serious reflections on the issue of sexuality. In a personal interview, Shohini Ghosh, writer, activist and academician affiliated to Jamia Millia Islamia, recalls,

> In Delhi, the autonomous women's groups, organisations like the Centre for Feminist Legal Research (CFLR) were opening up spaces for the discussion of gender and sexualities. It was not easy to create such spaces because a number of rather established feminists were struggling with queer ideas and finding it hard to decentre the heteronormative frame. Yet, queer ideas were emerging primarily through debates on feminism.

Ghosh's claim can be corroborated by the violent dissent on the resolution taken at the 1994 National Conference on Women's Movement in India. Ghosh was one of those who began to queer the academic pitch in the 1990s. Ghosh, who had been spending one semester every year at the Department of Communication, Cornell University (1991–95), was exposed to a whole spectrum of queer films unavailable in India at that time. She brought back those films as VHS tapes, especially works of Maya Deren (*Meshes of the Afternoon*) and Kenneth Anger (*Scorpio Rising*), and introduced them in her course at the Mass Communication Research Centre at Jamia. Two films in particular, Rob Epstein's *The Times of Harvey Milk* (1984) and Nishit Saran's *Summer in My Veins* (1998), left an indelible mark on her students: 'During the post-screening discussion, many students would say that *The Times of Harvey Milk* had made them think about gays and lesbians in a different way', Ghosh recalled in an interview.

While Ghosh was challenging the predominance of heteronormativity in university courses, Sumanyu Satpathy put together a course, 'Sexual Dissidence and Modernism: Oscar Wilde and After', for the Master of Philosophy programme at the Department of English, University of Delhi, in 1998. In the same year, a semester later, Hoshang Merchant introduced 'Gay Indian Poetry' at the Department of English, University of Hyderabad. This course which rediscovered many queer Indian poets, the most important of them being Sultan Padamsee, was later anthologised in *Yaraana*. Satpathy's course, on the other hand, consisted mostly of Anglo-European texts, with a specific aim. As he recalled in a personal interview,

> The course aims, by studying about ten authors and their works, to see how the subject of sexual dissidence is integral to our understanding of ideologies of modernism particularly by exploring the link between modernism and sexual dissent. It is also designed to study the correlation between the two realms of discourse, the "literary" and "non-literary" (the legal, for example) during the period 1885–1960, as also the representations of homosexuals in modern texts, and their changing images vis-à-vis other kinds of sexuality. Here the term, "dissent"/"dissidence" is used to refer to the questioning of essentialism, and notions which had resulted in viewing homosexuality as perversion or deviance from heteronormative perspectives.

While Merchant's course brought out of the closet several literary texts by enabling a queer reading (see Rath), Satpathy's course addressed the question of sexuality as a modern construction. The two courses made way for the formation of a new literary canon, consisting of both familiar texts of yesteryears and a new emergent literature which identified itself as 'gay' or 'lesbian'.

R. Raj Rao designed a course on LGBT Studies and proposed it as a Masters course at the University of Pune (Savitribai Phule Pune University) at the turn of the millennium, only to take it back. Rao writes, 'The Board of Studies in English (BSE), an academic body made up of politically rather than academically minded individuals, promptly singled it out and rejected it, remarking that *Indian* students did not need such a course!' (Rao and Sarma xi; emphasis added). It is not hard to see how the BSE felt the urgency to dissociate Indian nationality from queerness, unquestioningly subscribing to the anxiety-ridden postcolonial myth that gayness and lesbianism were 'corrupt Western imports' (xi). One may also mention here the objection raised by one of Satpathy's senior colleagues to his course on 'Sexual Dissidence': he objected to the course citing Section 377 of the IPC which criminalised homosexuality (which was in force till 2018 when the Supreme Court of India ruled that the Section was unconstitutional and irrational), thereby evoking the question of the national legitimacy of sexually dissident citizens.

In both these cases, where the hostility to the courses was of varying degrees, it is unsettling to see the repeated emphasis on the illegitimacy of same-sex love in India. Both these instances foreground a rhizomic power structure of a dominant ideology in which those who raised objections were interpellated. The abhorrence for any same-sex association and a cautionary evocation of a law that prohibits it are both inherited from a colonial culture. This kind of moral policing is a classic example of what Ashcroft calls, 'the very complex system of opposition and complicity which characterizes the relationship between postcolonial subjects and imperial discourse' (53). Discourses of 'mainstream' Christianity and colonialism, which 'rejected the presence of femininity in man as virtually the negation of all humaneness' (Nandy 43), were intrinsically intertwined with each other; and the colonising enterprise was popularly viewed as a religious and ethical duty. Under such circumstances, when the community of the colonisers obsessed over their 'self-image as a community of well-defined men, with clear-cut man-woman relationships' (Nandy 44), anything that hinted at a sexual ambivalence was mercilessly repressed. In fact, all markers of ambiguous sexuality were either eliminated or tactically concealed so as not to tarnish the colonisers' hypermasculine image. As a way of substantiating this, one may cite an interesting incident that took place in 2005 at Jadavpur University's Department of English, when a course entitled 'Queer Studies' was proposed as an optional for postgraduate students.

The 2000s: An Era of Light and Darkness

2000–2009

Focusing on the development of Queer Theory and the various aspects of the LGBTQ movement in India, the Queer Studies course at the Department of English, Jadavpur University, chose largely English, European and American texts as literary case studies, much like the one at the University of Delhi. The course proposer, Paromita Chakravarti, recalls in a personal interview, 'The course was passed without resistance; I believe few knew at that time what Queer Studies was all about. People were more familiar with Gay and Lesbian Studies then; the term "queer" was less available in the public domain.' However, resistance was to come. 'A colleague was uncomfortable with Tennyson's *In Memoriam* being taught on the course', says Chakravarti. This relatively 'old school' colleague, visibly distraught, requested her not to usurp Tennyson and place him under the rubric of Queer Studies. Chakravarti had designed the course in such a way so as to include one text from each of the 'ages' of English literary history, and thought *In Memoriam* (1850) was an important text, which while firmly located within the Victorian paradigm, revealed intensities of a deep homoerotic friendship in an age which moralised against and ruthlessly punished sodomites. But, eventually, on being repeatedly requested by the colleague, she had to let go of Tennyson and replace him with a more obvious Oscar Wilde.

Chakarvarti's anecdote, though amusing, is deeply disconcerting. In her colleague's bid to 'reclaim' Tennyson who had apparently fallen from grace by being taught in a course on Queer Studies, lies a profound anxiety about cogitating on homoerotic desires in sanctified canonical texts in the classroom. By including Tennyson in the Queer Studies course, Chakaravarti, it seems, was doing a disservice to an English poet laureate who could not *afford to be gay*, even though his epical mourning in *In Memoriam* could not perhaps have been less unequivocal about it. The colonial strategies of invisibilising the queer, as one can see, were being preserved by a postcolonial subject, a teacher of English literature, who stood guard against what she thought was an 'outing' of Tennyson whose identity as a queer poet, ironically, was no secret anymore. It was not a secret even in the Victorian period, though the general denigration of it was similar to that of Chakravarti's colleague's. For instance, Arthur Hallam's father, terribly disconcerted about the intense relationship between his son and Tennyson, held Shakespeare's sonnets responsible for sanctioning same-sex love: 'it is impossible not to wish that Shakespeare had never written them. There is a weakness and folly in all excessive and misplaced affection, which is not redeemed by the touches of nobler sentiments' (qtd. in Sinfield 128). Interestingly, long before Queer Theory provided tools for a contrapuntal reading of these sonnets, the well-informed Englishman had deep reservations for Shakespeare's celebration of the 'Fair Youth' which upset the heteronormative idea of love and romance.

Chakravarti shared with us an intriguing semi-autobiographical paper, 'Teaching Queer and Queering Teaching: Introducing Queer Studies at the University', which she had presented at a women's conference held in Lucknow in 2008. The paper emphasised the necessity of queering the curriculum, in order to contest the hegemony of heteronormative discourses in the university syllabi. With more than sixty students signing up for her course on Queer Studies (which still runs in the department and is co-taught by Kaustav Bakshi, one of the authors of this volume), Chakravarti rationalised the essentiality of having canonical texts and authors (such as Tennyson) on the course:

> Prescribing familiar texts which had been studied in other courses and contexts also allowed students to focus on the processes of "straight" and queer readings of the same text, illustrating differences in modes of appropriation. This indicated how "queer" or "non-queer" texts are not predetermined categories, but it is the processes of reading, reception, circulation and canonization which determine the meanings and status of texts. For many students this understanding was both new and empowering. It helped them to define their own locations as readers and understand the implications of their social and sexual identities in their textual negotiations. ('Teaching Queer and Queering Teaching' n. p.)

Chakravarti's view is somewhat corroborated by Ruth Vanita. Vanita, in a personal interview, says,

> When I teach a course where the title and main topic is same-sex desire or even gender and sexuality, I get a self-selected crowd of students. But if I teach it (as I do) in almost any course on any topic, then it reaches a wide cross-section of students who realise that it is part of everyone's life, not just those who identify as queer.

Shakespeare's sonnets, *Edward II*, *The Picture of Dorian Gray*, *In Memoriam* and *Orlando* have been taught across universities for decades. For instance, Swati Ganguly, a professor at the Department of English and Other Modern European Languages, Visva-Bharati, says it was impossible for her to teach *Orlando* in a course on feminist literature without alluding to its unequivocal queerness. She has recently developed a course on gender and sexuality, but she has always taught *Orlando* or *The Well of Loneliness* in courses on feminism although these texts were never part of specifically marked out courses on queer sexualities.

But the 1990s saw the formulation of a special category whereby these texts, just like sexually 'deviant' individuals, began to be clustered under the rubric of 'queer', much to the chagrin of the conservatives such as Chakravarti's colleague. Simultaneously, self-consciously written queer literatures (such as poems by Suniti Namjoshi, Hoshang Merchant and Vikram Seth; prose fiction by Firdaus Kanga and R. Raj Rao; or Mahesh Dattani's plays) also began to be produced, marketed, and included in syllabi as belonging to an emergent category. The discipline of Queer Studies is, therefore, caught in a curious paradox, just like dissident sexual identities – on the one hand, there is the necessity to *normalise* 'queer', as Vanita says in an interview with us, 'that it is part of everyone's life, not just those who identify as queer'; on the other hand, the formation of a unique category is also necessary for it provides a whole range of critical tools and rhetoric for oppositional readings and interpretations of already canonised texts and the emergent ones, to dismantle the *normal*, and its fragility and constructedness. Chakravarti's experience with her colleague reveals the anxiety that such categorisation can breed. On a positive note, it also reinforces the necessity of instituting such academic courses in order to open the closet of half-truths in which many queer literary artists had so far been confined.

While universities mildly or aggressively replicated state resistance to recognising homosexuality within the national register, throughout the first decade of the new millennium, the state's repressive apparatuses continued to unabashedly stage their homophobia on various occasions. For example, on 6 July 2001, the Lucknow offices of Bharosa Trust and Naz Foundation International, two NGOs working with MSMs, were raided by the police, under false charges of running 'call boy rackets'. And Naz Foundation's Public Interest Litigation demanding repeal of Section 377 of the IPC was dismissed by the Delhi High Court in 2004. Arvind Narrain's *Queer: Despised Sexuality, Law and Societal Change*, published in the same year, reflected on the nuances of the legal battle against the draconian anti-sodomy law, while historicising sexuality's contested relationship with law since ancient times.

In the first decade of the new millennium, the impact of the Internet revolution had begun to be felt in the Indian academia. Books, journals, magazines, newspaper reports, films, television series, videos and other databases and archives became available, owing to the democratisation of knowledge which the Internet paved the way for. Academicians and students had greater access to research material which a previous generation could not imagine finding in local university libraries. The Internet provided free spaces for unheard voices to emerge: social networking sites, blogs, portals and domains for uploading personal videos that allowed people to share their opinions and views, without having to go through the rigmarole of state censorship. Automatically, research in gender and sexuality, like in the case of all other fields, became relatively easier; and a simultaneity with the West was established in terms of knowledge production. International publishing houses began showing an increasing interest in South Asian histories and cultures; and easy communication with publishers, enabled by free access to e-mails, helped South Asian scholars and writers to pitch their research on an international platform with greater comfort. They need not be affiliated to Western universities in order to find recognition internationally. The first decade of the new millennium was remarkably prolific in producing queer scholarship of extremely high standards.

In 2000, the publication of Ruth Vanita and Saleem Kidwai's *Same-Sex Love in India: A Literary History* revolutionised Queer Studies in India. Vanita and Kidwai brought together ancient, medieval and modern Indian texts that dealt with homoeroticism, transvestism, transsexuality, and the *tritiya prakiriti* or third gender. The book wrote a history of sexuality in India by exploring a large number of cultural texts produced in different ages. It revisited folk tales, stories, songs, poems, myths and episodes from epics from a queer perspective, and showed them in a different light. The introductions to the various sections of the book provided a methodology of researching and teaching queer texts. *Same-Sex Love in India* broke new grounds in welding cultural studies with Queer Theory, bringing in its wake an astonishing range of studies on gender and sex.

While masculinity studies, following the works of Slavoj Žižek, Harry Brod, Michael Kimmel, Jeff Hearn and R. W. Connell, emphasised the necessity of perceiving men as 'gendered subjects', queer feminists, in the tradition of the successful convergence of queer and feminist scholarships in the Western academia, opened up interesting sites of enquiry into non-normative erotic economies and sexual practices. Breaking away from Western discourses of sexuality, identity politics and history of sexuality, large number of books from India, written by both activists and academicians, brought out the diverse manifestations of sexuality in Indian cultures, while challenging the conspiracy of silence surrounding sex and sexuality. Vanita and Kidwai's book was followed by a number of academic publications focusing on sexuality and gender in India, all of which extensively reinforced sexuality studies in India by inaugurating diverse fields of research – postcoloniality and queer sexualities, queer cultures and political activism, transnational queer citizens of colour, subaltern queers, construction of masculinity, and the digital world of queer lives and intimacies. Each of these books made significant contributions to the formulation of a queer pedagogy in Indian universities.

In 2002, two organisations working on human rights and sexuality issues – CREA and TARSHI (Talking about Reproductive and Sexual Health Issues) – started the annual Sexuality and Rights Institutes (SRIs). Shohini Ghosh observes in our interview with her,

> The SRIs have been for me the most important academic space for cutting-edge discussions on issues of sexuality. The SRIs left an indelible impact on many who would make significant contributions to the LGBT movement. Here, I had complete freedom to design sessions on the most provocative ideas engendered by feminist and queer thought in relation to debates on representation, spectatorship and censorship.

It was becoming increasingly difficult not to be a feminist, without being queer. Although, in the 1990s, feminists were rather wary of showing solidarity with their queer peers, the merging of the two movements which were technically not opposed to each other was inevitable. An urgency to talk about sex and sexuality was certainly being felt; and some things were changing, albeit slowly and almost imperceptibly.

One also needs to understand what was happening on the university campus around this time. A case in point would be R. Raj Rao's course which the English department at the University of Pune had refused to pass in 1999. The ban was eventually lifted in 2007, when Rao was allowed to teach 'LGBT Literature in India' under the rubric of 'Alternative Literature II'. 'Alternative Literature I' had 'Dalit Writing in India' under it: '[W]e were emphasizing the underlying connection between both these forms of marginal literature or literature of protest: we were suggesting that coalitions of oppressed groups was the need of the hour' (Rao and Sarma xiii). While such solidarity is certainly coveted, one problem of teaching queer texts under the rubric of 'Alternative Literature' is that it takes away the liberty to teach canonical texts – texts which had unambiguous queer markers in them, but were written long before LGBTQ literature became a separate category – on the same course. Unless the course included only those texts that are written by self-proclaimed gay, lesbian, bisexual and transgender authors, it might be difficult to establish the marginality of already canonised authors.

It would be impossible to establish, for instance, Shakespeare, Wilde or Woolf's texts as 'alternative', unless the course decided not to teach any of these unavoidable writers. Apart from that, the title of the course falls into the same trap of which Menon had already forewarned in her 1996 essay, 'Destabilising Feminism': 'alternative' is not a term that empowers queer literature; rather, it assumes and reinforces heteronormative narratives as the sanctified norm. Nonetheless, the need of the hour was to make a respectable space for LGBTQ Studies within the curriculum.

These events, such as the University of Pune's introduction of a LGBT course, look like huge progressive leaps when viewed in relation to the larger social picture. The year 2007 saw the introduction of a scheme for adolescent education programme (in other words, introduction of 'sex education') in the school curriculum, promoted by the National AIDS Control Organisation (NACO) and the Ministry of Human Resource Development (MHRD), Government of India. The proposition met with enormous opposition from all quarters. It seemed as if the nation was being stripped of the apparel of morality in which it had so far cloaked sex and sexuality. Several groups – religious, political, feminist – argued that sex education was not required in India for Indian children were not promiscuous like their Western counterparts, and that introduction of sex education would provoke them into becoming sexually adventurous. While several Indian states rejected the proposal on more or less similar grounds, West Bengal, then under the rule of a Left government, embraced it in an apparently progressive move. But what they did with the idea of sex education by adopting it into the curriculum was even more questionable; and it seems it would have been better if they had not introduced it at all.

Paromita Chakravarti, in 'The Sex Education Debates: Teaching "Life Style" in West Bengal, India', deconstructs *Life Style Education Manual*, a textbook for secondary education introduced in the 2006–07 session into the syllabus of all schools in West Bengal. The text, which was reminiscent of conservative Victorianism, ended up reinforcing 'the terms of nineteenth century *brahmacharya* debate' (392). Promoting an anti-globalisation rhetoric, the text contextualised its own emergence as a necessity to contest the '"rootless culture" (*Life Style* 2005, 3), erosion of values and dominance of the electronic media, all of which create a decadent atmosphere of unrestrained sexuality' (393). The text suggested abstinence from sex as the only way to contend this temptation to explore one's sexuality, a throwback to the nationalist emphasis on the conservation of semen. 'HIV/AIDS becomes a site for both moral outrage and gender stereotyping' (397) in the text, and there was barely a mention of contraceptives that could actually be the most effective measure to be undertaken in order to prevent the disease. Reinstating heterosexist marriage, with well-defined gender roles within it, as the only possible antidote to life-threatening STDs, the text, unsurprisingly, did not recognise the existence of non-normative forms of sexual associations at all. There was no mention of homosexuality, as if it did not exist in India.

What this *Life Style* text did was not very different from the outright denouncement of sex education by the conservative Right, and one may cite the report of the committee constituted by the Rajya Sabha to review the Adolescent Education Programme. The report released in 2009 concluded that sex education was not necessary in India, stating that the programme could cause irreparable damage to the future of the country by polluting young, impressionable minds, by encouraging promiscuity. Just like the *Life Style* manual published by the West Bengal government, the report upheld the need for conveying the message of 'no sex' before marriage among adolescents and declaring it as dissolute, unscrupulous and detrimental to health (Rajya Sabha Committee on Petitions, Web, n. p.). The general discomfort about sex education in schools persists even today.

In order not to offend protestors, a more conservative approach has been adopted by the government in recent years. The current existing program of sex education incorporated in the Indian curriculum is termed Family Life Education (FLE), which was proposed by the National AIDS Control Organisation and the Ministry of Human Resources and Development. The very title of the programme eliminates the possibility of any kind of sexual association or kinship ties other than those permissible within the heterosexist framework of sexual and emotional attachments. The debate around sex education which took the nation by storm also brought to the fore the suppressed hostility which surrounds any form of sexual expression, heteronormative or queer – in fact, towards the word 'sex' itself. It was as if contact with the word 'sex', if mentioned anywhere in the curriculum, would pollute educational institutions and the process of education.

Within this generally hostile environment in post-globalisation India, literature and cinema, however, continued to contribute positively to addressing queer issues. If *Fire* (1998) had brought the Indian lesbian out of the closet, a number of overtly queer films had begun to be made around that time, though none of these stirred up a hornet's nest like *Fire* did. Small films with limited viewership such as *BOMGay* (dir: Riyad Vinci Wadia and Jangu Sethna, 1996), *Bombay Boys* (dir: Kaizad Gustad, 1998), *Split Wide Open* (dir: Dev Benegal, 1999), *Mango Soufflé* (dir: Mahesh Dattani, 2002) and *Gulabi Aaina/The Pink Mirror* (dir: Sridhar Rangayan, 2003) found wide circulation in film festivals and through informal networks. The early 2000s also saw the making of extremely competent films from the South: Santosh Sivan's Telugu film *Navarasa* (2004), a sensitive take on the Araavani community of South India, and Ligy J. Pullappally's Malayalam film *Sancharram/The Journey* (2004), which told a deeply emotional tale of a lesbian couple's predicament in a small village of Kerala. Shohini Ghosh's documentary *Tale of the Night Fairies* (2005) also made a significant contribution to queer narratives in India: focusing on five sex workers based in Kolkata, Ghosh's documentary, though not dealing with specifically gay or lesbian sex workers, unravelled the complex moral knots in which the debates over decriminalisation of sex work were embroiled.

On a larger scale, Onir's *My Brother . . . Nikhil* (2005) released to critical acclaim, while Nikkhil Advani's blockbuster *Kal Ho Na Ho/ Tomorrow May Never Come* (2003) raised much controversy for its homophobic comedy of errors involving its two male protagonists. Yet, *Kal Ho Na Ho* did not offend as much as Karan Razdan's *Girlfriend* (2004), which established lesbianism as a psychological disorder, an abnormality from the monstrous clutches of which the male protagonist rescues his lover. Bombay Cinema, the most powerful medium of entertainment in India, continued to be largely homophobic, although positive images of gay or lesbian people appeared in small-budget films. One example could be *Rules: Pyar ka Superhit Formula* (dir: Parvati Balagopalan, 2003). In 2007, a LGBTQ film festival, Dialogues, was launched in Kolkata by the non-profit organisation Pratyay Gender Trust, in association with Sappho for Equality and Sanhita, hosted by the Goethe-Institut Max Mueller Bhavan. In that very year, Sridhar Rangayan released his second gay-themed film, *Yours Emotionally*, a UK–India co-production.

Two novels, Anita Nair's *Ladies Coupé* (2001) and Manju Kapoor's *A Married Woman* (2002), portrayed positive pictures of lesbian women, challenging heteronormative templates of friendship and coupledom. Vijay Tendulkar's Marathi play, *Mitrachi goshta* (A Friend's Story), originally written in the early 1980s, was translated into English along with his other plays, in 2001. Set in pre-independence India, the play revolves around a homoerotic relationship between two women, Sumitra and Nama, at a time when the term 'lesbian' was not widely known in India. Dayanita Singh's *Myself Mona Ahmed* – an extremely touching tale of a Delhi-based *hijra* who told her own story without demur or pretence – was published in 2002. The book sustained the enigma of the *hijra* community, never giving away the real truth which researchers and journalists had been trying to unravel for years. It is an important text which, told in the voice of Mona, successfully brought out the intricacies of relationships and power dynamics, misgivings and anguishes, of a marginalised community which has always been there, either as 'gifts of gods' or money-extracting hypocritical men trying to pass themselves off as women. But, as Mona repeatedly says, no one, no researcher, has ever been able to penetrate their soul. The same Mona Ahmed was to return as Anjum in Arundhati Roy's *The Ministry of Utmost Happiness* in 2017.

It appeared that alternative spaces were gradually opening up for the articulation of queer politics, desires and intimacy, although the 'mainstream' remained largely oblivious of, or deliberately invisibilised, the queer. These isolated but not unrelated cultural events allowed universities to expand their pedagogical framework for teaching gender to include sex, sexualities and queer discourses.

In 2008, Niladri R. Chatterjee proposed a course entitled 'New Gender Studies' in the University of Kalyani, West Bengal. This was indeed an extremely courageous step, given that Chatterjee was to offer this course to students who mostly came from peri-urban locales. Unlike Jadavpur, Delhi, Pune or Hyderabad, Kalyani University is not located in a metropolitan centre, but is a good forty-three-kilometre train ride from the nearest metropolis, Kolkata. However, Chatterjee, an alumnus of Jadavpur University and working in the field of sexuality studies for years, did not encounter any resistance from his colleagues or administrative authorities – the course opened in July 2009, thirteen days after the momentous Delhi High Court verdict on Section 377 of the IPC. The course, which is still running successfully with an increasing number of enthusiastic students signing up for it every semester, is described by Chatterjee, in a personal interview with us:

> The course attempts to understand queering as a politics of reading, seeing how the queer can exist overtly or covertly in culture. While by no means exhausting the ways in which queer can function in culture, the course was meant to be a mere introduction to the ways in which gender/sexual subversion can be used as an anti-patriarchal tool by repeated questioning of imputed stable identities.

In an interesting way, Chatterjee, from the very outset, broadened the rubric of 'queer' by incorporating in the syllabus the chapter on masculinity from *Genders* by Cora Kaplan and David Glover, and Firdaus Kanga's *Trying to Grow* (1990), because '[He] wanted to keep disability as a crucial part of queer studies'. In other words, while challenging structuralist ideas of stable and coherent identities, Chatterjee also thought it necessary to include other forms of marginal, non-normative identities which are not essentially sexual. Within a year of launching this course, Chatterjee began a Facebook page under the same name, on 25 June 2010. With more than 13,000 members and counting, the 'New Gender Studies' page has garnered extraordinary popularity among students, teachers and activists – both queer and non-queer Facebook users. Today, the page, on the wall of which members regularly post personal anecdotes, opinions, events, photographs, and links to relevant articles, reports, films, videos, etc., has become an online archive of sorts, scrolling down which one can find interesting pointers regarding the course the LGBTQ movement has taken in the last few years.

2009–2018

The Delhi High Court verdict that read down Section 377 of the IPC on 2 July 2009 saw in its wake a surfeit of queer texts from well-known publishing houses as well as relatively newer ones. *Leaving India: My Family's Journey from Five Villages to Five Continents* (2010) by Minal Hajratwala, *Quarantine* (2011) by Rahul Mehta, *The Exiles* (2011) by Ghalib Shiraz Dhalla, *A Life Apart* (2010) by Neel Mukherjee, *Vivek and I* (2012) by Mayur Patel, *My Magical Palace* (2012) by Kunal Mukherjee, *Six Metres of Pavement* (2012) by Farzana Doctor, and *Too Close: The Tranquebar Book of Queer Erotica* (2012) written by both expatriate and local Indian authors, came out in quick succession. V. Geetha translated *The Truth About Me: A Hijra Life Story* (2010), A. Revathi's autobiography, from Tamil. Whatever their literary merit, all these books carried tremendous political currency at that hour, and continue to be politically and socially relevant. Another significant development was the foundation of Queer Ink by Shobhna S. Kumar. The 'About Us' page of Queer Ink, introduces it as,

> Established in April 2010, Queer Ink started off as an online retail platform, catering to Indian queer content. We aimed to bridge the market gap that prevented access to queer resources and content. Although our initial business focused on publishing and distributing literary works, we have since expanded to short films, documentaries, experimental theatre, and more. In 2016, Queer Ink decided to act as a catalyst for the creation of Indian queer content through the medium of crowdsourcing. For the next four years, we aim to provide a platform for diverse queer Indian voices, thoughts, and ideas. (Web, n. p.)

There were no publishing initiatives in India solely dedicated to the LGBTQ cause and that promoted queer art without fear. In 2012, Queer Ink brought out one of its first publications, *Out! Stories from the New Queer India*, edited by Minal Hajratwala. The online bookstore, which has a real presence in Mumbai, sells books related to queer issues and showcases a range of writers, from globally acclaimed authors such as E. M. Forster (*A Passage to India* or *Maurice*) to budding talents such as Arun Mirchandani (*You are Not Alone*, 2010; *The Week I Wish That Wasn't*, 2015). Another bookstore, Azaad Bazaar, which started its journey in Bandra, Mumbai, in December 2009, branded itself as the 'first LGBT pride store'. Apart from books, the store showcased an iconography of consumer products celebrating sexual minority rights.

The KASHISH Mumbai International Queer Film Festival was launched in 2010, and today it has grown into one of the primary queer film festivals of India, garnering support from the Mumbai film industry. Showcasing world queer cinema, KASHISH introduced awards in different categories, judged by a panel of eminent jury members. While mainstream Bombay Cinema continued its ambiguous relationship with queer subjects, sometimes handling it sensitively and sometimes with offensive mockery, KASHISH made space for a new kind of cinema to emerge, making way for a counterdiscourse to enter the mainstream. However, Bombay Cinema's regressive stance was countered by three Bengali films, *Arekti Premer Golpo/Just Another Love Story* (dir: Kaushik Ganguly, 2010), *Memories in March* (dir: Sanjoy Nag, 2011) and *Chitrangada: A Crowning Wish* (dir: Rituparno Ghosh, 2012), all of which released in mainstream theatres, generating a public discourse – supportive or otherwise – which could be compared to that engendered by *Fire*. These films, which became a vehicle for Bengal's cultural icon Rituparno Ghosh to 'come out' and audaciously assert his identity as a sexual non-conformist, were not taken off screens but, for the first time, 'brought queerness out of the closet to dwell in the middle class living room' (Datta, Bakshi and Dasgupta 17), much to the discomfort of the conservatives and the less-informed. In a candid interview with Kaustav Bakshi, Ghosh said,

> I have indeed estranged a section of my audience . . . the middleclass audience, we were talking about . . . I am aware of the loss. A lot of them are wary of my cross-dressing in public! In fact, the respect I used to command has been seriously affected by my decision to proclaim my sexuality. (247)

But these films became points of reference for queer subjects who, for a long time, had been waiting for a powerful media such as cinema to talk about queerness sensitively. In the same interview, Ghosh said,

> You were asking me whether I would ever take part in LGBT activism. Let me share this experience. *Arekti Premer Golpo* premiered at Priya Cinema. I was there, and I noticed young boys coming in, self-assuredly crossdressed! I could tell from their body language, they felt at home . . . the attitude was it was *their* film! I was so deeply touched! At least for a day, I had been able to hand over to them the ensign of victory! Isn't that activism too? (247)

Ghosh passed away in 2013, leaving the LGBTQ community of Kolkata mourning the loss. Soon after, in late 2015, Sangeeta Datta, Kaustav Bakshi and Rohit K. Dasgupta brought out an anthology, *Rituparno Ghosh: Cinema, Gender and Art*, published by Routledge. It was the first volume ever to be dedicated to the works, aesthetics and cultural activism of an Indian queer filmmaker who has emerged as a queer icon. The book, which garnered extremely positive reviews, was marked out by the reviewer of *Sight and Sound* as a 'timely' publication, 'at a time when India's conservative right is having a resurgence' (Ray n. p.).

The line quoted above was the closing sentence of the *Sight and Sound* review of *Rituparno Ghosh: Cinema, Gender and Art*, and put in perspective, it resonated with the disappointments and misgivings of the queer citizens of India, who were again outlawed by the Supreme Court judgement pronounced on 11 December 2013, exactly six months and eleven days from the day Ghosh passed away. The Supreme Court of India overturned the Delhi High Court ruling on the Naz Foundation v. Govt. of NCT of Delhi case, and reinstated Section 377 of the IPC. This judgement did not find Section 377 unconstitutional, and surprisingly, did not consider it important to protect the rights of gay and lesbian citizens, branding them as a 'miniscule minority', without revealing the data based on which they arrived at such a conclusion. The judgement invited protests from civil society, criticism from lawyers and judges, and condemnation by the United Nations. A curative petition was soon filed. This judgement left the LGBTQ community with little hope, for within a few months, the Bharatiya Janata Party formed the NDA government, following a landslide victory. The general perception was that it would be almost impossible to ever read down Section 377, given the party's unabashed right-wing ideologies and homophobic disposition.

On 15 April 2014, the Supreme Court's verdict on the National Legal Services Authority v. Union of India, famously known as the NALSA judgement, declared transgender people as a 'third gender', affirming that the fundamental rights granted under the Constitution of India will be equally applicable to transgender people, while giving them the right to self-identification of their gender as male, female or third gender. While this judgement was welcomed by the transgender community, loopholes in the judgement soon became evident when various Indian states began forming transgender boards, following the passing of the Rights of Transgender Persons Bill, 2016. Two major issues at stake were the 'directions' and the question of self-identification. Firstly, the definition of transgender according to this bill was contestable; secondly, the proposal to conduct psychological tests on trans persons to determine whether he or she is rightfully 'trans' was found unacceptable.

However, a major triumphant moment for the LGBT community of India came through the Supreme Court judgement on 6 September 2018, when Section 377 of the IPC was read down, with the five-judge bench clearly expressing disapproval of leaving the decision on decriminalising homosexuality to the Parliament. This became a watershed moment in the history of queer lives in India, opening up 'legitimate' spaces for the voices of a queer minority to emerge. It remains to be seen, however, how the decriminalisation of homosexuality actually transforms lives of queer citizens of India, given that amendment of a law cannot change mindsets or eliminate age-old prejudices.

Even before Section 377 of the IPC was eventually read down, universities had continued to expand their courses on gender studies to include queer discourses. In fact, among several factors contributing to the reading down of Section 377 of the IPC, university campus activism and expansion of gender studies to include queer studies in university curricula had an important role to play in the formation of a positive opinion in favour of decriminalising homosexuality. Apart from the courses mentioned above, a few others were also launched. One such course was 'Theories of Women's and Gender Studies' introduced in 2013 at the Indira Gandhi National Open University (IGNOU) as a part of the Master of Arts in Women's and Gender Studies (MAWGS) in the School of Gender and Development Studies. Anu Aneja and Nilima Srivastava, programme coordinators for MAWGS, led a team through several sessions, and edited, vetted and finalised the self-learning material (SLM) for the programme. In a personal interview with us, Aneja said, 'In MWG 001, there are two entire blocks – one on queer movements and another on Queer Theory. Each block has around 4 to 5 units (each unit is like a chapter of about 5000 words). In several other courses, issues related to queer and lesbian sexualities and identities are taken up across various units.'

The MAWGS course, unlike the ones offered to regular learners at universities, catered to less privileged, relatively less 'meritorious', marginalised learners from metropolitan centres as well as rural and peri-urban sectors. One of the major challenges of meaningfully reaching out to the learners was the 'lack of personal contact' and 'lack of space for validation of individual, subjective experiences which may emerge in synchronous, participatory classroom discussions' (Aneja, 'Blending In' 3). A sensitive issue like sexuality demands interpersonal contact and constant dialogue between the uninitiated learner and the teacher. 'Theories of Women's and Gender Studies' was nonetheless introduced; but the course remained under strict surveillance, 'reflective of higher education's dominant fiduciary rationale as well as a general suspicion of gender studies – perceived as either not important enough to merit academic stature, or associated with limited interest groups (read, too radical or idiosyncratic)' (9).

The real distance between the learner and the teacher was bridged to some extent by recruiting counsellors at local IGNOU centres, and most importantly, through an asynchronous online discussion forum hosted on the institution's server in 2013. Aneja writes, 'The forum has become the primary means of undermining the masculinised materialities of SLM through free discussion and debate on any of the topics studied' ('Blending In' 16). A survey of students' responses to the course revealed that the modules addressing non-normative sexualities turned out to be particularly helpful to the less-informed and uninitiated students. One student said that the readings made him realise the importance of 'liberty not only for the women folk, but also for Queer/LGBTI community, Ghetto and Black liberalism'. Another saw feminism as 'a breakaway from traditional definitions of masculinity, of machoism, when all sexes can live, . . .' (qtd. in Aneja, 'Blending In' 18). Both these responses validate the course's success in meaningfully widening the horizon of feminism, within which queer people, coloured folk, both heterosexual and homosexual, and men, as a gendered category, have all found place.

The current scenario of Queer Studies in urban Indian universities seems to suggest that a change in the mindset of institutional authorities and students is underway. Some of the older courses mentioned above, such as the Queer Studies course at Jadavpur University and 'New Gender Studies' at the University of Kalyani, are still running successfully. Three other courses which have been introduced in the past two years also deserve to be mentioned here.

Shivaji K. Panikkar, a well-known scholar of queer art who has been running a popular blog, *Queer-Way-Art,* since 2009, introduced a course titled 'Queer Theory, Activism and Cultural Practices' in the School of Culture and Creative Expressions at Ambedkar University in Delhi, in 2015. In a personal interview, Panikkar describes the course thus:

> Taking exemplary instances from Euro-American and Asian contexts, the course will focus on the critical perspectives inherent in the formulation of the concept of 'queer', the poststructuralist understanding of sexual and gender differences and identity formations, and the cultural practices that reflect these shift-overs. Their radical breakaway points from the heteronormative status-quo positions will be the focus of the course. The course will focus on the practices that push the boundaries of what is accepted as the norm, or as the statusquo.

In 2016, the Centre for Women Studies at the Jawaharlal Nehru University (JNU) introduced a course entitled 'Public Formations of Sexuality'. The course, like Panikkar's, proposed to challenge formulations of sexuality in deeply entrenched binary oppositions that eliminate other forms of sexual expressions and intimacies or uphold them as unnatural. Working around the idea that sexuality should not be concealed within the 'private realm', but needs to be discussed as 'central to the making of the modern individual, the family and the state', the course made way for analysing sexual scripts that govern everyday lives and problematise the 'dominant paradigm of sexual repression and violence and maps the contested, pervasive and multi-layered terrains of sexuality'. The course proposed to bring together apparently diverse fields of political and social movements: interestingly, it proposed to locate the idea of family planning within discourses of political movements such as mobilisations by sex workers and queer organisations, and public health discourses on HIV-AIDS.

The Ashoka University website, while introducing its Centre for Studies in Gender and Sexuality, states how such centres are policed in every society in the world. They are issues of universal import that also take on different dimensions depending on their local setting. In India, the policing of gender and sexuality forms the cornerstone of many inequalities perpetrated in society. Equally, sexuality is relatively free when compared with the West, while gender seems more repressive. The Centre for Studies in Gender and Sexuality (CSGS) at Ashoka University is the first such centre in the country to study the nuances of these issues concerning both gender and sexuality. The scholarly, policy and media approaches required for this study must be pioneered by educational institutions which rigorously focus on these inter-related issues. CSGS sees itself as fulfilling this global requirement while being fully responsive to local needs. The Centre was set up in August 2015 and focuses on three areas of activity: scholarly research, social outreach and media consultation. Scholarly research at CSGS has developed major and minor programmes in gender studies and sexuality studies that have been offered to students from the 2017–18 academic year.

The latest addition to the list of academic courses in Queer Studies is the newly introduced course on gender studies in the departments of English and Tamil at the American College in

Madurai. This college, which has been coordinating a course on transgender studies since 2008, has recently expanded their course to identify 58 different genders – a wide spectrum of sexualities – inspired by the book *Maraikkapatta pakkangal* (*Hidden Pages*) by Gopi Shankar Madurai, published in 2018. This book, written in Tamil and then translated into English, took four years to see the light of day, since the author (as told in an interview with *The Times of India*) found it difficult to convince publishers in the Tamil publishing industry that such a book was a need of the hour (Gautham, Web, n. p.).

***

As we were writing this chapter, the Supreme Court of India upheld the right to privacy (protected under Article 21 of the Indian Constitution) as a fundamental right. The arguments in favour of this ruling critiqued the Court's earlier verdict that reinforced Section 377 of the IPC. The Court said, 'It is an individual's choice as to who enters his house, how he lives and in what relationship. The privacy of the home must protect the family, marriage, procreation and sexual orientation which are all important aspects of dignity'; it added, 'One's sexual orientation is undoubtedly an attribute of privacy' (qtd. in Venkataramakrishnan, Web, n. p.). This Supreme Court ruling came as a rejoinder to the rise of right-wing majoritarianism and controversial debates around food habits. The judges specifically mention this in their ruling, alluding to the controversy surrounding eating beef, which had reached an aggressive level in the preceding two years. The pretext of this ruling was, however, the government's enforcement of the world's largest biometric project, the Aadhar, which had implications for the privacy of every Indian citizen since it made it mandatory for them to share their photographs, fingerprints, iris scans, etc. The critics of the project argued that the data thus collected could be used as an easy device for mass surveillance. In declaring that every Indian citizen has a fundamental right to privacy, the Supreme Court made way for sexual identity to be protected and honoured under Article 21.

This ruling, which is yet to become a judgement, seemed to ease the struggle to de-constitutionalise Section 377 of the IPC. But a piece of news which followed the 'privacy' ruling upturned the optimism which had been building within the LGBTQ community. The NDA government, on 3 September 2017, nine days after the ruling, refused to acknowledge transgender persons as the 'third gender' in the country's labour law framework. The Wages Code Bill categorises the country's forty-four labour laws into four codes; the Labour Code on Wages Bill drafted in 2015 had provisions prohibiting discrimination against transgender persons in matters of wages. But the Law Ministry objected to adding a separate clause for transgender persons, which infuriated the community. Amid these disappointments, the writ petitions for striking down Section 377 of the IPC began to be heard by a five-bench judge on 10 July 2018; the four-day hearing ended on a positive note, with the judges articulating progressive views in favour of decriminalising homosexuality. And, as mentioned above, the five-judge bench read down Section 377 of the IPC in one of its most progressive judgements ever, on 6 September 2018. The whole purpose of recalling the preamble to this judgement is to underline the fact that larger battles are yet to be won. The reading down of Section 377 of the IPC is only the beginning.

However, one may mention here that academicians across India, particularly those who teach Humanities and Social Sciences courses, are finding it difficult to work with a conspicuous curtailing of funds by the current government, especially in the case of public universities. The introduction of Choice Based Credit System by the University Grants Commission in universities across India in recent times also comes with the apparently autocratic directive to have a uniform syllabus for undergraduate courses. While some universities have already accepted this recommendation without demur, a few others are trying to resist it as long as possible; for the introduction of a uniform syllabus, controlled by the state, takes away the university's freedom to introduce courses which maybe more progressive than the prescribed ones. The argument in favour of the uniform syllabus is that it would facilitate students' mobility across universities in the country; but the dangerous implication it has is not hard to see. Under such circumstances, when higher education in India is under serious state vigilance, sexuality studies cannot possibly be introduced at the undergraduate level. Yet, a thin ray of hope is the inclusion of a contemporary queer classic, *Funny Boy* by Sri Lankan–Canadian author Shyam Selvadurai, in the CBCS English Honours syllabus in the module on popular literature. No matter in which module it has been included, it is impossible to teach *Funny Boy* without discussing same-sex desires. However romantic it may sound, teachers should more vehemently exercise their agency in the classroom in interpreting texts and events or raising awareness against various forms of discrimination, in ways which cannot be controlled by the state. However, one cannot predict the degree of state monitoring that classroom lectures may be exposed to in the near future. It largely depends upon where a person is teaching, among other factors. The academia, which plays a significant role in shaping the worldview of the country's future citizens, is therefore further burdened with the responsibility of dismantling heteronormative frameworks of knowledge-sharing.

NOTES

[1] One of the most notable among these is Shohini Ghosh's monograph on the film, *Fire* (2010), which delineates in painstaking detail the social, political and cultural environment that led to the production of the film and the Hindu fundamentalist opposition to the screening of the film.

REFERENCES

'About Us (Queer Ink)'. *Queer Ink*. Web. 27 November 2018. <http://queer-ink.com/about-us/>.

Aneja, Anu. 'Blending In: Reconciling Feminist Pedagogy and Distance Education across Cultures'. *Gender and Education.* 29 September 2016. Web. 29 November 2018. <10.1080/09540253.2016.1237621>.

---. Personal interview. 13 August 2017.

Ashcroft, Bill. *Post-colonial Transformation*. London: Routledge, 2001. Print.

Chakravarti, Paromita. Personal interview. 12 July 2017.

---. 'Teaching Queer and Queering Teaching: Introducing Queer Studies at the University'. 2008. TS.

---. 'The Sex Education Debates: Teaching "Life Style" in West Bengal, India'. *Sex Education: Sexuality, Society and Learning* 11.4 (2011): 389–400. Print.

Chatterjee, Niladri R. Personal interview. 9 August 2017.

Datta, Sangeeta, Kaustav Bakshi, and Rohit K. Dasgupta, eds. *Rituparno Ghosh: Cinema, Gender and Art*. New Delhi: Routledge, 2015. Print.

Ganguly, Swati. Personal interview. 23 August 2017.

Gautham, Komal. 'Madurai College's "Intersex" Course to Cover 58 Genders'. *The Times of India*, 25 August 2018. Web. 7 December 2018. <https://timesofindia.indiatimes.com/city/chennai/madurai-colleges-intersex-course-to-cover-58-genders/articleshow/65537361.cms>.

Ghosh, Shohini. Personal interview. 13 September 2017.

John, Mary E, and Janaki Nair, eds. *A Question of Silence?: The Sexual Economies of Modern India.* 1998. London: Zed Books, 2000. Print.

Joseph, Sherry. *Social Work Practice and Men who Have Sex with Men*. New Delhi: Sage, 2005. Print.

Majumdar, Ajay, and Niloy Basu. *Samaprem: Samakamita bishoyok ekti samaj-monostwatik anweshan* [An Equal Love: A Socio-Psychological Investigation into the Subject of Homosexuality]. Kolkata: Deep Prakashan, 2005. Print.

McNaron, Toni A. H. *Poisoned Ivy: Lesbian and Gay Academics Confronting Homophobia*. Philadelphia: Temple UP, 1997. Print.

Menon, Nivedita, ed. *Sexualities*. New Delhi: Women Unlimited (Kali for Women), 2007. Print.

Nandy, Ashis. *The Intimate Enemy*. 1983. *Exiled at Home*. New Delhi: Oxford UP, 1998. Print.

Panikkar, Shivaji. Personal interview. 11 October 2017.

Rao, R. Raj, and Dibyajyoti Sarma, eds. *Whistling in the Woods: Twenty-one Queer Interviews*. New Delhi: Sage, 2009. Print.

Rajya Sabha Committee on Petitions. Rajya Sabha Secretariat. 'Hundred and Thirty-fifth Report on Petition Praying for National Debate and Evolving Consensus on the Implementation of the Policy for

Introduction of Sex Education in the Schools'. Web. 12 April 2012. <164.100.47.5.8080/newcommittee/reports/EnglishCommittees/CommitteeonPetitions/135 Report.htm>.

Rath, Akshay. 'Either Sink or Swim: Interview with Hoshang Merchant'. *The Challenge* 23.1 (Jan–Jun 2014). Web. 23 November 2018. <http://www.thechallenge.org.in/contents_3.html#>.

Ray, Debika. 'Review of *Rituparno Ghosh: Cinema, Gender and Art*'. *Sight and Sound*, December 2016. Print.

Report on Lesbian Meeting. National Conference on Women's Movement in India, Tirupati, 1994. *Sexualities*. Ed. N. Menon. New Delhi: Women Unlimited (Kali for Women), 2007. 298–300. Print.

Satpathy, Sumanyu. Personal interview. 18 October 2017.

Sinfield, Alan. *Alfred Tennyson. Rereading Literature*. London: Blackwell, 1986. Print.

Tarun. 'Heteronormativity in Educational Institutions'. *Sexualities*. Ed. N. Menon. New Delhi: Women Unlimited (Kali for Women), 2007. 128–38. Print.

Thadani, Giti. *Sakhiyani: Lesbian Desire in Ancient and Modern India*. London: Bloomsbury, 1996. Print.

Vanita, Ruth. Personal interview. 19 July 2017.

Vanita, Ruth, and Saleem Kidwai, eds. *Same Sex Love in India: A Literary History*. Rev. Ed. New Delhi: Penguin Books, 2008. Print.

Venkataramakrishnan, R. 'What Does Privacy Actually Mean? Excerpts from the Supreme Court Judgment'. *Scroll.in*, 24 August 2017. Web. 28 August 2017. <https://scroll.in/article/848349/what-does-privacy-actually-mean-excerpts-from-the-supreme-court-judgment>.

Glossary of Select Terms

Androgyny: The word 'androgyny' comes from the Greek word '*andro*' meaning 'man', and '*gyny*' meaning 'woman'. Androgyny therefore means 'of having both male and female characteristics'. The term applies to people who do not want to be identified by their gender.

Gay Liberation Front: The Gay Liberation Front (GLF) comprised a number of gay liberation groups, the first of which was formed in New York City in 1969, immediately after the Stonewall Riots in which the police clashed with gay demonstrators. There was also a GLF group in London, UK, which was formed in the basement of the London School of Economics (LSE) in October 1970.

Gender-queer: The term denotes or relates to a person who does not subscribe to conventional gender distinctions; but identifies with neither, both, or a combination of male and female genders.

Heteronormativity: Michael Warner is credited for coining the term in his essay 'Fear of a Queer Planet' (1991), based on Gayle Rubin's idea of the 'sex/gender system' and Adrienne Rich's notion of 'compulsory heterosexuality'. Heteronormativity assumes every person to be 'heterosexual', and that sex, gender and the body are in line with one another. It stigmatises and marks out any sign of deviation from this alignment as a sin or pathological abnormality, thereby generating a deep-seated phobia for those who challenge this hypothesis.

Homitern: A portmanteau word formed by conjoining 'Comintern' (an international communist organisation) and 'homosexual', 'homitern' is 'a joke, a nightmare, or a dream, depending on one's point of view', as Gregory Woods writes in *Homintern: How Gay Culture Liberated the Modern World* (2016). It refers to a practice that a group of gay men and lesbian women engage in to control the world of arts from behind the scenes, in which they privilege the work of their lovers, ex-lovers and would-be lovers, diverting taste away from the 'natural' and 'wholesome'. Nobody knows who invented this term. But Cyril Connolly or Jocelyn Brooke or W. H. Auden could have coined this term in jest. However, it has been adopted seriously by many who are antagonistic to queer people.

Homonationalism: 'Homonationalism' and 'homonormativity' are closely linked in the neoliberal, capitalist integration of LGBTQ rights movement into the mainstream. Homonationalism is not an identity, but a process by which some homosexual bodies are identified as worthy of protection by the white supremacist Western state, while marking out other bodies as dangerous. As Jasbir Puar has shown, it is a name for different processes by which some powers promise protection and right to life to the LGBTQ community in order to validate racist and xenophobic positions, especially against Islam, basing them on the prejudice that migrant people, especially people religiously affiliated to Islam, are necessarily homophobic as against a progressive, tolerant, egalitarian, white, Christian West.

Homonormativity: The neo-liberal integration of LGBTQ citizens into the mainstream promotes adoption of monogamy, marriage, raising a family, etc., at the expense of abandoning radicalism. If one wishes to enjoy state benefits and protection, one needs to be 'homonormative', an unquestioning replication of heteronormativity. As Lisa Duggan famously said in her article 'The New Homonormativity: the Sexual Politics of Neoliberalism', homonormativity is a form of depoliticised gay culture which is anchored in domesticity and consumption, extremely enticing for many sexually marginalised citizens. Trans people, queer of colour, single queer people with multiple sexual partners – all these people are outside the homonormative fold and are detested by the state which is determined to promote a demobilised gay constituency, by 'normalising' queer people.

Homophile: 'Homophile' is a dated term for homosexuality. It has now gone out of fashion. The word '*phile*' emphasises 'love' rather than 'sex'. The term was coined by the German psychoanalyst Karl-Günther Heimsoth in his 1924 doctoral dissertation. The term was in common use in the 1950s and 60s by homosexual organisations and publications, until it was replaced by new terminologies and concepts.

Homophobe: This term is used to denote a person who dislikes or is prejudiced against homosexual people.

Lavender Scare: The term, borrowed from 'lavender lads' referring to gay boys, refers to the witch hunt and firing of homosexual citizens in the United States in the 1950s. The term was popularised by David K. Johnson's book *The Lavender Scare: The Cold War Persecution of Gays and Lesbians in the Federal Government* (2004). In 2011, a similar kind of witch hunt was spearheaded by TV9, a Telugu channel, which threatened to 'out' and publicly shame closeted gay citizens of India, by recording their phone conversations and displaying on the channel photographs of members from a gay social networking site without seeking their consent.

Mattachine Society: One of the earliest American gay movement (or homophile) organisations, the Mattachine Society began in Los Angeles in the winter of 1950. It was formed by Harry Hay, a leading gay activist and former Communist Party member, along with seven other gay men. The name refers to the Société Mattachine, a French medieval masque group. The name was meant to symbolise the fact that, as Hay commented, 'gays were a masked people, unknown and anonymous'.

Pink Money or Dorothy Dollar: Pink Money or Dorothy Dollar refers to the purchasing power of the LGBTQ community – their power to participate freely in the consumerist market, while also having enough disposable income to donate to political movements. The recognition of the buying powers of the LGBTQ community is one of the primary reasons behind the capitalist state's celebration of LGBTQ rights, particularly in the West. Pinkwashing of Israel as a paradisiacal site for gay tourism was only made possible because LGBTQ people with sufficient money to spend on 'good life' were ready to comply. The state offers a series of consumerist enticements to the LGBTQ people, knowing well their ability to purchase those enticements; and conformist, homonormative, homonationalist LGBTQ citizens often fall into the trap, sometimes willingly.

Pink Triangle: Originally, the inverted pink triangle was used as a badge for marking out male homosexuals in Nazi concentration camps. This was later reclaimed by the AIDS Coalition To Unleash Power (ACT UP) along with the slogan 'SILENCE = DEATH' as its logo, after it was founded in New York City in 1987. The inverted pink triangle is now a global symbol of Queer Pride.

Pinkwashing: Pinkwashing, a term coined in 1992 to name a state practice of supporting people with breast cancer while actually reaping profits from their ill health, has been appropriated by dissident queer discourses. The term is closely linked with homonationalism and homonormativity. It is an eyewash of sorts, by which LGBTQ people are made to think that they are being integrated by the state, whereas the state actually uses the excuse of protecting LGBTQ rights to advance its racist and xenophobic policies in modifying their immigration laws and spreading phobia against the non-white, non-Christian migrant, particularly Muslims. Pinkwashing is also seen in the ways in which the state targets moneyed LGBTQ people to promote tourism industry in places such as Tel Aviv in Israel, by projecting them as gay paradises. In this sense, Israel's location, in close geographical proximity to other Muslim-dominated states, makes it a place of investment, because by endorsing it as 'queer-friendly' the American state can highlight the homophobia of the rest of the middle-eastern countries by contrast.

Queer Nation: Queer Nation is an LGBTQ activist organisation founded in March 1990 in New York City by HIV/AIDS activists from ACT UP. The organisation was founded in response to the escalation of anti-gay and anti-lesbian violence on the streets and prejudice in the arts and media. The group is known for its confrontational tactics, its slogans and the practice of 'outing'. It stands in contrast to the assimilationist politics of other organisations such as the Human Rights Campaign.

Rainbow Flag: Originally carrying eight stripes, the current Rainbow Flag used worldwide as a symbol of LGBTQ Pride now has six stripes – red, orange, yellow, green, blue and violet. Each of the original eight stripes, initially designed by Gilbert Baker and Lynn Segerblom in San Francisco in 1978, was coded with meaning: hot pink – sex; red – life; orange – healing; yellow – sunlight; green – nature; turquoise – magic or art; indigo – serenity; violet – spirit. There are various theories regarding how the original idea of this flag emerged. Baker could have been inspired by Judy Garland's song, 'Over the Rainbow', Garland being one of the most sought after queer icons; or he could have conceived the idea from the

Flag of the Races popular in American campuses in the 1960s; or he could have borrowed the idea from the Hippie Movement of the 1960s and 70s.

Stonewall Riots: Stonewall Inn Riots is a series of disruptive demonstrations that took place in the Greenwich Village in New York City in 1969. It is considered an important moment for LGBTQ organising as the confrontational encounter with a largely homophobic police force served as a catalyst for modern LGBTQ activism.

Further Reading

A further reading list for Queer Studies can be quite exhaustive; and at the point when we were compiling this, it was becoming quite unmanageable and growing into almost an entire bibliographic book in itself. In the end we decided to limit the scope of this list to a few key works, given that each chapter has a comprehensive reference list.

Abelove, Henry, Michele Aina Barale, and David M. Halperin, eds. *The Lesbian and Gay Studies Reader*. New York: Routledge, 1993. Print.

Ahmed, S. *The Promise of Happiness.* Durham: Duke UP, 2010. Print.

Banerjea, Niharika, Debanuj Dasgupta, Rohit K. Dasgupta, and Jaime M. Grant, eds. *Friendship as Social Justice Activism: Critical Solidarities in a Global Perspective*. Chicago: U of Chicago P, 2016. Print.

Barton, Bernadette. *Pray the Gay Away: The Extraordinary Lives of Bible Belt Gays*. New York and London: New York UP, 2012. Print.

Benshoff, Harry M., and Sean Griffin. *Queer Images: A History of Gay and Lesbian Film in America.* Lanham: Lexington Books, 2006. Print.

Berry, Chris, Fran Martin, and Audrey Yue, eds. *Mobile Cultures: New Media in Queer Asia.* Durham: Duke UP, 2003. Print.

Bose, B, and S. Bhattacharya, eds. *The Phobic and the Erotic: The Politics of Sexualities in Contemporary India*. London and New York: Seagull, 2007. Print.

Butler, Judith. *Bodies That Matter: On the Discursive Limits of 'Sex'*. New York and London: Routledge, 1993. Print.

Carter, David. *Stonewall: The Riots that Sparked the Gay Revolution*. New York: St Martins Press, 2004. Print.

Chiang, Howard. *Sexuality in China: Histories of Power and Pleasure.* Seattle: U of Washington P, 2018. Print.

Corber, R. J., and S. Valocchi, eds. *Queer Studies: An Interdisciplinary Reader*. Malden: Blackwell, 2013. Print.

Dasgupta, Rohit K. *Digital Queer Cultures in India: Politics, Intimacies and Belonging*. London: Routledge, 2017. Print.

Datta, Sangeeta, Kaustav Bakshi, and Rohit K. Dasgupta, eds. *Rituparno Ghosh: Cinema, Gender and Art*. London: Routledge, 2015. Print.

Dave, Naisargi. *Queer Activism in India: A Story in the Anthropology of Ethics*. Durham: Duke UP, 2012. Print.

de Lauretis, Teresa, ed. *Queer Theory: Lesbian and Gay Sexualities*. Spec. issue of *differences* 3 (1991). Print.

Doty, Alexander. *Making Things Perfectly Queer: Interpreting Mass Culture*. Minneapolis: U of Minnesota P, 1993. Print.

Edsall, Nicholas C. *Toward Stonewall: Homosexuality and Society in the Modern Western World*. Charlottesville: U of Virginia P, 2003. Print.

Engebretsen, Elisabeth. *Queer Women in Urban China*. London: Routledge, 2015. Print.

Evans, David. *Sexual Citizenship: The Material Construction of Sexualities*. London: Routledge, 1993. Print.

Ferguson, Roderick. *Aberrations in Black: Toward a Queer of Color Critique*. Minneapolis: U of Minnesota P, 2003. Print.

Foster, David. *Queer Issues in Contemporary Latin American Cinema*. Austin: U of Texas P, 2004. Print.

Foucault, Michel. *Discipline and Punish: The Birth of the Prison*. 1975. Trans. Alan Sheridan. 2nd Edition. New York: Vintage Books, 1995. Print.

---. *History of Sexuality* Vol. 1. 1976. Trans. Robert Hurley. Victoria: Penguin, 1984. Print.

Giffney, N, and M. O'Rourke, eds. *The Ashgate Research Companion to Queer Theory*. London and New York: Routledge, 2009. Print.

Goldberg, J., ed. *Queering the Renaissance*. Durham and London: Duke UP, 1994. Print.

Gopinath, Gayatri. *Impossible Desires: Queer Diasporas and South Asian Public Cultures*. Durham: Duke UP, 2005. Print.

Gray, Mary. *Out in the Country: Youth, Media, and Queer Visibility in Rural America*. New York: New York UP, 2010. Print.

Grossman, Andrew, ed. *Queer Asian Cinema: Shadows in the Shade.* London: Routledge, 2000. Print.

Haggerty, G. E., and M. McGarry, eds. *A Companion to LGBTQ Studies*. Malden: Blackwell, 2007. Print.

Halberstam, Jack. *In a Queer Time and Place: Transgender Bodies, Subcultural Lives*. New York: New York UP, 2005. Print.

Halperin, David. 'The Normalisation of Queer Theory'. *Journal of Homosexuality* 45: 2–4 (2003): 339–43. Print.

---. *Saint Foucault: Towards a Gay Hagiography*. New York: Oxford UP, 1995. Print.

Haritaworn, Jin. *Queer Lovers and Hateful Others: Regenerating Violent Times and Places.* London: Pluto, 2016. Print.

Hawley, John C, ed. *Postcolonial, Queer: Theoretical Intersections.* New York: State U of New York P, 2001. Print.

Henderson, Lisa. *Love and Money: Queers, Class and Cultural Production*. New York: New York UP, 2013. Print.

Herek, Gregory M., and Kevin Berrill, eds. *Hate Crimes: Confronting Violence against Lesbians and Gay Men*. Thousand Oaks: Sage, 1992. Print.

Hinsch, Bret. *Passions of the Cut Sleeve: The Male Homosexual Tradition in China*. Berkeley: U of California P, 1992. Print.

Hoare, Philip. *Oscar Wilde's Last Stand: Decadence, Conspiracy, and the Most Outrageous Trial of the Century*. New York: Arcade Publishing, 1997. Print.

hooks, bell. *Feminist Theory: From Margin to Centre.* Cambridge, MA: South End Press, 1984. Print.

John, Mary E., and Janaki Nair, eds. *A Question of Silence?: The Sexual Economies of Modern India.* 1998. London: Zed Books, 2000. Print.

Joseph, Sherry. *Social Work Practice and Men who Have Sex with Men*. New Delhi: Sage, 2005. Print.

Katyal, A. *The Doubleness of Sexuality: Idioms of Same-Sex Desire in Modern India*. New Delhi: New Text, 2016. Print.

khanna, akshay. *Sexualness*. New Delhi: New Text, 2016. Print.

Kuhn, Betsy. *Gay Power!: The Stonewall Riots and the Gay Rights Movement, 1969.* Minneapolis: 21st Century Books, 2011. Print.

Liu, Petrus. *Queer Marxism in Two Chinas*. Durham: Duke UP, 2015. Print.

Livia, Anna, and Kira Hall, eds. *Queerly Phrased: Language, Gender, and Sexuality*. New York: Oxford UP, 1997. Print.

Luibhéid, Eithne. *Entry Denied: Controlling Sexuality at the Border*. Minneapolis: U of Minnesota P, 2002. Print.

Lyons, H., and A. Lyons, eds. *Sexualities in Anthropology: A Reader*. Malden: Wiley-Blackwell, 2011. Print.

Majumdar, Ajay, and Niloy Basu. *Samaprem: Samakamita bishoyok ekti samaj–monostwatik anweshan* (An Equal Love: A Socio-psychological Investigation into the Subject of Homosexuality). Kolkata: Deep Prakashan, 2005. Print.

Marhoefer, Laurie. *Sex and the Weimer Republic: German Homosexual Emancipation and the Rise of the Nazis*. Toronto: U of Toronto P, 2015. Print.

Martin, Fran. *Backward Glances: Contemporary Chinese Cultures and Female Homoerotic Imaginary*. Durham: Duke UP, 2010. Print.

---. *Situating Sexualities: Queer Representation in Taiwanese Fiction, Film and Public Culture*. Hong Kong: Hong Kong UP, 2003. Print.

Menon, Nivedita, ed. *Sexualities*. New Delhi: Women Unlimited (Kali for Women), 2007. Print.

Mosse, George L. *The Image of Man: The Creation of Modern Masculinity*. Oxford: Oxford UP, 1996. Print.

Mowlabocus, Sharif. *Gaydar Culture: Gay Men, Technology and Embodiment in the Digital Age*. Farnham: Ashgate, 2010. Print.

Muñoz, José Esteban. *Disidentifications: Queers of Color and the Performance of Politics*. Durham: Duke UP, 1999. Print.

Naphy, William. *Born to be Gay: A History of Homosexuality*. Gloucestershire: Tempus, 2004. Print.

Puar, Jasbir, K. *Terrorist Assemblages: Homonationalism in Queer Times*. Durham: Duke UP, 2007. Print.

Pullen, Christopher. *Gay Identity, New Storytelling and the Media*. London: Palgrave Macmillan, 2009. Print.

Rao, R. Raj, and Dibyajyoti Sarma, eds. *Whistling in the Woods: Twenty-one Queer Interviews*. New Delhi: Sage, 2009. Print.

Rich, B. Ruby. *New Queer Cinema: The Director's Cut.* Durham: Duke UP, 2013. Print.

Riordon, Michael. *Out Our Way: Gay and Lesbian Life in the Country.* Toronto: Between The Lines, 1996. Print.

Reddy, Chandan. *Freedom with Violence: Race, Sexuality, and the US State.* Durham: Duke UP, 2011. Print.

Reddy, Gayatri. *With Respect to Sex: Negotiating Hijra Identity in South India*. Chicago: U of Chicago P, 2010. Print.

Rich, Adrienne. *Blood, Bread and Poetry: Selected Prose*. New York: W. W. Norton, 1986. Print.

Rodríguez, Juana María. *Queer Latinidad: Identity Practices, Discursive Spaces*. New York: New York UP, 2003. Print. Sexual Cultures.

Schneider, David. *A Critique of the Study of Kinship*. Ann Arbor: U of Michigan P, 1984. Print.

Schoonover, Karl, and Rosalind Galt. *Queer Cinema in the World.* Durham: Duke UP, 2016. Print.

Sedgwick, Eve K. *Between Men: English Literature and Male Homosocial Desire*. 1985. New York: Columbia UP, 1992. Print.

Shahani, Parmesh. *Gay Bombay: Globalization, Love and (Be)longing in Contemporary India*. London: Sage, 2008. Print.

Sharma, Maya. *Loving Women: Being Lesbian in Unprivileged India*. New Delhi: Yoda Press, 2007. Print.

Shuttleton, D. D. Watt, and R. Phillips, eds. *De-Centring Sexualities: Politics and Representation Beyond the Metropolis*. London: Routledge, 2000. Print.

Sinfield, Alan. *Alfred Tennyson*: *Rereading Literature*. London: Blackwell, 1986. Print.

Smith, Paul Julian. *Queer Mexico: Cinema and Television Since 2000.* Detroit: Wayne State UP, 2017. Print.

Spurlock, John C. *Free Love: Marriage and Middle-Class Radicalism in America.* New York: New York UP, 1988. Print.

Tang, Denise. *Conditional Spaces: Hong Kong Lesbian Desires and Everyday Life*. New York: Columbia UP, 2011. Print.

Vanita, Ruth, and Saleem Kidwai, eds. *Same Sex Love in India: A Literary History*. Rev. Ed. New Delhi: Penguin Books, 2008. Print.

Weeks, Jeffery. *Sexuality and Its Discontents: Meanings, Myths and Modern Sexualities.* 1985. New York and London: Routledge, 2000. Print.

White, Patricia. *UnInvited: Classical Hollywood Cinema and Lesbian Representability.* Indiana: Indiana UP, 1999. Print.

Yosef, Raz. *Beyond Flesh: Queer Masculinities and Nationalism in Israeli Cinema*. Detroit: Wayne State UP, 2004. Print.

Other books in the series

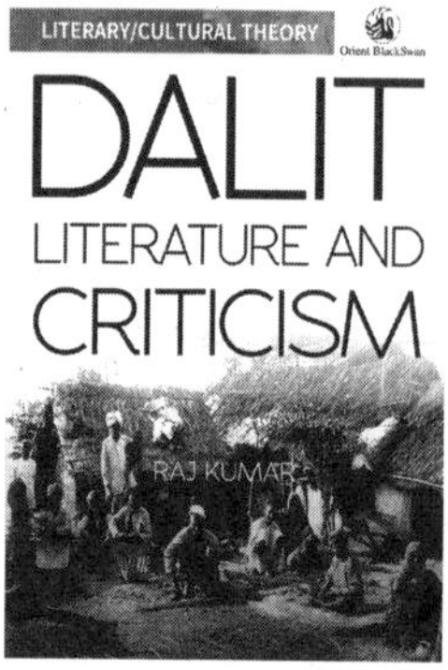

For more information, visit www.orientblackswan.com